HOW TO GET
FROM JANUARY
THROUGH DECEMBER
— IN —

POWER-
BOATING

BOOKS BY MARTIN LEVIN

Love Stories
Hollywood and the Great Fan Magazines
Five Boyhoods
The Phoenix Nest
The Bedside Phoenix Nest
The Saturday Review Sampler of Wit and Wisdom

HOW TO GET
FROM JANUARY
THROUGH DECEMBER
— IN —
POWER-
BOATING

Edited by Martin Levin

Illustrated by Alan Williams

HARPER & ROW, PUBLISHERS

New York / Hagerstown / San Francisco / London

My thanks to the editors and publishers of the boating magazines—*Boating, Motorboat, Motor Boating & Sailing, Rudder* (now combined with *Sea*), *Yachting*—for guiding me from January through December these many years, and for their help in bringing this book to fruition.

Copyright acknowledgments appear on pages 199 and 200.

FIRST EDITION

Designed by Nora Sheehan

Library of Congress Cataloging in Publication Data
Main entry under title:
How to get from January through December
in powerboating.
   1. Motor-boats—Addresses, essays, lectures.
2. Boats and boating—Addresses, essays, lectures.
I. Levin, Martin.
GV835.H63   1978   797.1′25   77-11815
ISBN 0-06-012558-6
78 79 80 81 82 10 9 8 7 6 5 4 3 2 1

C O N T E N T S

HOW TO GET
FROM JANUARY
THROUGH DECEMBER
— IN —

POWER-
BOATING

CASTING OFF
The Displacement Principle

Seasoned boatmen know that the priceless ingredient in pleasure boating is anxiety. You don't take up boating to *relax*. Relaxing is for stamp collectors. You take up boating to *displace* workaday tensions with new and exotic obsessions. Given enough marine problems, the dedicated boatman doesn't have any room left in his head for onshore anxieties. How can you worry about losing your job in a month or two, when *today,* right before your eyes, water is oozing up along the garboards?

Furthermore, boating is rife with unresolved choices. One engine or two? Wet storage or dry? Fiber glass or wood or aluminum or ferro-cement?

The fact is that the natural habitat of a pleasure boat is not the water. It is a cradle in a showroom, where it can be protected from hostile elements. Sharks and alligators thrive in water. Boats dissolve. Wood rots, steel rusts, fiber glass flexes and crazes. Electrical wiring goes *kaput* from condensation; metal fittings corrode; pumps and blowers jam. The battery dies. If the engine is not used often enough it may seize up. If it is run too hard, it may need a valve job. The stuffing box can leak, the cable controls can fail, and do you know what can happen if you plug in to a dockside outlet the wrong way? Don't ask.

The question then is, Can a boatman find happiness in the midst of creeping disintegration and unanswered questions? The answer is *Yes!* His workaday worries displaced by a new list of maritime problems, the boatman can replenish his energies by *creative coping.* Creative coping explains the euphoria that pervades the boatyard or marina. Visit your local boatyard and the chances are 100 percent that you will run into a boat owner with a problem. Like that man in grease-stained chinos looking for a new impeller for his raw-water pump. Is he downhearted? No! While he is taking his pump apart on Sunday, he cannot think of the nastier realities that lie in wait for him on Monday. The *Displacement Principle* is working beautifully, even though his engine isn't. Or just because it isn't.

And once you leave your mooring for another port of call, the Displacement Principle continues working for you. Even if you are only going across Long Island Sound from New Rochelle to Louie's restaurant on Manhasset Bay, there are bilges to sniff, lines to cast off, wind and current to judge, compass to check, landmarks to look out for, and a landfall to make. It adds spice to the chowder. Returning after dark guided by lighted buoys and structures requires your undivided attention. Especially if you encounter a tug or two with barges in tow. You tie up to your mooring renewed and refreshed, having emptied your head for a few hours of everything but the particulars of a safe voyage.

Now, in order for the Displacement Principle to do its best for you, it's helpful to accumulate as much marine lore as possible. Creative coping requires a knowledgeable coper. Hence this almanac, with a line of beacons, to see you safely from January through December.

Huguenot Y.C.   MARTIN LEVIN
New Rochelle

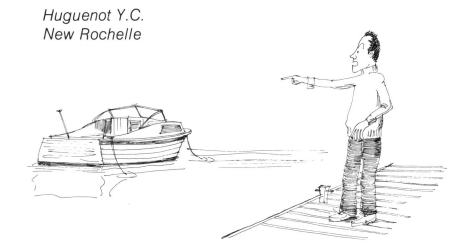

Boat show time

May 1 is frequently proclaimed as the start of the boating season. Nonsense!

Any boatman knows that the season is cyclical, and it may as well begin in January when the boat shows are launched.

Some snobs profess to be turned off by the carnival atmosphere of a boat show. Not me. The smell of fiber glass mingled with singed hot dogs, the eternal hope in the eyes of the dealers, the working models of bilge pumps and ship's wheels that your kids delight in, the huge diesel that is a thing of beauty and monstrous expense—all of this is part of an elixir as potent as the circus. No—more potent. Few of us aspire to be acrobats, lion tamers, or clowns. But anyone who buys a ticket to a boat show can hope to be a captain. At the most recent boat show I visited, there were 200 boats under

$5,000 and the bottom price was $49 for a 7'2" inflatable dinghy. So much for J. P. Morgan's widely quoted advice that you have no right to own a yacht "if you have to ask how much it costs." (As a matter of fact, Morgan did not even succeed in discouraging the man he gave that acerbic answer to, an oil baron named Henry Clay Pierce. According to Bill Robinson, editor of *Yachting,* Pierce thereupon commissioned an opulent steam yacht designed by Clinton H. Crane, a leading naval architect, which included such extras as gold-plated hardware and gold fittings in the bathroom, and some 150 special items.)

When the world of power boating was young, at the turn of the century, there was only one boat show, in New York's Grand Central Palace. Now there are dozens, from the New York Coliseum to Seattle's Kingdome—some indoors, some in the water. With 5.9 million outboards in use, and 950,000 inboards, the proliferation of boat shows is not surprising.

What is the magic that draws the public into the boat show in increasing numbers? It is the promise of instant adventure. Not on the level of Tristan Jones, the world's champion single-handed circumnavigator, but in a mundane way that is also accessible to all of us. From his boat, the yachtsman gets a horizon to look at and a fresh view of even the most familiar environment. Living in Manhattan, I had thought that the rivers were things to be crossed, via the city's bridges. But what a different view you get cruising down the East River in your own sea skiff! The industrial seascapes of New York are breathtaking, the U.N. building is a spectacular sight (never mind what goes on inside!), and the harbor is a never-ending source of refreshment. The boat owner gets a whiff of this when he cases the boat show. The boat owner-to-be gets a hint of a mysterious, untapped source of pleasure. Plus a plastic bagful of brochures and some free tide tables that the donor (an oil company) hopes he may find a use for.

For the boat show shopper who may have been infected by boat fever, turn the page for some advice on how to choose wisely.

R/ FOR BOAT FEVER

By Joe Gregory

january

Webster doesn't define the term, but *boat fever* is an infection that starts in the head and bursts in the wallet. The symptoms are flushed face, rapid breathing, expressions of anxiety and agitation, and occasional drooling. Your temperature rises when your favorite boating magazine arrives, when someone mentions the word "boat," or when your eight-year old won't release the boating section of the Sunday *Times*. Striking primarily the male members of a family, the fever appears each year after the January boat shows, worsens as spring nears, continues through the summer, and tapers off in September to lie dormant during the winter.

The man infected with a serious case of boat fever is in sad shape. He's so filled with desire and anxiety that he buys the first boat offered—anything that floats and often things that don't float. He seldom questions cost.

Sometimes the disease can be warded off if female members of the family constantly remind the affected male that the status of the budget prohibits buying the remedy. This treatment,

however, often has the adverse effect of increasing the victim's agitation and discomfort. And although temporary relief may be found by visiting yacht yards, dealers' showrooms, and boat shows, or by bumming rides on friends' boats, the only cure is—buy a boat.

The major prerequisite for a satisfactory boat-buying campaign is fever control. You must remember: There are plenty of boats available; builders have not and will not stop building and selling boats; the boat you are looking at is not the only one of its kind in the world; and there are not ten thousand other buyers clamoring for that particular boat. Condition your mind.

Before you buy, consider seriously.

Although the unmarried boatbuyer may have to consider only friends or pickup crew, the married buyer must plan for the family. He may need a deep cockpit to contain children safely. He should not want a deep main-cabin sole. Three- and four-year-olds spend much of their cruise time climbing companionway ladders, and a pitching yacht can easily toss a child from the ladder to the forward bulkhead. A cabin with a two-foot ladder is safer than one with a five-foot ladder.

When considering children, remember they frequently want milk, soft drinks, and sandwiches. A deck-loading icebox can save the cook many trips in and out of the galley. If there are teenage girls and boys in the family, remember they like and need privacy, so enclosed heads and separate sleeping compartments should be considered for sons and daughters.

The accommodation—bunks, galley, head, and clothes and gear stowage space—deserves serious thought.

It's desirable to have a berth for each member of the family or crew, but a boat that lacks the required number of bunks shouldn't be ignored. In summer, particularly in the southern latitudes, the best sleeping location is the cockpit. On a sailboat, a foam cushion under the protective cover of a boom tent edged by twinkling stars and enclosed by mosquito netting becomes a fascinating place for the older children to sleep. When considering a cruiser that has too few bunks, choose one that has wide cockpit seats and high coamings or monkey rails to prevent sleepers from rolling overboard.

Galley space is seldom adequate. Usually the work area is crowded into a corner or crammed under a side-deck, barely accessible. A galley located off center, fore-and-aft, allows more working space than one built athwartships. Gimballed stoves are useless when installed athwartships, except under power in a head sea. The trend is to install the stove in a recess in the countertop. However, this often limits the movement and angle-of-dangle of the stove and that can cause hot spills.

The hanging locker is one of the most useful parts of a boat. Nothing is more disconcerting on a cruise than having to keep clothes crumpled in sea bags or in jumbled heaps on bunks. In boats under 31 feet in length, you seldom find more than one locker per boat, but Pullman nets and coathooks rigged on bulkheads in each berth space, will satisfactorily disperse the surplus.

Boats under 25 feet in length often have the heads (if any) installed under a berth or under a seat in the cabin. This arrangement may be necessary because of limited space but it's undesirable, particularly at night when the berths are occupied. The best arrangement is to have a head compartment isolated from living quarters by closed doors. That compartment definitely should be equipped with an opening port or vent; and an exhaust blower is a nice feature.

When to Buy

A knowledge of the boat market, as it is affected by the four seasons of the year, will save you money. The best time to buy a boat is at the end of the season. Season's end is determined primarily by the weather. On the east coast of the United States, from Delaware north, cold weather, snow, and ice arrive soon after Labor Day, and after October 1st only the frostbiters and the boats heading south are still in commission. Most others are swinging on winter moorings or are up in the yards.

From Maryland to South Carolina, the boating season extends into October, and into November for serious sailors and rockfishermen. Along the coast of Georgia, throughout Florida and the Bahamas, the activity seems to never end, but it does fluctuate with the movements of yachts from the north.

In the fall, many dealers find themselves overstocked. Some of their surplus may have been on cradles or at their docks for several months. The dealer may be renting the dock space, or paying high interest rates on the money used for purchasing the stock. Right now he could use cash to order new boats for the next spring. If he holds his excess stock at list price, he'll probably have the same boats on hand all winter. So what does he do? He offers discounts.

In areas where the boating season ends in the fall, it is not unusual to find boats available for 10 percent, 15 percent, even 25 percent below spring and summer prices. And some of these bargains are loaded with extras, which means you get the goodies at a discount too.

During the winter, prices remain approximately where they were in the fall, until the dealer's stock is pretty well depleted. And if the boat you want isn't in stock, the dealer can save you money by placing your order with the builder, with delivery delayed until spring. Many plants build on speculation during winter months but they prefer to have concrete commitments and cash binders. The builder's operating costs and bills from vendors are no less in the winter than in any other season, so they adjust prices to attract orders. Dealers and brokers are cognizant of these policies and will gladly advise you regarding off-season prices.

Spring is the expensive time to buy a boat. Everybody's been to the boat shows and caught boat fever—it spreads like wildfire. To make matters worse, the Show issues of boating magazines have been thumbed through a thousand times, and the fitting-out issues are now on the stands.

The yacht clubs and boat yards are humming with activity. Sailors are tuning rigs and making trial runs around the buoys; powerboat skippers are painting, polishing, and installing hardware. Fishermen are checking gear and cleaning bait boxes, getting ready for the blues or a first run out to the Gulf Stream. Dealers' cash registers are playing a merry tune. Demand is high and prices are high.

Except in the deep south, summer is the height of the boating season. During July, boat prices average about the same as in the spring. The month of August, though, brings summer sales and end-of-the-season closeout sales to clear the floors for next year's models. Dealers, too, feel the boat fever cooling and begin offering discounts. Then, as the days get cooler and slightly shorter, we again reach the end of the grand circle of boating—fall.

Where to Buy

After you have decided on the make or kind of boat you want, check the classified ads of all the newspapers and boating publications you can lay your hands on. Many libraries rack out-of-town papers and national boating magazines. Besides location of boats, the classified ads will give you a good briefing on current prices. Other sources are boat directories, yacht club bulletin boards, local boatyards, boat shows, and the yacht brokers and dealers listed in the magazines. Bought through a broker, the price of a used boat will include a brokerage fee ranging from five to ten percent of the sale price. The fee is paid by the individual selling the boat, when the sale is completed. A reputable broker will charge you nothing for sending listings. He can supply both new and used boats, and lists hundreds. Definitely, do not overlook the yacht broker. Write or call every broker in the book who advertises your kind of boat. Keep a log of details regarding the location of the boat, asking price, freight charges, equipment, etc., then compare offerings for the most desirable buy.

Don't be afraid to bargain and don't let the word *firm* frighten you away. Regardless of how firmly a price has been set, there is no broker, no owner desiring to sell, who won't at least think about a lower price, particularly if you are speaking in terms of cash.

Most yacht brokers are straightforward, high-principled businessmen, but if you happen to choose one whose scruples are somewhat flexible, there is one pitfall to avoid. It's a device which binds the prospective buyer to the broker who then may hold the prospect in suspense for an indefinite time.

The trap: You call a broker and make him an offer for a particular boat he has listed. He tells you that for a fee (not to be confused with a deposit on a confirmed sale, or an option to buy), he will forward the offer to the owner for approval. If you pay the fee, you won't get a refund if that deal falls through. Eventually, you'll buy the boat at a price determined by the broker, you'll buy a different boat that he wants to sell, or you'll lose your remittance. Yet you can't consider any other source for a boat because you're committed financially to the one broker. In effect, you have commissioned the man to find you a boat; *any boat* are the words the broker will use. If this happens, remind the broker that his fee for selling the boat has been charged already to the present owner, is normally included in the sale price, and that he, the broker, has the responsibility for relaying your offer to the seller.

The broker may say that you must get on his hook and stay until he has contacted the seller, etc.—he doesn't want you free to deal with other brokers or boatowners. You wouldn't shop for an automobile, a house, or a trailer by paying a procurement fee, would you? No, nor should you for a boat!

Consider the Extras

Builders' and retail dealers' price lists for services, extra equipment, and options are lengthy, and the items are costly.

Most builders classify as extra or optional everything except the boat hull, the mast, the boom, and the rigging. With powerboats it's the hull, and the smallest engine she can use. Listing and pricing in this fashion puts the apparent cost of a boat in an attractive light. Many boats, particularly sailboats, can't be moved from the dock without at least one or two of the optional items—engines or sails. And, when you take your new boat on her first cruise, you may learn that items such as winches, anchor rode, and anchor are not matters of choice at all.

Read the dealer's list of optional and extra items carefully. Evaluate each item. Do you need this gadget for operating the boat? Is it essential, or simply a decoration? Can the item be bought from another, less expensive source, though a hardware dealer or a reputable discount house? Do you have the time, the tools, and skill to install the items yourself? Check prices and installation costs. Often the builder or the dealer can supply and install the equipment better and less expensively than you can.

As mentioned previously, a man suffering boat fever seldom questions the cost. But his fever may cool when he reads his bill, because there are costs which should not only be questioned but also investigated. Let's check a few: freight, cradles, and commissioning.

Freight

Although carriers vary their policies, freight charges are usually based on the size of the boat, the value, and the distance carried. If you have a boat that exceeds 20 feet in length, shipped from the factory directly to you, have the carrier's office verify the freight charge. Why? Well, an audit of unpaid bills conducted this year by a national carrier revealed that various builders over-charged buyers $100 to $275 each, for freight. Some builders said that the excessive charge was due to the cost of notifying and scheduling the trucker—but are telephone calls that expensive?

If you buy a boat from a dealer's stock there is little chance of checking the freight bill—the boat is already delivered. On the other hand, if you're placing a factory order and taking delivery through a dealer, confirm the shipping charges with him—*prior* to ordering. The reason? Because you may have a dealer who likes to jockey freight bills. For example: One dealer, interviewed recently, told how he had used a freight bill for his own advantage. His words: "I had a buyer for a $9000 boat loaded with extras. The customer was happy with the price of the boat but refused to buy because of a $90 cradle charge. We argued heatedly. To save the sale, I agreed finally to throw in the cradle for free. Later, when the boat was delivered, I sandbagged the guy by ballooning the freight bill—90 bucks."

Cradles

These are not a must. There are returnable and non-returnable cradles. If you base your boat in a freeze zone or have other reasons for winter haul-out, buy a cradle; you can use it. But if you don't need a cradle, don't buy it, argue the point!

Cradles are built primarily for transporting the boat to the buyer. While most cradles are stoutly constructed and adequate for temporary use, some won't last six months after delivery. Some cradles are nothing more than a few dollars worth of sapwood, plain nails, a few black iron bolts, and about $20 worth of labor. Cradles have been known to fall apart and drop a boat on delivery day. Yet, depending on size and value of the boat, manufacturers charge from $75 to $300 for cradles. For the price paid, cradles could and should be built of construction-grade fir, secured with galvanized or cadmium-plated fastenings, and prime painted.

Commissioning

Often an optional item, commissioning ranges from $75 to $175 for boats under 30 feet in length. For larger vessels, the cost is higher and variable. In Navy parlance, commissioning is the act of accepting ownership of a vessel, manning it, and putting her in service. Before the Navy commissions a ship she is outfitted and all machinery and equipment is installed and tested. Only minor outfitting and stores are held until later. The vessel has passed several Dock Trials and Preliminary Acceptance Trials, and a Final Acceptance Trial before the builder and the Navy are satisfied the ship is ready for commissioning. Even then, when the ship makes its shakedown voyage the builder's guaranty man is aboard to observe and record for later correction any malfunction in equipment or failure in structure.

Commissioning should have the same significance for boatmen as it has for the United States Navy. For all pleasure boats, large or small, a modified version of commissioning as noted above should be conducted. Even an 18-foot outboard should have at least one checkout at the dock and one sea trial under the dealer's cognizance, before the sale is closed. A conscientious dealer with a mind for increasing his sales and his list of happy, back-again customers, will give a boat a proper commissioning. Beware of the dealer who simply grabs your check, drops a boat into the water, and says, "Shove off, buddy. Your boat is commissioned."

Prior to the actual commissioning of your boat, the dealer should check the hull and all through-hull fittings for leakage. He should service and check engine operation, instruments, controls, lighting systems, and auxiliary equipment like pumps and generators. He should inspect the furnishings and the hull exterior for defects or damage suffered during shipment and outfitting. He should brief you on the operation of the engine and any other items of equipment that may require special operating procedures.

Before you pay the commissioning fee, inspect and operate the boat yourself. Accompany the dealer during his checkout of the boat. Ask questions, punch, probe, and operate everything you see. Shake all hose lines. Feel for loose hose clamps. If the boat is afloat, open the sea valves to flood the lines. Then, using a paper towel, wipe all water connections such as lower end of cockpit drains, head inlet and outlet, sink and icebox drains, and engine cooling water piping. Fill the fuel tanks and wipe their lines, too. Your paper towel will pick up even a weep, but don't mistake condensation for leakage—wait a few minutes, then wipe again.

If the boat is constructed of fiberglass, check the outside of the hull. Examine the paint coating or gel coat for cracks and blisters. Gel coat blisters may occur when the boat is one, two or more years old, but at least be certain you don't buy them with a new boat.

Stand off and run your eye around the sides of the hull. Are her lines fair? Quite a few boats come out of the mold showing flat spots in their sides, concave areas in the bilges, or other asymmetrical features. Don't make the mistake of buying one.

In addition to veneer hatch covers that peel and warp, and fiberglass decks that burp when walked on, a common complaint of boat owners is water leakage through decks, ports, and fittings. Builders of wooden boats learned long ago that the best guard against wet bunks and ruined gear is the generous and proper application of sealers and bedding compounds, but to judge by the frequency of complaints from owners, plastic boat manufacturers have not yet perfected the art of sealing hull joints and fittings.

The majority of leaking joints, when investi-gated, are found to be the result of sealers being absent or used in insufficient quantities. The basic cause is carelessness and poor quality control on the part of the builder.

To forestall leakage on fiberglass boats, all mechanically fastened joints, such as hull-to-deck at sheer, and all through-fastenings for fittings, trim, hatch framing, and window framing, should be sealed well and leak-tested.

Since it is not practical to seal the entire boat and pressurize the interior with air for a soap test, then a water hose test simulating severe rain, spray, and boarding seas, should be applied. Even then, in spite of all the pressure you can muster, a light summer-shower will show leakage where you proved none could be, but try—before you commission, and before you write the check.

Some boatmen make a hobby of buying and selling boats. They go through the procedure of thumping hulls, buying and outfitting each year, and probably derive more pleasure from the choosing than from the using of a boat. Others continually buy and sell because of an unsatisfactory performance or other intolerable faults in their boats.

It doesn't matter how skilled you are in the art of selecting *the* proper yacht, how many leaks you've stopped, how many times you've bought too small or too large, how much money you've spent on well-found boats or wasted on clunkers—when the fever strikes again, you start all over again. But if you don't let the fever get the upper hand, you can win more times than you lose.

GETTING THE MOST POWERBOAT FOR YOUR MONEY

By Jim Martenhoff

january

Getting the best powerboat buy means more than haggling with a salesman to knock a couple hundred dollars off the sticker price. It means shopping the boat shows scientifically and evaluating each boat from a quality/design/price point of view.

What's the best way to size up a powerboat? We consulted two eminent designers, Dick Cole (father of the tri-hull) and Jim Wynne (deep-V specialist and inventor of the modern sterndrive), on how you can get the most boat for your money.

According to Wynne, the first step should begin before you even get to the show. Foremost, you should decide what you want to do with the boat. Make a list of the activities you want to use the boat for and zero in on the type that best suits your needs. In other words, don't buy a runabout to placate the family if you're really going to fish with it.

Wynne also believes boat buyers waste money on excessive power options. "Everybody thinks they want to go fast in a boat," he states. "They

say, 'I want to go 40 miles an hour,' but very few people go 40 miles an hour very often because you can't do it. It's too uncomfortable and in congested areas it can be downright dangerous."

He cites the typical power options that might be offered with a 22- or 23-foot boat: a pair of 130 or 140 hp sterndrives, single 165, 188, 230 or 250, even a pair of 165s or 188s. "That's a tremendous range of power," Wynne says. "How does a guy decide what he's going to get?"

For fishing, he suggests a pair of 130s or 140s with dual-engine reliability, or a single 165. A waterskier may want a single 188 or 230. "But getting up to a pair of 188s, or two big V8s over 200 hp in that size boat is generally pretty ridiculous," he says. "It becomes somewhat of a hot rod, there's too much weight in the stern for the boat to perform properly unless it's running really fast or you have big transom flaps."

Once you've determined the basics—the type of boat and amount of horsepower you need—you're ready to hit the shows and compare the boats that fit your needs and price range. Instead of the traditional hull-thumping, however, Cole offers this method of general evaluation: compare the weight of any particular boat to others of the same approximate class and dimensions. Weights are normally provided in sales brochures. You can collect a handful of pamphlets and study the weights.

"Don't assume that just because it looks like a big boat but weighs very little that you're going to get any great efficiency," Cole says. "In all probability it means a light layup, or a copy of some other boat." Such boats could have what he refers to as "dents" in the bottom, not apparent to the eye, but capable of affecting performance very badly. "Don't assume that a light boat is necessarily a bargain," he warns. "It is usually the other way around."

Cole's designs have been widely copied, and he doesn't mean the legitimate way in which another designer may have been inspired to borrow some of his lines. He means the "pop" copy, where a boat is borrowed, turned over, and a fiberglass mold made from the hull. The popped mold is put into production, with only minor cosmetic changes. Cole says you should be wary of copies, but admits they're hard to spot.

"It might," he suggests, "be a good idea to ask the salesman if it's the same kind of hull as the hull it looks like—like a Glastron, for instance, which is regularly copied. Then don't pay any attention to his answer until he uses the word 'modified,' and then you know it's a copy. After that, ask all sorts of questions."

Cheap copies of better known brands, apart from being significantly lower in price, can have invisible defects. Stringers, the strengthening members found in most hulls, may not be fully encapsulated in glass. "The ignoramus just bonds the hull to the stringers thinking it's going to stick," says Cole. Obviously you would have to take the salesman's word on this question, but there are other things.

"Some have decks that will move if you jump on them. They will get gel coat cracks," he says. Such boats are so lightly laid up they may even break up although, he notes, "you usually see these problems before they get dangerous."

Once you've checked the hulls, you're ready to give the boats a thorough going-over. Here are some of the items to inspect. "Look at the little things," says Wynne. "They're important. For example, even on a well-built boat, if there's no way you can get on the bow deck without crawling on your belly, you're going to be unhappy with it."

"Check the wiring," he adds. "You can see the general quality of what has been done. Look in the engine compartment to see if the wiring is all clipped up, or left laying in the bilge. See if the bilge pump hose is clamped up so it won't lie around loose. These are examples of some of the little things that can indicate general, overall quality."

Five Ways to Judge Five Powerboats

Runabout or Ski Boat

1. Does it have good lateral stability?
2. Is it big enough to ride the whole family comfortably?
3. Is the engine powerful enough to pull two skiers?
4. Does it have a boarding ladder?
5. Is the cockpit well thought-out, with enough storage space?

Weekender

1. Are the cuddy cabin accommodations and galley facilities adequate?
2. Is the cuddy cabin well ventilated?
3. Does it have a head?
4. Can it be equipped with a camper top?
5. Is there enough storage space for gear?

Cruiser

1. Is the hull seaworthy?
2. Are the accommodations suitable for long cruises?
3. Does the galley have a large work area, adequate refrigeration and cooking facilities?
4. What's the fuel and water tankage capacity?
5. Does the helm provide good visibility?

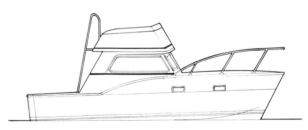

Sportfisherman

1. Does it have a good self-bailing cockpit?
2. Does the helm provide a good view of the cockpit?
3. Is there adequate rod, gear, bait, and fisher stowage?
4. Can you boat fish easily from the cockpit, and are cleats recessed so you can't snag youreself?
5. Is the hull seaworthy?

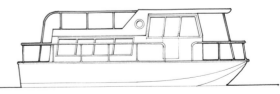

Houseboat

1. How maneuverable is it with single versus twin screws?
2. Are the accommodations well thought out, with a good galley area and private berths?
3. Does it have a boarding ladder?
4. Does it have a shallow draft for gunkholing?
5. What's the fuel and water tankage capacity?

Cole zeroes in on hardware. "Pot metal," he says, "should not be allowed anywhere on a powerboat except in the carburetor." He is turned off by cheap alloy castings that are dressed up with chrome and installed as cleats, chocks and other allied deck items. Such items, he suggests, should be good quality bronze, chrome-on-brass, stainless or highly developed alloys like Marinium.

The two designers disagree somewhat on one question—carpeting. "Out of deference for polite society," says Cole, "try not to get sick as you look at the carpet in the cockpit, which is asinine. Unfortunately, it is getting almost impossible to avoid. It might be a good idea to ask the salesman if the boat is useable when you take the carpet up—which it never is—just to aggravate the idiot for putting it there in the first place.

"There's no excuse for putting upholstery up all over everything. When you think about the dead shrimp, and the guts from the fish and the indiscretions of the dog, it's totally ridiculous. Nobody who knows anything about a boat should do anything like that, but they do it. The things should now be done with molded inner liners."

Apart from questions of his own personal taste, Cole feels carpeting complicates maintenance problems. Wynne doesn't fully agree, but he prefaces his comment by pointing out that boats are used in different waters and different ways. "The serious boatman using a boat on coastal waters," he says, "needs a boat that's easy to keep clean." In such cases, he believes, carpeting is not such a good idea. But for a man on an inland lake who buys a small boat like a sports car, uses it only occasionally and then tows it home, "carpeting is not so much of a problem," he says.

Another item to check on any size boat is how you are going to reboard it after skiing, diving, swimming or whatever. "A lot of boats now have transom ladders," says Wynne. "It's important to have something to hang onto." On some boats he has seen, though, you'd have to claw with your fingers at the hinge on an engine hatch because adequate handgrips or rails weren't included.

There are other factors any buyer can evaluate for himself. Consider the question of safety. Those side decks Cole mentions, for example, which provide easy access to the bow deck area, should have nonskid surfacing. Toe rails, which keep you from slipping overboard, are desirable—and you'll find them on the better boats from the boards of more thoughtful designers.

There's an old adage, "one hand for the ship, one hand for yourself," but the hand you employ to assure your own security in a sea must have something to hang onto—so look for grab rails strategically located. On the smaller, console-type fishing boats such rails should surround the windshield, if there is one. Grab plexiglas when the boat lurches and there is risk of both damage and injury.

Another point to consider is watertight integrity. If there are through-hull fittings, can you get at them and are they fitted with seacocks? Can you get into the bilges forward, toward the bow? Water sometimes does accumulate there, and if the boat at rest is slightly down by the bow the water can't flow to the bilge pump aft. You should be able to pump it out at the bow, or make sure it can flow aft. Should you strike some submerged object and knock a hole in the hull forward, you really want to get at the water—and the hole to plug it.

If you're an all-weather skipper, and many anglers are, you would find a self-bailing cockpit a blessing. It is especially important on smaller fishing boats, which might be docked at a fishing camp overnight while you sleep ashore. Heavy midnight rains can swamp such craft if they lack self-bailing capability or if you failed to snap on a cockpit cover.

And small outboards used in occasionally rough seas should have motor wells, even if they are self-bailing. Otherwise a sea can slop over the transom, leaving you up to your ankles in water. Lacking that splashboard protection can even mean swamping. "Dump ports" are also helpful. You find them on some boats. Take green water aboard, and you get rid of it by hitting the throttle. The water surges aft, and by its own weight opens a port in the well, flowing out to sea quickly. It's a small-boat adaption of a big sportfisherman trick, where skippers use the transom door—ordinarily installed for boating large gamefish—to spill a flood of water overboard.

Ask the salesman how the deck unit is secured to the hull. If just bolted, you can expect occasional sheets of water to spurt in between deck and hull as you plunge in a sea or across a wake. There should be adequate bonding, perhaps with fiberglass; or any one of a number of methods that assure integrity here.

Another point to check is stowage, and you don't have to be an expert to see that Boat A has far more places to put things than comparably sized Boat B. On small boats look for dry lockers; on open boats look for hatches protected by coamings or guttering that drains overside. Such lockers can be dry. And the boat that has them doesn't cost much more than a boat that doesn't.

Another way to compare Boat A with Boat B is to check the fuel and (on larger craft) water tank capacities. Nothing proves so dismal as short cruising range and constantly halting at fuel docks; or continually running out of fresh water. Again, the cost differential may not be great between two similar boats, yet one is obviously superior to the other.

Always check a boat's list of standard equipment against a competing make. Some builders include many items as standard that are options on another offering. The first boat may seem more expensive, but can be a bargain in the long run.

When it comes to accessories and options, don't be afraid to dicker. It is still a wheel-and-deal world, perhaps more so these days. To sweeten a sale and clinch it, they may discount accessories or options substantially below the list price.

According to Wynne, before you sign any dotted lines, the final step is to arrange a demonstration ride—and not just in one boat. Try several boats, he suggests, so you can compare them, and how they ride; how wet one boat may be, or dry; how hard or soft the ride may be in a chop.

"See how hard it is to get on a plane," he said. "Put a couple of people in the back of the boat. Take some friends with you, so you simulate the load you would normally have. Will the boat get on a plane easily, or will it mush along, bow high in the air, before getting on plane?"

Pick a choppy day or find the wakes from passing boats. "Going out on a flat, calm day," says Wynne, "is not going to tell you much at all. There is a tremendous difference in hull designs, and the ultimate means of evaluating a boat is to go out and try it."

SEX AND THE SINGLE BOATMAN

By Martin Levin

january

It is the dead of winter and young men's fancies are being turned on again by the boating industry.

Hardly a marine product is on the market that is not being hustled by pictures of sex objects in bikinis. In the lush multicolored ads in the glossy boating magazines, stunning manikins pose alongside outboard motors or are seen loafing languidly aboard craft of all sizes—in the bucket seats of runabouts, in the cockpits of cruisers and damn near anywhere else.

The idea here is, women are good to have on boats and that time can be made with women on boats. If that's what you have in mind when shopping for a boat—forget it. Unless, that is, you plan to have a professional crew aboard to handle all details except the loving.

Take your typical ad for a cabin cruiser. It shows a boat anchored in tropic waters at sunset, while the skipper and his lady enjoy a frosted drink on deck. That's how it is in the ad.

In real life, the skipper has just finished dropping the hook, and his hands are covered with slime. He wipes them on a rag and gets two beers from the cooler. As he and his friend are taking their first sip—there is a funny vibration felt along the hull. The anchor is dragging!

Half an hour and a few buckets of slime later, the anchor is set, and the skipper and his L. F. finish two cans of warm beer. He puts his arm around her and looks deeply into her eyes, as she says,

"Do you smell gasoline?"

By the time he has found the source of his trouble or gone in search of a mechanic, the chemistry has been altered by infusions of adrenalin caused by fear.

You may think that this experience is untypical. Okay, let's take a more ideal situation. The boat is properly moored and there is no engine funny business. Ever try to make out on the V-bunks in the bow of a boat? If you have taken contortion training on a bed of nails, you may like this kind of thing.

The other possibility on most cruisers under 40 feet is the dinette. This makes up into a bed. Yes, after you clear the dinette of food, fishing tackle, shopping bags, duffle bags and the garbage underneath and then lever it into place, sliding the seat and the back cushions together.

All this time, she has been watching you and wondering what the hell you're doing. Planned Parenthood is wasting a lot of time; they should promote boating.

Don't get me wrong. I am not saying that women have no place on a boat. What I am saying is that women are not just playthings on a boat. Ashore, a red-blooded male looks at a female's legs with admiration. Afloat, a skipper looks at a girl's legs to see if she's wearing sneakers.

Look at any pair of singles on a boat tied up at a marina. Chances are the woman is sitting in a captain's chair, reading a magazine and the guy is haring all over the boat, swabbing it down, checking bilges and gas gauges, buffing the fiber glass, filling the water tank, reading charts, getting a weather advisory.

What's a woman to do? Well, for one thing, she can look in the cruising guide for a convenient motel.

WHAT KIND OF DRIVE FOR YOUR BOAT?

By W. A. Connor

january

A potential powerboat buyer—whether he's looking for a runabout or a cabin cruiser—faces a bewildering array of engine choices and drive options. If the buyer has some background experience in various hulls and drive options, the selection of the most appropriate drive is relatively easy, providing he visualizes the conditions under which he will be operating his new craft. On the other hand, if he has no prior experience in boating, the choice of the best drive for his particular hull becomes a real problem and, considering the number of options available, the odds are against his picking the right one.

The most appropriate drive will depend to some extent on the size of boat being considered, so the following observations start with small powerboats and progress to the largest cruisers.

Single Outboard Drive

A single outboard drive is almost universal for smaller hulls—skiffs, runabouts, and smaller cruisers. For this class of boat, the outboard provides the ultimate in flexibility and the maximum in maneuverability, at the least first cost.

Notwithstanding these advantages, most outboards now on the market are two-cycle engines that have inherent shortcomings not yet overcome by the excellent engineering of the outboard manufacturers. These engines must be lubricated by oil added to the fuel, because the operating cycle does not permit the use of an oil-filled crankcase or sump. The oil-fuel mixture does an excellent job of lubricating the engine, but some of it accumulates on spark plugs and a lot of oil escapes out the exhaust. As a result, spark plugs foul up with carbon and the engine produces some air and water pollution. Also, because the two-cycle system is less efficient than the four-cycle, most outboards are relatively heavy fuel consumers.

The four-cycle outboard seems to offer a more efficient means of small-boat propulsion because fuel and oil consumption is significantly lower, spark plugs seldom foul and only a small amount of oil escapes out the exhaust. However, four-cycle engines are more complicated mechanically and therefore cost more.

Considering the advantages of the four-cycle type, it might be worthwhile to make the following comparison of the two types before buying: Estimate the annual fuel and oil cost by multiplying the total hours of operating time by the predicted hourly fuel consumption of the engine; multiply the result by the per-gallon cost of fuel. Then do the same for a two-cycle outboard, remembering to add in the cost of oil. Subtract the estimated annual fuel and oil cost of operating a four-cycle outboard from the cost of operating a two-cycle engine—the difference is the annual return of the extra investment required by the four-cycle.

While the single outboard drive is the best option for most boats up to about 25 feet, this leaves a lot to be desired if you are considering a houseboat. These big craft present a relatively large, flat area to wind from almost any direction and because of this, and their big pontoons or large and relatively flat hull form, they are tough boats to maneuver in close quarters. Even when they are under way, a beam wind can present a steering problem. As a matter of fact, a houseboat with a single outboard drive can find itself "in irons" as the old saying goes. It is practically

gives the skipper much more assurance on long runs in open water. While two engines also multiply potential engine troubles, the likelihood of both engines failing at once is quite remote. So the skipper is pretty sure of getting where he is headed. A second engine adds practically nothing in the way of slow-speed maneuverability, however, unless the boat is quite large.

Twin outboards on skiffs or runabouts look like too much of a good thing unless the boats are used for racing. The second engine adds a lot of weight to the hull and the two engines will burn appreciably more fuel than a single one with equivalent total power. The combination of two engines will give a lower center of gravity than a big single, but it is doubtful that this will make an appreciable difference in the boat's stability. Probably the only advantage of twins is when pulling up water skiers, because in coming up to speed, the twins will deliver more thrust. Even so, it's doubtful that the time saved justifies the extra expense of twins.

One Inboard Engine— Direct Drive

Most stock cabin cruisers up to 30′ offer a single inboard engine with direct drive as the lowest-cost option. A new boat buyer may not know that this drive option has a shortcoming which is quite pronounced when maneuvering at slow speed, particularly if there is wind.

A typical current model single-engined, direct-drive cruiser has a relatively light hull. The light hull, combined with an engine of a couple of hundred horsepower, means it is a fast combination. On this account, the rudder will likely be quite small and while adequate for speeds above, say, five mph, will definitely be too small for quick response at slow maneuvering speeds. This will become uncomfortably evident to a green skipper when he first attempts to dock the boat, for example. He will certainly get a rude shock if there is a wind, because wind compounds the problem enormously and can lead to great embarrassment, if not some damage. The fact is, of course, that rudder control becomes more sluggish as speed drops—and the smaller the rudder the more marked is this effect. The same applies to going astern; actually, steering capability is practically nil when backing up.

the same situation as square-riggers faced in the last century when they were unable either to come about or fill away. A houseboat with a single outboard is particularly susceptible to the condition if it is underpowered.

In calm weather, the single-engined houseboat usually tends to steer to one side, which must be countered by applying opposite helm. When a beam wind adds to this effect, the extra helm needed increases hull resistance and slows the boat. If wind velocity increases sufficiently, the skipper can find himself with the helm hard over to counter it and the boat almost dead in the water. He then has only two choices: hang there in irons until all his gas is burned up, or turn and go with the wind.

One or two experiences of this type will convince even the most stubborn skipper that an outboard-propelled houseboat cannot have too much power and that two outboards are far better than one.

Twin Outboard Drive

Twin outboards are quite common on larger outboard cruisers because the second engine

All this means that the skipper of a single-engine, direct-drive boat must be fully aware of the limitations imposed by that drive and take all these into consideration before maneuvering at slow speed. Generally, it is best to keep forward motion as long as possible so as to maintain steerageway until the last minute. Skippers of single-engine, direct drive boats must be considerably more skillful than their counterparts with other drives.

Twin Inboards—Direct Drive

Twin engines usually mean that the boat's skipper does not consider first cost and running cost too important. Twins give the boat more speed and maneuverability, and much higher fuel consumption.

Twin engines make slow-speed maneuvering a pleasure; the craft can be turned around almost in her own length, even when dead in the water. Positive control is maintained down to dead slow by forgetting the rudder at speeds below about five mph and using engine throttles and gearshifts for steering. Usually the skipper will use just the throttles down to about three mph and the shifts alone for slower speeds—with his throttles at idle. Some skill is needed to do the thing right, but the demands on the skipper are far less than when operating a single-engine craft.

Twin engines do, however, introduce the need to synchronize engine speeds so as to avoid pulsing vibrations in the boat and irritating exhaust beats between the two exhaust systems. Synchronizing engines used to be a problem, but the advent of tachometers and synchronizers has solved this.

Direct-drive boats, both single- or twin-engined, share a common problem: vibration in the boat at all speeds, but particularly at higher ones. The direct drive means that the propeller speed is the same as that of the engine and this makes for a fair degree of vibration in the boat, which can be annoying on long runs. Modern inboard engines have a performance peak in the upper rpm range; therefore, a fairly high speed is needed in a direct-drive boat to get the best out of the engines and usually this is undesirable because of vibration.

Reduction Gears

Reduction gears permit engine speeds in the maximum efficiency range—that is, relatively high—while propeller speed stays fairly low. The low-speed wheels on reduction-gear boats are therefore quite a bit larger in diameter than the propellers on direct-drive boats. For example, a reduction-gear boat with a gear ratio of 2:1 (which is common), will have wheels about twice the diameter of the propellers on a direct-drive boat with the same power.

The difference in vibration between the two drives is almost as striking—vibration at speed in the reduction-gear boat will be only a fraction of what it is in the direct-drive boat. In fact, the skipper of a reduction-drive craft will feel something like the pilot of a 747 jet, while the skipper of a direct-drive boat will feel like the pilot of a 1950-model, piston-engine, propeller-driven airplane.

Fuel consumption is also lower with reduction gears, despite friction losses in the gear box, and control of the boat at very low speeds is much more positive than with direct drive. The big wheels on the reduction-drive boats retain their grip on the water right down to nearly dead slow, and very slow-speed maneuvering is easy. The same system of maintaining low-speed control is used with reduction-gear craft as with direct-drive twins.

The combination of more efficient engine speeds and larger, slower-turning propellers with low slip and better grip on the water suggest that reduction gears should be given serious consideration when buying larger boats. Usually the extra cost of reduction gears is justified by improved performance and operating economy.

One more point should be noted in connection with twin inboard engines: Their propellers should be counter-rotating. Even a single engine produces some turning effect that must be countered by the rudder. Twin engines rotating in the same direction produce twice as much turning effect, of course, and that's too much. Counter-rotating engines and propellers neutralize the turning effect so the boat will stay on a straight course with helm amidships. Thus, counter-rotation of twin inboard drives is worth the extra cost.

Inboard-Outboard or Sterndrive

The sterndrive option is a godsend to skippers of single-engined boats because it eliminates all the disadvantages of a direct drive. With a sterndrive, the propeller housing and propeller turn together with the helm. There is no separate rudder in the usual sense and propeller thrust does most of the steering. The sterndrive permits the boat to be swung while dead in the water; this is sometimes a very handy feature. The sterndrive also gives some reduction in speed between engine and propeller and, as already described, this is a very fine feature because it reduces vibration in the boat.

A boat with two sterndrives will not be significantly more maneuverable than a boat with one, but it will of course, have more power and speed. As is the case with any twin installation, they should preferably be counter-rotating.

Twin sterndrives will not likely match twin inboards with reduction gears in the matter of vibration because you can buy a greater reduction ratio for the latter option. Consequently, for equal horsepower in similar hulls, the inboard reduction gear option will have greater fuel economy than the sterndrive. A careful buyer might find the higher cost of the inboard hull with its longer shafts, stuffing boxes, and rudders justified by greater fuel economy and lower vibration level when under way at speed.

A Caution about Single Engines

All boats—outboard, inboard, and sterndrive—share a common feature which is worth noting. This is the fact that the engine not only propels the boat but also provides the brake. Sometimes the importance of the engine as a brake is overlooked, as the following example makes clear.

The boat in question was an elderly 37′ cruiser of some 11 tons, with a single-engine, direct drive. This skipper did not know the boat, because he had taken her over only two days before and was therefore ignorant of the idiosyncrasies of both hull and engine. He followed another cruiser into a canal lock. The other cruiser, a gleaming new boat with a brand-new

fiberglass dinghy slung on davits across the stern, was stopped and secured to the lock wall, ready for the lift. Her proud owner was standing on his fancy command bridge, watching the old boat approach.

The skipper of the older boat was being very cagey. He was entering his first lock, so his speed was dead slow. He carefully lined up the bow of the old boat with the lock wall, pulled the manual shift to neutral, and let the old boat slide silently towards the gleaming new cruiser. At that point his 11 tons of boat was gliding through the water at about one mph.

At the appropriate time—about 20 feet from the stern of the new cruiser—the skipper of the old boat pushed his big manual shift lever into reverse, with the old engine idling. The engine promptly stalled out and refused to restart! Meanwhile, 11 tons of old boat continued ghosting forward, bow aimed dead center at the new fiberglass dinghy hanging across the transom of the new boat. Finally, the bow of the old boat and the side of the dinghy met and the little boat bent in under the impact. At first it seemed that the dinghy would split along her keel, but the dink slowed the big boat to a stop, then pushed her back as the dinghy returned to her original shape.

In the end there were only some scratches to mark the affair and a very clear moral: In a single-engined boat, make sure the engine will take a quick reverse when it's idling. If not, raise the idling speed so the shock of a sudden reverse won't stall it.

A Caution about All Drives

Once upon a time, almost all powerboats had skegs that protected propellers and skippers therefore didn't need to be particularly concerned about underwater obstructions. The skegs were usually quite substantial and the average powerboat could be driven up on a beach without much damage because the skeg functioned like a steel-shod ski. Those carefree times are long gone and today's propellers are now right out in the open—waiting, as it were, to hit something. In most cases the propeller is just about the most vulnerable part of the craft and invariably when a propeller hits something, damage results, usually costly.

Outboards and sterndrives tip up when they hit something solid and it might at first seem that they avoid damage this way, but actually they do so only if speed is quite low and they strike soft sand. If they strike a deadhead or a rock, the propeller shaft and gear housing may fracture even if the propeller escapes damage. Actually, the assembly will survive striking a hard object unscathed only if speed is quite low. The best that can be said is that with tip-up drives, the hull of the boat will not likely be damaged.

The same cannot be said about inboard drives of any type. Striking a hard underwater object with propeller or shaft can cause very serious damage; in fact, this can sink a boat, though the object never touches the hull. If this seems impossible, read on.

The accident happened in a well-buoyed channel meandering between rocks. The boat, a 40-footer with twin engines and reduction gears, was proceeding up the channel at a moderate speed of possibly six mph. At one point the channel took a 90-degree turn, where the neophyte at the wheel misread the tall marker at the heel of the turn, failed to consult the chart, and took a short-cut across the bend towards the next two stick markers in the channel.

He was barely into the short-cut when one propeller hit a rock. The impact drove the propeller back against its rudder, which promptly bent up the back like the screw and cut right through the transom of the boat. The propeller pulled the shaft with it, out of the reverse gear coupling and out of the stuffing box. At the same time, as the wheel and shaft were driven back, the boat rode up on the rock so that the shaft and shaft strut took the boat's weight. The load on the strut pushed the strut pad up through the bottom of the boat. Thus, when the hatches were pulled up to assess damage, the boat was well on her way to the bottom.

Fortunately the channel wasn't wide and a smooth shelving rock was nearby. Also, one engine and its drive were still intact, and were used to drive the boat up on the shelving rock where she canted over about one-third full of water. Later, the holes were plugged by a diver, she was pumped out, and towed to the nearest boatyard.

The moral is that whatever drive you choose, it is still a very vulnerable part of the boat and that the best protection against damage from underwater objects is frequent reference to a dependable chart and a constant awareness that submerged objects are very dangerous.

UNDERSTANDING JET DRIVES

By Jim Wright

january

Pity the jet drive: born in New Zealand, taken to the U.S. while still in infancy and raised amid a bunch of hot-rodding Californians, people so adrift from the mainstream of boating they think Power Squadrons can be found only in Orange County.

Before long, the jet got stereotyped as a high-performance drive—it could rocket drag boats out of the hole as if shot from cannons, it could pull a brace of skiers with ease, but would you want your daughter to own one?

The jet drive has come of age now and, alas, all it wants is to be understood and accepted. If its growing sophistication and popularity give any indication, it's well on the way. In 1964 there were only 4000 jets around; last year the number passed 100,000. Some 200 boatbuilders now install jets on their products' sterns, from runabouts to bass boats, from center consoles to houseboats.

For all the attention paid it, a jet drive is essentially a simple beast. At its heart is a pump, not unlike the common agricultural irrigation pump, driven by a conventional inboard engine. The pump takes water through an intake in the keel and pushes it much faster by means of an enclosed impeller out a steerable nozzle mounted on the boat's stern. Enter Newton's Third Law—for every action there is an opposite and equal reaction—and the force of the water thrust out the nozzle pushes the boat forward.

Jet drives have a space-age name, but the principle behind them has knocked around for centuries. In 1730, for example, a doctor named John Allen experimented with an 11-inch model boat that had a small cylindrical tank of water that could be pumped out the stern, creating a forward speed of $1/5$ mph. On a larger scale, inventor James Rumsey successfully demonstrated a steam-powered, water-jet-propelled boat on the Potomac River in 1784 and 1787. It traveled 4 mph against the current.

Just prior to the turn of this century, the British used jet drives on several of their gunboats. A few years later, Germany, Italy, Russia, New Zealand and the U.S. tried jets also, but poor efficiency ultimately made them abandon their efforts.

A turning point came in 1953 when New Zealand sheep farmer William Hamilton devised a jet pump for a boat to navigate the shallow, rocky whitewater rivers of the high country. He started selling them two years later, but it wasn't until 1960 that his unit gained wide-spread attention. That year Hamilton's son Jon in *Kiwi,* a test boat powered by four jet drives, tackled the Colorado River through the Grand Canyon, first running downstream then turning around for a nine-day thrash up the 350 miles of rapids to become the first man to conquer the Colorado.

1960 also marked Berkeley Pump Co.'s entry into the marine jet market. Berkeley engineers saw a jet boat at the San Francisco Boat Show and decided they could build a better one based on a standard Berkeley deepwell turbine impeller. On its first test run, it pushed a 15-foot plywood hull at 40 mph. In 1962, Jacuzzi, another commercial pump manufacturer, entered the market, and these two companies have sold 95 percent of all marine jets now in use. More recently, Chrysler, Mercury, Turbo-Marine, Drake, Castoldi and Panther have introduced units in the U.S.

What's the fuss? Because of its design simplicity, the jet offers certain advantages over the

I/O, its main competition for boating dollars. First, since the entire jet unit is enclosed and above the keel line, it offers an added safety factor. There's no exposed prop to endanger swimmers, divers or skiers or chew up anchor lines, fishing lines or tow lines.

The jet is the ideal shallow-water drive. You can go anywhere the hull floats and, with a little prudence, not worry about submerged rocks, weeds or stumps because there's no shear pin to shear, no prop to mangle or lower unit to crunch. Likewise, beaching, launching, retrieving and trailering are a cinch because there are no appendages to get in the way.

The jet is also a low-maintenance unit. Most jets have no gearbox or clutch to contend with, and there are few moving parts—basically just the nozzle, the impeller and its shaft, which is usually connected to the engine by a U-joint. The impeller moves in only one direction since reverse is a redirection of thrust outside the boat (a hood-like device called a deflector descends over the nozzle and redirects water flow downward and forward). This reversing method also acts as an effective brake at high speeds.

Maneuverability is another jet hallmark. The nozzle steering allows jet boats to turn 180 degrees in a little more than their own lengths since there is no rudder or strut drag.

Finally, jets have rapid straight-line acceleration, which makes them ski boats *non pareil*. Most jets have an enclosed direct-drive system (the impeller is inside a bowl) and acceleration is torque-free and directly proportional to rpm. A jet will beat an equally matched I/O in a drag race any day.

With all this going for it, you'd think the jet would send the I/O manufacturers packing, but the fact is I/Os are seven times as popular as jets. A major reason is that the jet drive has not yet overcome the uneven reputation created by the fledgling jets of the '60s, and a rash of misconceptions held by prop-oriented boatmen still abound.

Like scotch, jet drives are an acquired taste. If the only powerboats you've driven have props, the initial switch to jets is a substantial one. The first time I drove a jet was a hasty affair, 20 minutes behind the wheel during a press demonstration with little supervision. The results were far from satisfactory. Leaving the dock at no-wake speed, the boat handled like a bumper car at an amusement arcade, moving willynilly toward the open water on an unintentional slalom course. The thing drove me crazy.

With this for a background, I dared the brain trust at Berkeley Pump Co. in Berkeley, Cal., to teach me how to drive a jet properly. It took them 45 minutes. Last November Berkeley's Robert Donelson and Clyde Holloway and I trailered a 20-foot Sea Ray SRV 200 deep V with a Berkeley 12JC pump teamed with a 460-cubic-inch Ford marine inboard up the Sacramento River Delta to Walnut Grove, a small general-store/diner/marina set-up in the heart of the delta.

Launching the Sea Ray was easy enough. We just backed the trailer down the ramp until the intake was submerged, Clyde gave the throttle a shot in reverse and the boat slid into the water.

Once we were out of the marina, I took the wheel and, lo and behold, I felt like I was back in a bumper car. I was instructed to keep the tach

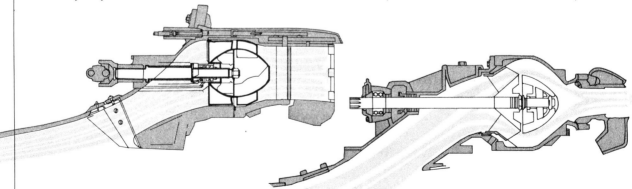

The two most widely used pump designs are the axial flow (left) and the mixed flow (right). The axial flow pump, with its larger intake and nozzle, pumps a large volume of water straight through the pump at lower velocity. The mixed-flow pump pushes the water axially and centrifugally (outward) from the shaft. With its smaller intake and nozzle, the mixed-flow pump moves less water at higher velocities.

around 1500 rpm and pick a point on shore in the distance and head for it, trying to anticipate any swing in the bow and compensate for it before the swing actually occurred. I did a heck of a lot of steering those first few minutes, but I found afterwhile that if I really concentrated I could anticipate with a minimal amount of wheel work. I'm told that once you drive a jet a few times, it becomes second-nature—steering a jet at low speeds is certainly no big deal, but at first it seems, well, *mushy*.

Understanding why a jet handles the way it does at low speeds is also helpful. A jet hull has no underwater appendages to give it complete directional stability at low rpm, and the thrust from the jet on a 20-foot hull at displacement speeds is minute compared to friction. Hence, it helps to run the boat at slightly higher rpm than you would with an I/O to keep the boat straight.

At planing speeds, the Sea Ray handled like a sports car for me immediately, with very positive steering and excellent control. (Clyde compares it to turnpike driving.) One trick I picked up quickly is to maintain rpm even in the sharpest turns. My first reaction going into a corner too fast was to get off the throttle, but like on a sports car you lose some control if you decelerate through a turn. Moments later, running at 2800 rpm, I shoved the throttle abruptly into reverse and the boat stopped neatly with zero spray and no gears to grind.

As we headed up Snodgrass Slough (pronounced *slew*) and I got accustomed to how the Sea Ray handled, I finally got a chance to check out the scenery along the delta, a 1000-mile maze of winding sloughs and slender rivers. The area is almost a California everglades, with miles of fertile farmland stretching beyond the shrubs, willows and blackberry bushes that cluster along the waterway's steep banks.

After we stopped for lunch at Terminous, another way station for boatmen along the delta, I tried a maneuver unique to jet drives called walking a boat, ideal for negotiating close quarters or docking in a tight space. With a great deal of coaching and a few false starts, I gradually developed a coordinated procedure for moving the hull from ten yards off the dock to the pilings with a minimum of forward movement. With the dock directly to starboard and the engine in idle, I turned the wheel hard right and gave the throttle a quick burst into forward,

swinging the bow dockward. Without hesitating, I then put the wheel over hard to port and gave the throttle a spurt in reverse, which spun the stern toward the dock. After repeating the procedure four times, the hull nestled nicely against the dock.

You can walk a jet because power can be applied instantly in forward and then shifted immediately into reverse since there are no gears to grind. You can't walk an I/O-powered boat because the lower unit prevents the stern from sliding sideways.

As the afternoon wound down, I tried other nifty jet maneuvers. I looked for some rapids to run, à la Hamilton, but had to settle for such tricks as running the Sea Ray up on a strand of beach and driving over submerged logs without lifting an outdrive or mangling a shaft. After we put the boat back on its trailer and headed back to Berkeley, I couldn't help but come away liking the jet drive immensely. I had finally acquired a taste for the jet, and maybe next time I'll be able to try it over the rocks.

Jets have been a long time coming, considering the first modern-day models appeared in the U.S. about the same time as I/Os. Jet sales didn't really surge until 1969, when I/Os were in short supply and, more important, engineers started to assess hull designs with the jet in mind. When they found that the jet was compatible with a lot more hull types than just the California ski boats, particularly deep Vs and trihulls, the jet sweepstakes was on. Sales have jumped 30 percent annually since 1969.

Though jets are compatible with several planing hulls, slight changes in hull design are the key to efficiency. Most hulls are designed to run with props. The center of thrust is therefore below the boat, making it high by the bow and reducing wetted surface at planing speeds. With a jet unit *inside* the hull, the line of thrust is higher, which puts a prop-oriented boat's bow down and increases drag. When a jet drive is thrown in an average boat, it often doesn't reach the efficiency it's capable of.

Jet engineers have found that if the bottom lines of a hull are rocked up more in the transom and have slightly more bow rise, the boat will maintain a planing angle that's more efficient for a jet. Many boatbuilders employing jets—Glastron, Fabuglas and many California ski-boat builders, for instance—have designed hulls especially for the jet drive.

A jet is only as good as its hull, and designers say that only 50 percent of all powerboat hulls between 16 and 24 feet are adequate for the jet. Boats with deep forefoots, for example, are frowned upon because they have a tendency to hook in turns when jets are employed. Similarly, the hull bottom should have no hooks or wedges aft to affect the angle of plane.

Many jet designers contend that the deep V is the ideal hull for the jet drive. The deep V offers less chance of aeration, puts the intake deep enough in the water to prime the pump at idle, and has longitudinal strakes to improve handling in turns. Flat bottoms are a cardinal sin.

Designing an efficient jet is as exact a science as watchmaking. The intake, the impeller and the nozzle make a jet tick, and the slightest change in one of them can alter efficiency drastically. One manufacturer who had trouble with handling characteristics of one of his jets shaved ⅜ of an inch off the intake ramp and the jet ran great. Engineering over the past decade has improved the jet's lot by perfecting the size and shape of the drive's innards.

Since jet performance can vary so significantly from hull to hull and from drive to drive, it's tough to make accurate comparisons with an I/O, but most manufacturers concede that the I/O is slightly more efficient. Chrysler and OMC, who offer both jet and I/O packages, have run tests using identical hulls and engines that give the I/O better marks for gas consumption, particularly at the mid-range speeds, 25 to 40 mph. Top speed and upper-end fuel consumption were almost identical; the I/O required less horsepower to get up on plane; and the jet could plane with more passengers aboard and out-accelerate the I/O.

Another problem with jets is the confusion generated by the variety of methods manufacturers employ to pump the water. Jet theory may be simple, but in practice it has more variations than a pro football defense. The simplest method is the single-stage axial-flow pump (built by Chrysler, Hamilton and Castoldi). A solitary impeller—Castoldi dubs it a propeller in a tube—forces the water picked up by the intake into a path almost parallel to the impeller axis and pumps it past a stator, which takes the swirl out of the stream of water to make it flow straight out the nozzle. To match impeller rpm to different engines' power and rpm, the single-stage axial-flow pumps employ either a gearbox (Castoldi), or the units are designed around specific engines (Chrysler).

Multiple-stage axial-flow pumps (Turbo-Marine, Hamilton) work much the same way as their single-stage cousins, but employ two or three impellers and stators to boost pressure (and thus speed) and accommodate the varying horsepower inputs of a range of larger engines. Generally, axial-flow pumps push a large volume of water straight through the impeller at low speeds.

Another type is the radial (or centrifugal) pump, which takes water from the intake and forces it outward at almost 90 degrees to the shaft as it goes through the impeller. Flow is then redirected 90 degrees as it goes through the stator and straight out the nozzle. The centrifugal force created by churning the water outward creates high velocity, but so much efficiency is lost by routing and rerouting the water through the unit that no jet-drive manufacturers use this method solely.

The last and by far the most popular design is the single-stage mixed-flow pump, a cross between radial and axial-flow designs (Berkeley, Jacuzzi, Mercury, Drake and Panther). When water enters the impeller, it is pushed through the pump both centrifugally and axially, enabling the pump to move a lower volume of water at extremely high speeds, making it ideal for high-speed planing hulls.

The future of the jet seems solid. It will never replace the I/O, not by a long shot—the jet will never be quite as economical and isn't suitable for as wide a range of boats. There will, however, be a lot more jets on the water in the next couple of years. The East Coast market is virtually untapped, more boatbuilders are designing their craft around the jet unit, and jet manufacturers are now working on jet drives for the lower-horsepower ranges. And now that they're understood, who knows. . . ?

WHAT TO LOOK FOR

In most cases when you shop for a jet, it is part of an entire new-boat package, so your decision as to which jet to buy is often tempered by the hull you choose, but there are certain features to check before you buy.

The Hull. The most important aspect of the jet is how well-suited it is for the hull. Generally, high-performance jets run best in planing hulls up to 24 feet long and 3500 pounds with single installations, up to 28 feet and 6500 pounds with twins. Twin installations are rare because the jet is basically a trailer drive—corrosion and marine growths can hurt performance when the boat is left in the water.

Theoretically, jet manufacturers take care when they agree to sell their unit with various hulls to ensure that the drive will perform well in each hull, but make sure you go for a test ride and talk to owners of similar boats to avoid problems later. When you go for a test ride, here's what to check: How easy is the steering and shifting? How well does the unit run in reverse? Is the water flowing evenly through the jet? If you hear a gravelly sound, it means there's cavitation.

The Engine. Inboard match-ups have been fairly well determined by the jet builders, with each pump designed for a specific horsepower range. Companies such as Mercury, Chrysler and Berkeley often sell the engine and jet as a single unit. Engine manufacturers Waukesha, Hardin and OMC sell inboards matched with Jacuzzi pumps.

The Impeller. Most pump manufacturers offer a variety of impellers with each jet model, with graphs charting each impeller's performance in relation to engine horsepower and rpm to simplify selection. If you run mostly in salt water, jet drives with stainless steel impellers have a slight edge over aluminum-alloy ones.

The Unit. Here are some items worth checking: Repairability and maintenance—is the unit easy to lubricate and easily accessible for repairs? In the event weeds or other substances get sucked into the impeller, can you remove them easily by taking off the hand-hole cover? Is the hand hole above the waterline? If it isn't, hand-hole extensions are readily available. A good boat should have an extension if the hand hole isn't above the waterline, otherwise you'll take on water every time you clean out the impeller bowl. Is the intake adapter flush with the hull? If it isn't the drive will run rough. Check both the intake and transom adapters to see if they're properly sealed and the workmanship is good.

The Price. As a rule, jet-drive packages are quite competitive with equivalent I/Os, sometimes offering more horsepower for the same money. Things to look for when comparing prices of jets is to weigh standard equipment versus options—features such as jet trim (especially nice for skiing), rudders (helpful for displacement-speed handling and trolling) and weed grates (to cut down impeller debris). One final item to compare is the warranty—how long is it and what does it cover?

Decisions, decisions

FEBRUARY

If you have a boat and have put it to bed for the winter, the Displacement Principle (see page 3) is still working for you. With a boat, out of sight is never out of mind. A gale wind has just blown the roof off a string of newly built houses adjoining your marina. (You call the boatyard office and of course there is no answer.) Subnormal temperatures have iced up the entire creek where you are in wet storage. (A fellow member tells you that the ice is crushing the piers and pilings. No, he did not happen to notice how your boat was faring.) You drive out on a nasty Saturday morning to inspect your boat. It's okay! But what about next week?

If you are shopping for a boat, February is a month full of sunshine, whatever the weather bureau says. This is when you make the transition from boat show to showroom. It's a heady experience that should be tempered with caution, because a wrong first boat can be dampening.

Ideally, you will have had a demonstration ride in the boat of your choice in the past summer. Barring that, you should have spoken to yachtsmen who have had some experience with the make of your choice. You should have also checked the yachting magazines for boat tests that may have covered it. In any event, you can always make a deal contingent on a demonstration ride in a similar boat as soon as weather permits.

Once you make up your mind, and agree on the basic price and financing (see "How to Get Boat Financing" by W. A. Knegendorf, page 31), there's the matter of "optional equipment." As Joe Gregory pointed out in January, optional equipment can include anything but the hull and power plant. But most cruisers over 24 feet will include a reasonable number of basics such as a dinette, galley and minimal safety equipment. Extras generally fall into two categories: comforts of home and needs afloat.

In the first category, you will find everything from water pressure system, which many two-armed people can't do without, to an electric ice-making machine. Needs afloat include:

BOW RAIL AND TAFFRAIL

Usually, you'll be considering a longer one than the one that comes with the boat. Think of your probable passenger list. Picture each person aboard and the likely and unlikely situations they may be getting themselves into. Especially if you're expecting some very young or elderly passengers.

BILGE PUMP

Most boats come with one electric bilge pump. An extra bilge pump is an excellent idea, installed where the original pump isn't. A pump at the stern will exhaust water from the bilges better when the boat is under way than when it is lying dead in the water. A pump in the forward section will not work too well when the boat is on plane. And if you want to be prudent, one of your bilge pumps will be manual, so that it will work even if your batteries don't.

BILGE BLOWER

This is an exhaust fan in the event gasoline fumes accumulate in the bilges. If your engine hatches are located beneath the cockpit sole, opening the hatches to ventilate the bilges will do quite well.

MUFFLERS

Mufflers reduce noise. They also may reduce engine efficiency by causing back pressure.

EXTRA BATTERY WITH VAPORPROOF SWITCH

Absolutely.

ZINCS

Zinc anodes, attached adjacent to your rudder and propeller shaft, will prevent disintegration due to galvanic action. The zinc plates divert the electrolysis by sacrificing themselves instead.

SPRINGLINE CLEATS

These are the cleats that you will find on deck, amidships. You can't tie in to a dockside slip properly without them.

SEACOCKS AND GATE VALVES

Every through-hull fitting should ideally come with seacocks, lever-operated valves with bronze ground seats. If not seacocks, the through-hull fittings (raw-water pump intake, head intake and outlet, etc.) should have gate valves, which operate like a water faucet. Gate valves are not as foolproof as seacocks because the thread can fail, especially if it is a zinc alloy and the zinc leaches out. If your boat is not already equipped with one or the other, see whether this safety device is offered as an extra.

TWIN ENGINES

Before deciding, read the upcoming advice by Jerry Hart, "The Case For the Single Screw."

You find in the month of February the Displacement Principle operating at near capacity, even before you buy your boat. Mufflers? Pressure water? What, no gate valves? How can you think of anything else?

HOW TO GET BOAT FINANCING

By W. A. Knegendorf

february

Ken Myers leaned back in the driver's seat, caught a glimpse of his wife Sandy's smile of approval, and felt the tension from three months of searching slowly drain from his body. Driving all over the Great Lakes area looking for their "dream boat" had worn them both out. Financing had never been a key factor since Ken had just sold his interest in a clothing store and assumed they would pay cash. But Sandy did not like the idea of putting all their savings into a boat. She convinced Ken to investigate the cost of a loan.

Ken talked to his friend at the bank and received an $18,000 commitment for a personal loan for five years at a 12% interest rate. Another friend recommended he check with the lender used by several marine dealers. This source offered a seven-year loan at an 11.5% rate. Shopping around paid off. Not only did the Myerses find a loan easy to obtain, but they received terms that freed their savings and were acceptable to their situation.

If you are like the majority of Americans today, you too will finance a portion of your boat's purchase price. Comparison shopping has led you to the boat best suited to your needs, but comparing financing programs may prove even more rewarding in the long run. As Tom Bruton, the boat specialist at the Bank of America in San Francisco, emphasizes, "Shop and compare just as you do for a car or clothes. There is no standardization of rates."

An effective comparison of lending programs begins with an understanding of certain basic lending terminology. Money is available from many different sources and, as you consider each, be prepared for contradiction, inconsistencies and puzzling statements.

All lenders are interested in the same basic information: stability of situation and ability to repay. All lenders will check your credit references, credit bureau and their own records, so if you are behind in any existing obligation, bring it up-to-date before applying for additional financing.

A few minutes spent in preparation for a meeting with a lender may help greatly. Have facts and figures about the boat and both your boating and credit experience ready. Offer information rather than just reply to questions. While most lenders have done some marine financing, you might be better off seeking one with a "marine specialist" who has years of experience in both lending and boating. The guidance and assistance such an individual will give is a bonus to the boat buyer.

A lender may make a loan on an older boat at the same rates and terms as on a new boat. He will take into account quality, material, design, maintenance and equipment. The age, type and condition of machinery are extremely important on powerboats. Sail inventory, hull and standing rigging are critical on sailboats. Older, more expensive boats may have to be documented to obtain financing. This means a search to get clear titles for every owner since the boat was built.

But the most important consideration is you. A lender is more interested in investing in the person than the product. Says George Giamalis of FinanceAmerica, a diversified finance company that does a substantial amount of marine lending, "These are not hock-shop loans. We want to get a good person on our books."

How Much Can You Afford?

Certain financial information should be determined before any customer with a fixed income decides on a possible purchase. He must determine how much of his excess cash can be designated for the boat purchase and maintenance. Most lenders will state emphatically that fixed monthly obligations must not exceed 40% to 50% of an individual's disposable income. The basic fault in this reasoning is illustrated below, with two families having an expense/income ratio of 60%.

FAMILY "A"

Net monthly income	$2,000
Fixed monthly expenses (60%)	1,200
Funds for living expenses	$ 800

FAMILY "B"

Net monthly income	$600
Fixed monthly expenses	360
Funds for living expenses	$240

Family "A" with two children has ample cash flow to handle an additional obligation. Family "B" with two children has no extra funds at this time. Each family's situation is unique, so do not hesitate to explain your condition in detail.

After determining the amount of excess funds that you have available, your generally affordable price range can be easily figured. In a survey of more than 40 lending institutions nationwide, a maturity of seven years and a range from 10% to 15% of annual percentage rates (APR) were found to be average. For initial computation we can use seven years and 12% APR. Down payments averaged 20% of the purchase price. For example, let's determine how much boat you can get for $300 per month.

Amount Financed	Monthly Payment
$16,000	$282.45
17,000	300,10
	—desired payment
18,000	317.75

Since an average down payment is 20% of the purchase price, the amount financed after the down payment represents 80% of the purchase price in our example.

$17,000 = 80% of anticipated purchase price
Purchase price = $21,250
Down payment = $4,250

If you can obtain an offer to finance a purchase with only 10% down, it will certainly lower your immediate cash needs. However, we have determined that we only want to spend $300 per month on the boat itself, so $17,000 is the maximum amount we can finance no matter how low the down payment might be.

Which has a greater impact on your level of financing, maturity or interest rate?

VARYING INTEREST RATE
—MONTHLY PAYMENT IS $300;
MATURITY IS SEVEN YEARS

Interest Rate	Amount Financeable
10%	$18,100
11	17,500
12	17,000

VARYING MATURITY
—MONTHLY PAYMENT IS $300;
INTEREST RATE IS 10%

Maturity	Amount Financeable
10 years	$22,800
7 years	18,100
5 years	13,200

car, travel trailer or appliances repossessed than lose a boat. As a result, many lenders will arrange some kind of a boat loan.

Different Types of Lenders

Boat manufacturers' lease purchase plans are few and far between. The advantage to the buyer is that he can get under way with less down payment. The boat manufacturer retains title to the boat until the last payment is made. Due to the lack of equity from not having a down payment originally, it is more probable that someone wishing to trade up will stick with the lease purchase program, creating repeat sales for the manufacturer's dealer.

The Pearson yacht-lease program, through the Paumanock Leasing Services, is available through Pearson dealers. Rates are slightly higher than bank rates, and the maximum maturity is seven years. It is noteworthy that a lease can be assigned without paying it off, making a subsequent sale easier.

To guard against the uninformed customer going beyond his means, Paumanock runs a very careful check to make sure the lease doesn't overextend him. They may even reject some applicants who might be approved by other lenders. On the other hand, because Paumanock knows the quality of the boats they are dealing with better than any other lender, they will be more liberal in the amount they lease.

Boat finance companies do not use their own money, but act as agents for a number of lending institutions. Because of the company's volume, the lender may be able to offer rates lower than those available in some specific area. With their knowledge of boating and boatmen, the specialists are less apt to let the borrower get into hot water by overextending himself. A specialist can often arrange financing for a boat that a commercial bank wouldn't touch. Yacht Finance, Inc., of Red Bank, N.J., in business since the early '50s, has secured financing for boats built as far back as 1898.

Savings banks may represent the simplest, quickest and least costly method of financing your boat. No credit investigation is needed, and your loan is processed immediately. The only requirement is, of course, that you have enough

Increasing maturities to ten years helps an individual's buying power significantly. Much has been written about the additional interest paid over this longer-term contract; however, the boat buyer has historically traded boats every five years or less. The American family mentally allocates a portion of its income to monthly obligations, and this generates a feeling of "we can afford to step up as our income steps up." The lower payment that comes with extended maturities gets the family out on the water and, if historical trends hold true over the next five years, the boat buyer will have built up an equity position due to the low depreciation rates for boats.

After determining you want a boat in the $17,000 range and have reconfirmed your choice at the boat dealer's, you are ready to shop for what seems to be the best financing arrangement. Some banks and financial institutions have discovered that lending money on boats is good business. They have found that the default rate on a boat installment loan is very low, lower than any other durables purchases. It seems that individuals would rather see their money in your savings account to cover the loan and the interest for the term of the loan. This account balance will secure the loan transaction. You may add to, or withdraw from, this account at any time, as long as the balance doesn't go below the loan balance. Interest is earned on the entire account, which makes your effective loan interest rate, usually stated at 2% over the rate paid for the deposit, extremely low. A 2% loan is quite a bargain in today's market.

Credit unions, usually restricted to a limited membership, offer a unique opportunity for those eligible. Qualified borrowers may find that credit unions will lend money on a payroll-deduction basis, even though they may not be experienced marine lenders. A long record of steady employment may be the primary motivator rather than the value of the boat purchased. Rates will generally fall in the 10% to 15% APR range of banks, and maturities of seven years are sometimes available. This is a valuable source of funds to consider, but don't expect to find a marine specialist at most credit unions, for their marine volume doesn't warrant it.

Commercial bank loans provide the vast majority of all money used to finance boats. Whether the manufacturer borrows the money for a lease program, a specialist borrows for another finance program, or the bank lends directly to the consumer, commercial banks provide the funds. The most common loan agreement calls for a 20% down payment, will run for seven years, and bears an interest rate of 12% APR.

Banks typically have the most extensive approval process, but you can speed it up by obtaining a "loan commitment" prior to shopping for the boat. These commitments are often only good for 30 days, but some may be made for up to six months. Most banks request evidence of full marine insurance coverage (both hull and protection and indemnity), and may suggest life insurance to cover the declining loan balance over the term of the loan. Bank lending policies are formulated on the well-known Cs of credit: character, capacity, collateral and conditions.

Be prepared to provide information that will assist the bank in evaluation of the boat as collateral. Due to a widespread lack of expertise on the part of bankers in estimating the collateral values of marine products, many loans are approached as an unsecured personal loan. A bank's thorough understanding of the product to be the collateral is critical if favorable rates and maximum maturities are to be obtained.

Boat-dealer-originated loans are often used for one reason: They are very handy for the customer since he normally will not have to run from lender to lender looking for better terms. For instance, Dick Seaman of *Time* magazine borrowed $10,000 several years ago when he was buying a new Westsail 32 from a Maryland dealer. The dealer arranged the loan and, according to Seaman, "All that was left to do was sign on the dotted line."

Each party has a stake in this type of transaction, so let's look at each person's participation in a typical indirect or dealer-originated situation:

The customer receives the money he needs to purchase a boat.

The bank receives an installment-loan contract which historically has the lowest delinquency and loss ratio of any installment loan a bank can make, as well as a lead on a new bank customer relationship. Giamalis says that the bank highly weighs the quality of the dealer. It wants to make sure that he will be the type of person who will stand behind his product.

The dealer sells the boat, hopefully making some margin of profit on the transaction. In many cases the dealer will receive a finder's fee for directing the customer to the bank. This fee is called "dealer reserve" and normally has no influence on the rate paid by the customer.

In some states the rates that can be charged through dealers are higher than those rates which banks can charge. In some states (Illinois for example) maturities through the dealer may also be longer (seven years) than maturities allowed on direct contracts (five years). In those states, assume that a large portion of the rate differential will be returned to the dealer in the form of a finder's fee or dealer reserve.

Don't think that dealer reserve is just an additional cost for the purchaser. You receive value for these dollars in several forms. The dealer has close ties to the lender, and will be able to favorably influence the lender on your behalf. The dealer will be able to offer much more detailed information about his products to the lender. The dealer may explain the different optional equipment and accessories to fully illustrate how each increases the collateral value. It is very important to include all anticipated options or extras in the initial purchase price so that these are included in the collateral value. Finally, the dealer may even agree to guarantee that the bank can't lose by agreeing to "repurchase" the contract should there be a problem down the road. In all situations where the rate difference is minimal, a customer financing through the dealer will not only hire the dealer as his representative, but may also receive noticeably better service in the future.

No one can tell you how much money you can afford to devote to boating. Each situation is unique. Not only do purchase prices vary, but mooring facilities and maintenance expenses are different. As you sit in your living room looking at brochures, or stand before your dream boat at the boat show, remember these basic considerations in financing the purchase:

• *Use your present earning level in planning the amount. Don't count on raises, bonuses or capital gains.*

• *Be sure to include all associated expenses.*

• *Attempt to measure possible savings generated from use of the boat for vacations, personal entertaining or, after verification of IRS guidelines, business entertaining.*

• *Be sure to include all financial obligations when determining how much of your income is really "excess funds" available for a boat purchase.*

• *Be prepared for the unexpected. Plan now for a medical or financial emergency. Just as you carry some form of life raft when cruising, prepare some form of emergency assistance in your financial plans. Limiting your purchase to a boat with universal appeal and high resale value would provide some measure of this protection.*

• *And, finally, don't overbuy. You will enjoy visiting more places in a smaller boat, rather than sitting at the dock ruminating about the burden of payments. A boat purchase that is properly financed will be fondly discussed and remembered for many years to come.*

THE CASE FOR THE SINGLE SCREW

By Jerry Hart

For long-range, displacement cruising boats, there is much to be said for the single screw. Although only a handful of trawler types and the fast lobster boats are single screw, custom boats with displacement hulls are frequently designed with a single screw, suggesting perhaps some serious thinking by experienced owners.

The Achilles' heel of the twin-screw boat is the vulnerability of the propellers themselves; more so when the radii of the screws extend well below the keel, where they are fully exposed to any obstruction that comes along. Where the keel does extend below the screws, it is sometimes chopped off forward of the props, so that the keel can slide over an obstruction, but the propellers can't.

Then there is the case of an accidental grounding on a falling tide wherein the underwater appendages could be bent when the full weight of the boat settles on them. Another inherent disadvantage of twin screws reveals itself in very heavy sea conditions when the props roll at least partially out of the water.

I believe I have seen at least as many instances of prop and shaft damage as I have of mechanical failures, which fortifies my opinion that unprotected twin screws invite just as many problems as they seem to avoid. Certainly the well-found twin-screw boat will carry a spare shaft, strut and a pair of handed propellers, and it must be said that, in the milder waters of the world, it is no great task to change a wheel with scuba or even snorkel equipment, especially on a small boat. But the job is progressively more difficult with larger craft, and becomes a serious problem if a shaft or strut is bent in a part of the world where machine shops and marine railways are few and far between.

Finally, on the negative side, a twin-screw boat on one engine is so utterly inefficient and difficult to handle that she'll have to head for the nearest repair port anyway—the cruise is over until the damaged wheel or inoperative engine can be repaired, and the chances of getting into that predicament are very real indeed. Even the most prudent skipper can, in a moment of inattention, or when running at night, hit a lobster-pot buoy or some other unidentified floating object. Then of course there is the 2 to 1 possibility of engine failure—but more about that later.

On the positive side, twin screws seem to insure against complete engine failure, and assuredly they make maneuvering infinitely easier, even in the tightest quarters. How often have we all seen the "master" helmsman slide his boat into a crowded marina, nonchalantly spinning his wheel and working his gear shifts at presumably precise moments, then turning his back on his levers while still manipulating them to graze the pilings as he backs his craft into the slip gracefully and perfectly parallel to it. If such an exercise gives satisfaction, then think how much more satisfying it can be to accomplish a similar maneuver with a single-screw boat in a cross-wind! Of course it isn't done so simply (usually you'll head into a slip and use a spring line), and it takes considerably more experience to do it smoothly, but the sense of accomplishment is thereby much deeper. It's like the fellow who sails up to his mooring instead of powering to it; the result is the same but the practiced skill stands out.

To be sure, in coastal waters where most twin-screw cruisers and sportfishermen are operated, these liabilities are rarely serious. Moreover, twin screw is the layout of choice for V-type hulls where a good turn of speed is important for weekend-cruising dashes and forays into distant fishing grounds. For owners of distance-cruising boats, such as me with a DeFever trawler type, single screw invulnerability makes sense—and here's why.

Skipping over the tedious graphs and formulas, no one who is familiar with the subject will question that a given amount of horsepower is more efficient when expended through a single slow-turning shaft swinging a big-diameter prop than through two fast-turning smaller wheels. Sometimes the fuel saving is not too significant, and one is willing to trade that off for easier maneuvering and more apparent reliability. But there is the nearly complete protection afforded to the single propeller by the hull and skeg. I can only say that in over 25,000 miles of running with our single-screw *Yellow Bird,* a 50-foot displacement type, we've never even nicked a blade. Fish-pot buoys that we've hit in the night simply get chewed up in our 42-inch-diameter wheel, and we've hit our share of bottom obstructions in the process, perhaps even more than our share because we dare to go where twin-screw skippers often fear to tread. In fact the owner of a twin-screw sportfisherman, a typical design with props extending lower than the keel, once made an interesting observation to me: He drew only 4½ feet but admitted he wouldn't think of going where we do with 6-foot draft. Quite rightly he wanted that extra foot and a half between security and real trouble!

The deeper draft that tends to go along with single-screw configuration is especially advantageous in a displacememt boat since it means more heft with correspondingly greater ability to handle heavy seas, and it also means considerably more interior space at no cost in length, which is the usual measure of a vessel's size and cost.

One further point: A single, slow-turning shaft, when properly aligned and bushed, is almost vibrationless—a strong plus for the off-watch on long night runs.

Now we'll move on to the consideration of one engine or two, which really boils down to one's opinion of the reliability of the modern diesel engine. We will not draw comparisons with the gasoline engine because most offshore men agree that long-distance cruising is not its best application, and there's the worry of the additional ignition system. The gas engine is lighter and cheaper, to be sure, but the crux of this discussion is reliability, so we'll stick with the diesel which, once it starts, has an amazing capacity to keep running as long as good clean fuel is fed to it. The diesel also tends to start complaining long before it quits and, if you learn to recognize the symptoms and how to repair ordinary deviations from the normal, you can be well assured of a faithful source of power. Maintenance is the name of the game and I submit that, human nature being what it is, a single-engine installation will get more loving care than a twin; or, to put it another way, a single engine is half as much trouble as two.

Maintenance, of course, requires an adequate supply of spare parts and tools, and at least a modicum of interest and skill in things mechanical. But there is hope, as we shall see later, for the single-screw concept even for those who lack mechanical aptitude and who feel impelled to head for the nearest repair port when one of a pair of engines quits.

Any engine can burst an oil or water line or lose a water-pump impeller, but these are failures that can usually be repaired at sea if you're prepared for them. If there's anything delicate about a diesel engine it's the fuel system, and when you have a problem there it almost invariably affects both engines of a twin-screw installation, so you are faced with a double job of replacing filters, bleeding the systems, and the sometimes-exasperating chore of priming each engine. This suggests that a little extra attention should be paid to the fuel system of a single-screw vessel, such as dual primary filters, so that they can be changed without having to shut down the engine, a place for tank sludge to collect and be removed at intervals, and, by all means, a fuel-pressure gauge to give warning of any abnormality in the fuel delivery, usually noticeable long before the engine falters.

One of the most overlooked aspects of single-versus twin-engine installations is the interior space saved, especially in the engine room itself. Twin engines are for contortionists, and even contortionists are hard put to get to the outboard side of an engine when trouble develops there, much less to notice any minor problems before they become big ones. In the engine rooms of most twin-screw yachts I've seen under

50 feet or so, proper maintenance is physically almost impossible. I might add that shallow draft and twin engines seem to go hand in hand, which further limits engine-room headroom to the extent that you have to get around on your hands and knees. No, there's nothing like an engine that sits in the center of the vessel and can be approached from all sides without having to clamber over a piping hot exhaust manifold!

Fishing Fleet Vote of Confidence

While the reliability of a single diesel certainly cannot be taken for granted, the sheer size of the world's fishing fleets—and virtually all of the smaller craft are single-engined—is some measure of the confidence that these toilers of the sea place in their power plants. Some of them spend 4,000 hours a year at their trade in all kinds of weather and farther at sea than most yachts cruise.

Having come this far with our comparisons, there may be those who are ready to trade maneuverability for near-freedom from shaft and prop problems, who would like more engine-room space, and might agree that taking proper care of one engine is half as much work as tending to two. But there is still that lingering worry about how to get home in case of complete engine failure. Fortunately there are ways to counter this eventuality, too, and sail is not one of them. A boat built for powering simply cannot get out of its own way under sail, except perhaps going downwind in a gale, and who knows what conditions will prevail if you ever have real engine trouble, or where the wind will be in relation to where you need to go?

The kinds of boats we are talking about are almost always equipped with 110 v/a.c. generators, so the motive power for emergency propulsion is usually ready and waiting. But harnessing this power to drive the shaft requires a certain amount of ingenuity and engineering, since there are no stock attachments made for this purpose (see "Consider Emergency Get-Home Power," page 39).

The Best of Both Worlds

Instead of using a small generator engine to drive the vessel in emergency circumstances, perhaps the best possible arrangement would be to use a pair of identical engines geared to a single shaft with a belt-driven power take-off (or hydraulic power-pump unit) from either engine to a separate generator. This would provide the best of both worlds by assuring reliability through a husky drive on the main shaft, substantial fuel economy (and added range) by shutting down one engine completely when under way in normal conditions, more than enough power for a 20kw generator if desired, a compact installation, and the advantage of a unified spare-parts inventory (plus the opportunity to cannibalize one engine if necessary).

To sum up the case for single screw, you have (a) maximum efficiency, (b) a propeller safely tucked up behind the keel and no exposed shafts or struts, (c) more interior space, especially around the engine itself, (d) less maintenance, and (e) reliability fully equal to twin screws if you decide on twin engines with a bull gear, or adequate security if you make use of a generator engine for emergency propulsion. All you lose is maneuverability, but as your ship-handling proficiency increases with practice, this gradually becomes a small price to pay.

CONSIDER EMERGENCY GET-HOME POWER

By Joseph Gribbins

february

For the single-screw skipper an engine failure at sea is an alarming prospect. But there is a way to provide emergency get-home propulsion without the considerable expense of going to twin-screw. The solution, favored by such noted designers as Arthur De-Fever and William Garden, among others, is to harness the boat's generating unit to the propeller shaft. This is a simple, effective means of bringing a crippled boat back to port, as the skipper of the 47-foot DeFever-designed *Pauhana* discovered when his reverse gear started slipping off Point Conception, Calif. Using generator power, the *Pauhana* aborted her trip to British Columbia and returned safely to home port in Santa Barbara.

There are three basic arrangements that can harness a generator to a shaft for get-home power: mechanical, hydraulic/hydrostatic and electrical. The shaft, as the diagrams indicate, can be the main engine's drive train or, less commonly, a separate shaft and prop.

Mechanical systems use V belts or chain drives running on pulleys, along with a clutch mechanism or idler pulley that can be backed off to slacken the belt or chain. Hydraulic/hydrostatic systems use a hydraulic motor driven by the generator which, in turn, drives the shaft. An electric-motor system devised by Willard Boat Works uses a five-hp, three-phase a.c. electric motor powered by the generator to turn the main-engine shaft.

Predictably, each system has its advantages. W. W. Shepherd, of Los Angeles' Shepherd Machinery Co. and Power Systems Associates, favors mechanical drives similar to the one his company installed on *Pauhana.* Another Shepherd installation brought the 50-foot offshore cruiser *Sisu* safely to La Paz in Baja, Calif. at three knots after the reverse and reduction gears packed up. Shepherd cautions that a drive chain should be installed and ready for use. As he warns: "If you stash the chain away in a box, inevitably five years later there'll be a real sea emergency and you won't be able to find the box." Shepherd also advises skippers interested in generators for get-home power to purchase a larger than normal generator drive engine.

Ben Hibbs, chief electrician at Kettenburg Marine in San Diego, likes a chain-driven hydraulic system because of its ease of installation. With it alignment problems are minimal and the hydraulic unit can be located about anywhere that is convenient in the engine room. A survey of dealers and owners who have had experience with the hydraulic-drive system offered as an option on DeFever Passagemaker offshore cruisers indicates that, although none has been challenged by a real emergency, both 34-foot and 40-foot DeFevers have tested out perfectly on dry runs. "We've installed six of them," reports DeFever dealer Jay Bettis of Seabrook, Texas, "and we get 3.7 knots with this system on the 40-foot DeFever. It's a real smooth operation—sounds like a sewing machine when it's running."

Willard Boat Works president Bill Tighue describes his company's electric-motor system as simple and efficient in both installation and operation. "A system like this runs about $1,700 for the belt, controllers, wiring and motor—it's a big motor. It will get you home *if* the weather permits. If the sea is calm you'll be able to do whatever five horsepower or so will do with that hull."

Burke George, part owner of the Willard Vega

40 *Domino,* is pleased with the electric-motor system installed by the boat's builder. "I've run it probably half a dozen times just to become familiar with it," he says. "We've even run around the harbor with it for an hour and a half and it's been very efficient."

With a generator running the propeller, no boat is going to be a speedster. But in calm seas the typical three- to four-knot speed is enough to get you home. Headway may be impossible in heavy seas, but generator power will at least enable you to maintain steerageway. As Shepherd summed it up: "We feel that any single-engine boat is definitely safer with an auxiliary drive that uses the generator engine or a second, smaller auxiliary engine."

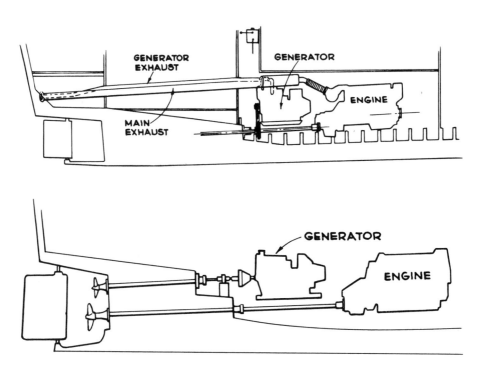

A belt drive (top) brings generator power to the shaft. Alternate system (bottom) uses separate generator shaft, prop.

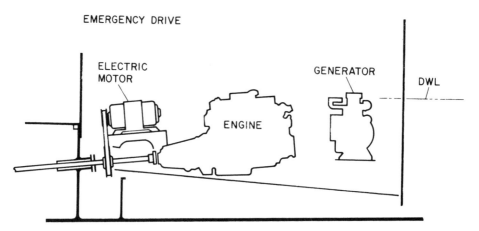

The generator-drive system devised by Willard Boat Works employs a 5-hp electric motor, powered by the generator, to drive the main-engine shaft in case of engine failure.

Where will you keep your boat?

If you already own a boat—this may be the time to sell it and look for the bigger (or smaller) one that you've been thinking of (see "Don't Sell your Boat Short" by Nancy T. White, on page 47).

If your new boat is already on order, this is the time to begin inquiring about delivery. Boat building may be booming, but it is still a cottage industry, and builders are not inclined to fill orders on time. Ask about the status of your boat from the nice salesman who took your order at the boat show in January or the showroom last month—if you can find him. If your deal was contingent on a trial run in a prototype of your new boat, the weather may be right for it.

And there are yet some things you must resolve before you can accept delivery. Shopping for boat insurance (covered on pages 44 to 46 by Arthur Blum) is one—so that when you finally get your delivery, a simple phone call will put the policy into effect. And you will have to find some complex of slime-covered pilings to call home for your new boat. Will it be a boatyard, a marina, or a yacht club?

You will be probably auditioning them by car. But let us imagine that we are inspecting them by boat.

THE BOATYARD

Here you will find none of the accoutrements of gracious living that you have seen in the magazine ads. The conveniences consist of a soft-drink machine and a candy-vending machine (referred to in cruising guides as "snack bar"), an ice dispenser (referred to as "ice"), a lavatory, including plumbing that spurts water from all joints (referred to as "showers") and a savage dog on a long leash (referred to as a "24-hour security guard").

But the reward for having to stumble, in addition, over marine railway tracks on the way to and from your boat is that the yard has a staff of craftsmen on call, able to fix a leaky stuffing box or a bent shaft in a trice. You hope.

Socially, boatyards lean heavily to families that cruise together and fish together. This gives a nice comradely feeling to the homeliest yard. Conversation among boat owners is frequently limited to:

"Have you seen Bob?" (Most mechanics are named Bob.)

"I just saw him drive away." (Mechanics are never seen arriving, only leaving.)

THE MARINA

We arrive at a waterside establishment, rich in striped awnings and dockside attendants. A smart-looking lad in starched suntans helps us tie in and asks for payment for transient dockage. From near and far, we hear cash registers ringing. We are at a marina.

The marina is a Southern invention that came North and made good during the past generation. It is based on the idea that owning a boat is no reason for not having a Good Time. A good time begins with a swimming pool, snack bar, restaurant, bar, picnic ground, ship's store, and sometimes such extras as trampolines.

Unlike the boatyard families, who are dedicated to boating, marina families tend more to hang around the marina, where they can idle a day away without leaving shore. Boat talk frequently concerns wives who want a bigger boat, wives who want a smaller boat, and wives who don't like boating at all.

THE YACHT CLUB

Leaving the marina, we now head across the darkening waters toward a Scott Fitzgerald house in front of which there is a flagstaff flying several ceremonial colors. As we approach, a piece of artillery goes off alarmingly close to us. This is the sunset gun, the signal for lowering the flag—one of many quasi-naval ceremonies that you can enjoy at a yacht club.

A salty old soul in dungarees helps us tie in. You're tempted to hand him a buck, after he's risked his life defending you against the strong current, which almost smashed your bow into the dock. But you don't. Tipping is *de trop* at a club, and besides, he is a bank president in mufti.

The chief occupation of yacht club members is racing (sail) and cruising (sail or power), and it is frequently a point of snobbery to reflect on how rarely one uses the shoreside facilities. Actually, if truth be known, cruise destinations of club members are frequently other clubs (which offer reciprocal privileges), where they use the swimming pools and tennis courts. No points lost for that, as long as you're using them elsewhere.

Curiously enough, the club frequently is the least expensive of the three facilities. The difference can be accounted for by the high profit motive of the marina and the nonprofit operation of the club. And even the break-even point of the club is substantially reduced by the members' willingness at many clubs to put in time on various managerial and housekeeping committees, which replace salaried employees at boatyards and marinas.

Oh, yes. In listing the three facilities, I forgot to mention a fourth. If you bought a trailerable boat, there's always your backyard.

SHOPPING FOR BOAT INSURANCE

By Arthur Blum

Insurance costs are going up. Inflationary pressure is probably the biggest single culprit. Boat costs, spare parts, labor costs, and medical costs have all increased, and these are reflected in the amount you have to pay for insurance. The best thing you can do to keep your insurance costs down is to know what an insurance underwriter looks for when he determines how much your insurance will cost—then, shop around.

Boat insurance—unlike home, life, auto or recreational vehicle insurance—is not a matter of cut-and-dried tables. Value judgments on the part of the underwriter are required to a far greater degree than almost any other form of insurance protection. These value judgments are very far from arbitrary. They are based upon sound insights as to what makes for safe boating, including the relative safety of boat types and equipment as well as demonstrated abilities of the skipper.

There are a number of rating factors which an underwriter will consider before arriving at a fig-ure for insurance costs which you will have to live with. These factors are as follows:

1. *Experience of the boatowner.* The accident record of a boatowner is a major factor to an underwriter in determining the risk (and therefore the cost) of insuring a boat. As you compile a good safety record, the cost of insuring your boat should go down. There are some companies which offer special graduated credit up to 20% for loss-free experience.

There are other ways of proving proficiency and these can pare your insurance costs. Have you taken a U.S. Coast Guard Auxiliary course? If so, what level have you passed? There is the U.S. Power Squadrons' course which parallels and may be taken in lieu of the U.S. Coast Guard Auxiliary course. The courses are a minor factor in insurance rating, however, since passing the courses demonstrates technical proficiency without proving that you will apply what you have learned.

2. *The boat herself.* While hull length is not a rating factor directly, the cost of the boat, which is a function of the length, is a definite factor. Most companies won't issue insurance for more than what the investment represents to the owner.

All other things being equal, insurance rates for a boat over five years old will be higher than for an identical boat that is new. The reasoning here is that the older boat has been exposed to a great deal more wear and tear and repair costs will be higher. Since most yacht insurance policies are all-risk (the inferior "named risk" policy is becoming something of a rarity), the added costs expected are reflected in higher rates.

An important consideration is "who made the boat." Was she constructed by an accredited manufacturer or was she put together by a backyard builder? Usually insurance rates are lowest on boats built of fiberglass.

Because of their better safety record, sailboats generally average 10–15% less in insurance premiums, all other things being equal. A diesel-powered boat will average 10–15% less in insurance costs compared with a gasoline-powered craft. If you have a sailboat with an auxiliary diesel, you will receive a premium advantage because of the sail and an additional advantage for the diesel powerplant.

The boat must meet National Fire Protection

Standards. Occasionally a company will request that something on the boat be changed—such as different fuel tanks or more lights installed.

Navigation and safety devices such as Loran, radar, depth sounders, gas sniffers, etc., are considered, but they are not a primary rating factor because they are only as good as the skill of the user.

3. *Where is the boat going to be used?* Insurance premiums for an ocean-going cruiser will be higher than if the boat is to be used on inland waters. Generally, areas are rated inland, coastal or offshore, with inland being the least expensive. Some companies use different rates for the same areas, so shop around. There are also geographical variations in rates.

4. *How many months of the year is your boat in commission?* Most policies in northern waters are based on the warranty that your boat will be in the water for seven or eight months of the year and laid up for five or four. If you know your boat will be in commission for less time, there might be a reduction for you.

5. *Where is your boat moored and laid up?* The underwriter will want to know where you keep your boat as some mooring locations are more prone to theft and vandalism than others. If the boat is going to be kept in the water all winter, the underwriter may check for a bubbler system. He will want to know where your boat is laid up for the off season. Some locations have proven to be more prone than others to ruinous fires which destroyed a number of pleasure craft located side by side.

6. *How is the boat to be used?* You may well be asked some question by the underwriter regarding your boat usage. There is an additional premium for racing boats. This reflects the inherent dangers caused by such punishing trials.

Do you plan to charter your boat to someone? The underwriter must know this because of the endorsement requirement. If you charter the boat once or twice a year, you will have to have special insurance for those weeks. If you plan to go into large-scale chartering, you will require a commercial policy with higher rates. since there is less control over the renter. (Most yacht policies include an omnibus clause which covers family and friends operating the boat.)

Other Points to Consider

To save money on your rates, consider going to a higher deductible. Depending on the company, the minimum deductible is usually $50 to $100. Going to the other extreme, you could realistically have deductibles from 1% to 4% of the insured value of the boat. Even with a larger deductible, you will be protected in the event of major loss—and this is what is really important. Protection against minor loss just succeeds in driving up your insurance costs. The only word of warning here is that you should never take a deductible larger than you can comfortably afford in the event of accident or loss.

A yacht policy is simpler than a homeowner's policy: It usually offers more all-risk coverage. The boat's hull as well as all equipment necessary for the maintenance and navigation of the vessel is included. The Protection and Indemnity (P&I) section of the policy covers all the liabilities of the owner with respect to property damage and loss of life or injuries to any individual in connection with the operation or ownership of the boat. Many good policies include medical payments coverage for people injured on the boat. Most people take out both the hull insurance and P&I although sometimes, for boats up to 26 feet, the latter is included in a homeowner's policy.

On the matter of small boats, craft which are easily transportable and are often kept in the owner's driveway are usually covered by a homeowner's policy—up to $500. However, this coverage is not all-risk, so you should see your agent to find out whether such protection is enough to meet your requirements. A small boat used as a tender will be covered under its mother ship's policy. (But remember your deductible. If your dinghy is a few years old and you have a high deductible, its loss probably won't be recovered.)

Larger runabouts, which fall somewhere in cost and size between the dinghy and the larger boat we have discussed, are insured in much the same way as large yachts. The only difference is that, since they are more easily divided by class, there are charts which would be used by underwriters in the determination of insurance premiums. The safety rules would still apply, but the underwriter simply does not have to go to the same lengths which are involved in determining the insurance rate for a large yacht.

A point to be aware of with marine insurance is that not every event is covered by a policy. Some of the main exclusions are: 1. wear and tear, gradual deterioration, and inherent vice; 2. marring, denting, and scratching while the boat is being transported by land conveyance; 3. electrolysis. Other exclusions, which some companies include and others do not, are mysterious disappearance of equipment other than boats or launches and their outboard motors; and loss, damage or expense due to or caused by ice or freezing while afloat.

Knowing what an insurance company uses in arriving at a premium is a good place to start in keeping your rates down. Once you know that, you can shop around to see which policy can best be tailored to suit your individual situation.

DON'T SELL YOUR BOAT SHORT

By Nancy J. White

march

She's been a good friend and served you well. All those summer weekends gunkholing with the kids—the sand trudged through the cabin, the Bain de Soleil rubbed into the cockpit sole, the night you dragged anchor and scraped Deadman's Ledge. She was forgiving through it all. You'll never forget the moonlit cruises or the two-week escapade through the canals. But the time has come, for whatever reason, to part company. You want to do it as pleasantly, quickly and economically as possible.

If you have plenty of time and the patience of Job, you might attempt selling your prized possession through classified newspaper ads. This route, however, may be the hardest on both you and your boat: Your boat is trampled upon by the only mildly curious and you provide afternoon jaunts for the sneaky freeloader. Most important, you run the risk of selling your boat for less than her current market value. Another idea is to advertise in the classified section of a boating magazine; the disadvantage is a lead time of about two months, but the advantage is that in-

quiries will be from knowledgeable people who generally recognize what they want.

The other option is to sell your boat through a broker. For his usual 10 percent commission, a broker will explain the realities of the market and undertake the time-consuming chore of showing the boat. The chances are good that you'll sell your boat fastest through a broker.

But whichever avenue you choose, your enduring old friend must be made ready for the marketplace. The little quirks you'd learned to live with, like the tach needle that hangs up until you hit the instrument panel, a stranger will not find so acceptable. All brokers agree that the cosmetic appearance of a boat is the No. 1 selling point. If a boat is dirty or untidy, the prospective buyer is immediately turned off, and will assume that the mechanics of the boat have also been treated in an unseamanlike fashion. As Bob Massey of Navesink Yacht Sales puts it: "It all rides with that first 30-second overall look. From that they know what to expect. If a boat is properly maintained, you can see it."

People would rather pay a premium for a boat that will require little work rather than do the commissioning themselves. Paul McIsaac, a broker at Stone Harbor Yacht Sales, explains, "Cleanliness has played an ever-increasing role in sales in the last two years. People want to spend their time enjoying the boat, not fixing it up. They want to run it away from the dock as if it were new."

So it is up to you to rejuvenate your boat. Nothing beats a consistent maintenance program, but for those too-often-overlooked details, here's some advice.

Any chipped or scarred exterior should be refinished—this would include painting the topsides and redoing the varnish. Joseph Baron, who overhauled his 33-foot powerboat under the guidance of a broker, believes that the work he did on the hull was the most important. The bottom was painted, the hull waxed, the props reconditioned. That boat sparkled, which caught the buyer's eye.

On a sailboat, check the rigging, usually the most neglected area. All cotter and safety keys should be taped. Any sail tears should be mended, but not necessarily a new suit made—the next owner may have his own preference in sailmakers.

All canvas and cushions should be cleaned

and any mildew removed. If dodgers and spray shields are tattered it may be wiser to remove them, as they will only detract from the overall appearance. All chrome and stainless steel must be gleaming. Any wiring ought to be neatly arranged—not looking like a bowl of spaghetti. All electrical connections should be operative and horn pressure checked—nothing is more disconcerting than to expect a resounding blast and get a mild bleat. Steering gear should be lubricated. Labeled stowage bins (both on deck and below) make for an organized boat. All lines and fenders must be in Bristol fashion.

Belowdecks, a clean and orderly engine room is the most important consideration. With a wire brush remove rust, flaking paint and salt deposits from all machinery and spruce them up with a fresh coat of paint. Richard Bertram, a well-known Florida broker, says to be sure the engine oil is clean. "When looking over engines, the first thing the prospect usually checks is the dipstick. Dirty oil may influence him to believe the engines have been abused." Engine pans should also be cleaned. Make sure no spare parts are scattered about. Flush out the bilge and give it a good soapy wash.

The interior also needs a face-lift. Carpeting, drapery and upholstery should be cleaned, or replaced if necessary. Those nicks and spots you've grown accustomed to in the woodwork must be rubbed with polish. Clean and re-oil any teak. In the galley make sure the refrigerator is clean and smells good. Scrub the stove and sink. Discard any nonessentials. All hardware should be corrosion-free, and the same applies in the head.

The extent of the preparation list will depend on the condition of your boat, but one definite rule to follow is: "Don't stint." Leaving something in poor shape to save money may prove to be a false economy. Peter Grimm of United Yacht Brokers believes that an expenditure of $1,000 can boost the overall price by as much as $5,000. The small details add up to the important total appearance, that first 30-second look. As Bob Massey emphasizes: "Boats are emotional purchases."

Prospective buyers are attracted to boats that are warm and friendly. Again, the accent is on the immediate appearance. Says Grimm: "Buyers can't visualize a boat's potential. They can't imagine how lovely a boat can look—they have to be shown outright."

When Sandy Hollister, a Great Lakes racer, was preparing to sell his Fastnet 45, he left nothing to the buyer's imagination. He hung pictures, bought matching dishes and glassware, put in bookends, even went so far as to leave a place setting on the dinette table. Hollister believes that his $228 investment in dressing up the boat netted him $10,000 more in the end.

Another rule is, "Don't pillage the boat." Certainly take anything you don't want to sell off the boat, but do include a few appurtenances in your inventory. An attractive ashtray, some colorful bunk covers, a clock and barometer set will go a long way toward an inviting ambience. The buyer will also feel he is getting something extra.

Of course, don't get carried away in constructing this warm feeling. Sometimes boats can be too personalized. One broker tells the story of a large motor yacht that was rather way out—the staterooms were paneled in leather, with hanging mirrors over the bed. The boat was, understandably, difficult to sell. Moral of the story: Try to see beyond your own taste.

Aside from appearance, the most important factor in selling is knowing the market—settling on a fair price to ask and understanding what will sell where. Sophisticated gear, for instance, is especially popular in coastal areas, where it generally returns 50 percent of its original cost, but in the Midwest it could serve as a hindrance to a sale. One man, thinking he was increasing the value of his medium-sized powerboat, added a tuna tower not long before putting her on the market. But what he actually did was limit his field solely to sports fishermen, and he sold her for a lot less than he could have.

Other selling hints include having clear photographs of the boat under way and of the interior. A well-kept logbook and a short history of the boat will give her added personality.

Preparing your boat for sale is a personal matter. You can try to sell her in disarray with the hopes of enticing an enthusiastic work fiend with the vision of a soothsayer. Or you can spend time and money fixing her up so you can be proud of her. And of yourself. One broker summed up: "I like to be able to point to a boat and say, 'Now you know the owner is a boatman.'"

Commissioning time!

Commissioning time. All over the waterfront, people are pottering about their boats in a cloud of dust and euphoria. Some are scraping, sanding or painting (see Twelve Painting Tips on page 56), some working on their engines (see all about recommissioning on page 54). Everybody looks glad to be right where he is. It's a pleasure of greater candlepower than you sense on a golf course. That's because boating is not a sport—it's an obsession that engages all your senses and whatever skills you have.

If your new boat has arrived when promised, that's good! But, inevitably, it will have a few bugs in it. That's bad. M. W. Johnson's piece on page 51 tells you how to rid your boat of some of them and how to assure yourself that everything is finally shipshape. That's good.

If you've had a wooden boat and have finally thrown in the sponge and bought fiber glass, some additional surprises await you. To wit:

THE ECHO CHAMBER EFFECT

Fiber glass has its own peculiar acoustics. Wood muffles sound; fiber glass amplifies it. A mild bump or a thump will sound to the ex-wooden boat owner like a stove-in hull. Not to worry.

THE CATHEDRAL WINDOW EFFECT

One sunny afternoon, the new owner suddenly discovers, with a sick feeling, that he can see clear through some unpainted areas of his fiber glass hull when it faces the sunlight. The light is streaming through his topsides as if they were rose windows. To a boatman who respects double planking, this translucence can be downright scary. Not to worry.

THE NUTS AND BOLTS MYSTERY

That collection of bolts, pipe joints, and assorted hardware in your brand new bilges. Does it all belong to some vital marine organ that the builder forgot to finish assembling? (See "Commissioning a New Boat" on page 51 for the answer.)

COMMISSIONING A NEW BOAT

By M. W. "Johnny" Johnson

Fitting out a boat carries the undercurrent meaning of refurbishing or repairing an older boat. But the truth is that it is the new boat or the first boat which needs the most preparation for her first season.

This may come as a nasty shock to the skipper who has bought his new beauty and now waits only for the warm and balmy embrace of Spring. But consider the following facts:

1. the new boat is one that is untested in service.

2. the new boat is the one with which you have absolutely no personal experience.

3. the new boat is one on which no supplies are available—not a roll of paper towels, not a beer can opener, not even a book of matches. Everything must be supplied from scratch.

The first discovery you're likely to make is that the suave, unhurried dealer who sold you the boat in the Winter (and perhaps bought you a drink afterwards) has become, by Spring, a harried, snappish fellow whose time is limited, and whose patience is strained. He will receive the boat from the factory, launch it, run a perfunctory check of equipment (or have someone do it for him), hand you the keys, and likely as not thank you for going on your way in order to make room for the next boat he has to deliver.

This, then is the second discovery of Spring—you are going to have to do a certain amount of preflight testing yourself; which enlightening leads directly to discovery number three: a boat is not a toaster you can plug into the wall and begin operating at once—it is much, much more complicated than that.

You should start your fitting-out by gathering all the individual instruction pamphlets that have been provided for the equipment installed aboard. Unless yours is an unusual vessel, you will not find a comprehensive owner's manual covering operation of the boat and all its gear. There's a reason for this: it would be too expensive to print. Customer-ordered extras vary greatly from boat to boat, and production line changes would probably make the manual obsolete before it came off the press.

Therefore, read the individual manuals you have collected and try out the equipment, one piece at a time. Check the toilet for leaks; work the lights and check the fuses; check the steering mechanism for excessive play, and roll the engines over and check the resultant oil pressure, temperature, and charge rate. If your boat is a complicated one with air conditioning, pressure hot and cold water, refrigeration, and the like, it may take a day or more to complete this check-up.

Don't be discouraged if you find a string of minor troubles. Although most boat manufacturers' warranties cover exclusively what they build (and they do not build engines, compasses, etc.), the boating business is a friendly and immensely cooperative operation. Most dealers will go to bat for you immediately, even if it means calling a distant supplier and air-freighting in some exotic part that you might require. Just make sure that you run a *full* check on the boat and that you tell your dealer quickly and *exactly* what appears to be wrong.

Incidentally, you should take time to fill out and mail in all the warranty registration cards that have come with the boat and its accessory equipment. Beyond assuring yourself of faster, better service, you also will have given the manufacturer of any piece of gear vital serial numbers and dates so that at some future time, he will know which model of equipment you have and what repair parts are needed.

When the boat is afloat and working mechanically, you will undoubtedly make the Spring's fourth discovery—it leaks. *All* boats leak, some through the stern tube, some through the bottom, some through the deck, and some through the hatches and portholes.

The experts in these dismal matters classify leaks this way: sitting-at-the-dock hull leaks; rain leaks (water coming down from above); underway hull leaks from engine vibration or misalignment; or deck leaks caused by spray moving *upwards* against the rails or, in sailboats, by immersion of the lee rails.

If you have a hull leak, you'll get better warranty service by finding it before you go snarling to the salesman or dealer. Knowing where the leak is obviously makes it easier to fix. Bail or pump boat dry and sponge the last of the water from the bilge. Then lie on your stomach, have a beer, and contemplate the wondrous mystery of trickling water under the floorboards. Hopefully, it will come from forward *or* from aft.

Having decided which end of your boat is leaking, pursue the stream back to its source so that you can report it accurately to the dealer. Difficult-to-spot leaks can sometimes be pinpointed by spraying inaccessible bilge areas with a pressure-can powder—it will paint out a nice white area which trickling water will cut a dark track through.

Also, try to spend a rainy night aboard, and do it as quickly as possible after delivery (or before it). You can hose-test a boat for hours and it may not leak a drop, but let a gentle Spring drizzle come along and watch—a malevolent drop of water will form in some maddening spot (usually over your berth where it can drip with Chinese-torture regularity into your right ear). It's strange but true—rain leaks appear only in the rain. Make an exact list of what you find for the dealer; help him by putting a piece of colored tape at any spot where you detect leakage.

Underway leaks are the most difficult to spot, or at least they seem to take longer to find. One reason is that in your first cruises, you'll be playing captain rather than going below and diligently finding out if and where the beast is taking water. You will have to force yourself to leave the bridge and spend some early underway time in the cabin, in the engine space, and hovering above the bilge to make sure everything is right and tight.

When it comes to leaks, be philosophic. There may be more than one, and you simply have to take the time and have the wit to run them down and fix them. You'll win without doubt—the modern boat may be a trifle hastily constructed, but it is eminently fixable. With a screwdriver, a tube of sealer, and some clean-up rags, you can do 80 per cent of it yourself (and you *will*, too, as the years go by).

One more word before we leave the world of bilges and leaks. In your various investigations under the cabin floorboards, you are likely to find a strange miscellany of items. New boats arrive from the factory with sandwich wrappers (some with parts of sandwich still in them), banana peels, wood shavings, fiberglass bits, the nipped-off ends of hoses, bolts and screws, and occasionally something valuable like a slightly rusty wrench or pair of pliers. Clean all of this out—it's not simply untidy, it can plug up your bilge pump at some critical moment.

Now you're ready to shove off—almost. Another day or so at the most will do it. *Now* is the time to check the finish of the boat. If it's a glass boat, you ought to wash down the topsides and apply a coat of wax to it (there are several waxes on the market specifically made for exposure to salt and sun). Though fiberglass appears to the eye to be as smooth-surfaced as window glass, it apparently has a somewhat dirty and stain-catching characteristic that is forestalled by wax. Waxed hulls also retain their original color longer because the wax keeps oxygen away from the paint and therefore curtails oxidization. Do not, of course, wax the deck. Slipping overboard can ruin the best of days.

If, in the close inspection of the hull that accompanies washing and waxing, you see little webs of cracks here and there, don't be discouraged. Star-cracking in fiberglass gelcoats is not serious, unusual, structural, or probably even avoidable. When an enormously hard and brittle gel is applied to a surface that flexes and bends (i.e., to a boat), it will crack microscopically.

At this point, with your attention directed to finishes and surfaces, you will make discovery five: if your boat has varnish trim, it hasn't got *enough* of it, that is, the varnish is thin and, likely as not, originally hot-sprayed. Before starting the season, join your brother yachtsmen who own older boats and put on an additional coat or two of varnish. If you have raw teak trim and it's bare, bronze-wool and seal it with any of the many teak-sealers available at marine stores. If you have teak and it's sealed and golden looking, make a note that you're going to have to redo it in about six to eight weeks anyhow. If you prefer to ignore teak and let it go grey, by all means do so, but bear in mind that it will weather-check and split when left unprotected.

If your new boat was in stock when you bought it, the bottom paint has probably lost a lot of its toxic punch. You can go with what you've got and plan to haul for a bottom job in late July (depending on the salinity of your water area), or you can have a fresh coat applied just prior to launching.

This is also a good time to talk with your dealer or boatyard man about installing zinc anodes underwater to protect against electrolysis. Stray electric current is a real danger, and is difficult to detect until too late.

Even with these items attended to, however, you're still not ready to sail. There remains the question of additional equipment: Coast Guard required items such as life jackets, fire extinguishers, and navigation lights. (You will find the requirements for your particular boat listed in this section on page 55.)

Not "required," but necessary are: two anchors, two anchor rodes with chain leads, four to six heavy, eye-spliced docklines, a boat hook, boat fenders and perhaps a fenderboard, several good flashlights with spare batteries and bulbs, and tools.

You will also want to carry flares; spare parts (for engine, stove, toilet, etc., usually purchased as packaged kits); foul weather gear for the family; boating shoes (discourage barefoot boating under way—bare feet slip easily and toes break like balsa); anchor light; extra battery (charged if your boat doesn't have a two battery system with multiposition switch); navigational tools—parallel rules, dividers, charts; dinghy or rubber inflatable raft; canvas/dacron goods such as awning, cockpit cushions, back and side curtains, cockpit dodger, sail cover; swimming ladder; first aid kit; manual bilge pump (if not included with boat), and cleaning materials.

For your first power run or trial sail, pick a good day with not too much wind. Plan only a short in-and-out trip with no long-range destination. On that first memorable occasion, moreover, do *not* take your mother, the seven wee ones, Aunt and Uncle Peergrass, or your chums from the office. If the boat is going to leak, sink, or heel over too far, or be more difficult to dock than you anticipated, you will need to give it your undivided attention.

While under way, check for engine vibration, leaks, and other peculiarities in operation. You can give a boat a complete dockside engine test only to have it wiggle out of alignment in the first few hours of actual operation. Make sure you do not exceed the recommended maximum rpms in the early hours of running, but do take the engine up to that maximum and hold it long enough to see that temperature, oil pressure, charge rate and tachs behave as advertised in the engine manual.

If time allows, find several buoys within easy sight of one another and try a few compass runs to see if you have unusual deviation. Before starting on a long cruise, you will want to have your compass swung and corrected for deviation.

Now, with the warm Spring sunlight dancing on the water and the boat purring along like a well-fed pussycat, you are ready for that first real cruise.

Some day the boating industry will produce true "sailaway" boats—ones that will require no more shakedown than today's new automobiles. Meanwhile, it is zany, amateurish and fun.

And that's discovery number six. Even if you had to hustle and got a bit closer to nature and cup grease than you wanted to, you'll pass that last sea buoy and head out into the green feeling it was well, well worth it!

COMMISSIONING THE BOAT YOU LAID UP LAST NOVEMBER

By Edward H. Nabb

Recommissioning is a case of "tilting the table," of undoing everything that was done last November. What was last becomes first, so we get the battery out, check it for charge and voltage, brighten up the terminal posts with steel wool, connect the clean-up cables and smear them with petroleum jelly or grease. We drain the oil or antifreeze from the engine's cooling system, unless we have a fresh-water system that merely needs checking. Remove and flush out the oil cooler core assembly and clean out any junk in the cooler body. Close all the drain cocks and replace the impeller in the pump, using a new gasket if necessary.

Rotate the engine several times with the spark plugs removed, to remove the oil which was squirted into the cylinders. Either replace spark plugs with new ones of the proper range and the right gap setting, or clean, sandblast, gap and install the old plugs. Replace all electric and ignition parts which were removed, or unwrap and clean those on the engine. It is best to have a good mechanic check points, rotors, distributor cap, and condensers; and if there is any doubt whatever replace the whole deal. They are among the most inexpensive parts on the engine—but they should be saved and carried along for troubleshooting spares. Clean and dry all distributor parts, lubricate the rotor cams and the felt wick under the rotor. Add a few drops of oil to the end bearings of the generator and the starter.

Check the outer parts of the engine for rust or rough spots, and paint if necessary. Check the engine lube oil and the connections around the filter and cooler. Realign the propeller shaft to .003″ in the water, after replacing the prop. Remove the rags from the exhaust outlets and be sure that the engine hold-down bolts are secure after the realigning job. Give all of the engine control rods and pivots a good inspection, and oil if necessary. Connect all the fuel system lines, clean all strainers and bowls, and fill the tank with a good grade of gasoline. Pump the hand lever on the fuel pump until the system is fully charged. Clean the element of the flame arrestor, for this will rob your power if clogged. Check the adjustment of the reverse and forward settings on the gears as prescribed in the engine manual. Be sure that the water intake line is hooked up and that the stop cock is turned to the "on" position.

Go ahead and crank her up, then check to see that water is circulating through the cooling system. Check up on the stuffing boxes at the rudder post and shaft log and tighten them enough to stop the flow of water but not enough to bind the shaft. It is recommended that a good mechanic, properly qualified to tune your engine, be taken on the first trial run. You will most likely be off to a good season if the power plant is well tuned early in the game. If your engine has been reconditioned during the lay-up period, you will have to take it slow and easy for a while. Many of the parts are new and require as much break-in as a new engine. Follow the manufacturer's recommendations for this running in period.

Just remember half of what you have read, and you will have many hours of happy boating—and extra years of efficient engine life!

MINIMUM MOTORBOAT EQUIPMENT REQUIRED ON U.S. WATERS[1]

Equipment	Class A	Class 1	Class 2	Class 3
Back-fire flame arrestor	One approved device on each carburetor of gasoline engines installed after April 25, 1940; not required on outboard motors.			
Ventilators	At least two ducted ventilators fitted with cowls or equivalent to sufficiently ventilate the spaces of every engine and fuel-tank compartment of boats constructed or decked over after April 25, 1940 and using gasoline or other fuel of a flashpoint under 110° F.			
Bell	None	None	One which when struck produces a "clear bell-like tone of full rounded characteristics"	
Lifesavers	One approved life preserver, buoyant vest, ring buoy or buoyant cushion for each person on board.	One approved wearable personal flotation device (PFD) life preserver or ring buoy for each person on board plus one throwable PFD.		
Whistle	None	One hand-, mouth-, or power-operated, audible for at least ½ mile	One hand- or power-operated, audible for at least 1 mile	One power-operated, audible for at least 1 mile
Fire extinguisher —portable. When no fixed fire extinguishing system is installed in machinery space(s)	At least one B-I type-approved hand portable extinguisher. None required on open outboards smaller than 26 feet		At least two B-I type-approved hand portable extinguishers; or at least one B-II type-approved hand portable extinguisher	At least three B-I type-approved hand portable extinguishers; or at least one B-I type plus one B-II type-approved hand portable extinguisher
When fixed fire extinguishing system is installed in machinery space(s)	None	None	At least one B-I type-approved hand portable extinguisher	At least two B-I type-approved hand portable extinguishers; or at least one B-II type-approved hand portable extinguisher

[1] *Adapted from official U.S. pamphlet CG-340.*

TWELVE PAINTING TIPS FROM THE PROS

april

Hard work isn't the first canon of a successful paint job. Patience is. A well planned day of painting that ends at 2 p.m., with a proper choice of brush and technique, is far more likely to win praise from a veteran boss painter than a work day stretching into the evening when dew fills the air. Attention to weather, wind conditions, "feathering in," paint consistency, even the way masking tape is applied—have far more currency with pros than the amount of sweat you put into a job. Patience is also the best protection against the common marks on the boats of amateur painters, marks which make professionals mutter ominous words like "laps . . . holidays . . . curtains."

You're asking a lot of your paint, a shield thinner than the thickness of this page, against all weather and sea conditions. So after you've prepared your surface properly and paid up to $70 a gallon, it pays to put it on professionally. Here's how the pros do it:

1. Use two cans for mixing paint. Nine complaints out of ten reaching the Baltimore Copper Paint Co., we're told, stem from the fact that paint wasn't mixed correctly. If you've found yourself griping that the paint comes out thin as bilge water, or that it dried to two different shades, you probably didn't mix it right. Here's how: "Tip off the top oil," says Clay Gritman, work-finishing foreman at Connecticut's Yacht Haven. "Stir up the mass that's left. Add the oil gradually until the can is mixed. It'll take at least five minutes." Stirring should be done with a lifting motion of the paddle. Even after the paint appears uniform, continue to mix it by pouring it back and forth between your two containers.

After mixing, pour only the paint you need into a separate container; seal the original can to keep out dust. "Whenever you prepare a surface, no matter how hard you try to clean it—with a vacuum or tacking it down or anything—you're going to pick up surface dirt and that's going to be put back into the paint or varnish," explains Gerry LaMarque, vice president of Nichols Yacht Yard in Mamaroneck, N.Y. "So we use disposable paper tubs, and when we're through with a job, we throw them away without contaminating the original supply of paint."

2. Run the flat edge of a putty knife along masking tape to force out air and prevent "bleeding." "Your hand won't ever be able to press hard enough to keep the tape down," says Al Merritt, president of his own boat yard in Pompano, Fla. "The knife treatment will give you a perfectly straight line." Other experts warn that masking tape should be taken up as soon as paint has set; the longer it sticks, the harder it is to strip.

3. Use a short-bristled full-bodied brush, no wider than three inches for most jobs. "I've never seen an amateur use the right brush and take care of it properly," says Maynard Bray, the man in charge of maintaining more than 150 classic boats at Mystic Seaport in Connecticut. "For hi-gloss work or varnish, we're talking about a $10 brush with fine bristles, maybe 2½" wide. Badger hair is probably the best you can get. Ours come cut to a chisel edge. Using the right brush eliminates brush marks." For bottom work, where cosmetics may be less important, the experts agree that a wider brush could be used for speedier application. When a painting session is done, separate white from colored paint brushes and hang them—by drilling a hole in the handle for doweling or wire—in a bath of turpentine so

around the boat, backing up. "You can always tell an amateur painter," says one Massachusetts yard man with 40 years' experience, "if he's right-handed and starts anywhere but the starboard bow or port stern." Working clockwise provides the best chance to watch for "holidays" and "sags" while controlling your brush. Paint from the top of the boat down; work on the bottom should begin at the keel and work out.

6. Keep the brush close to your body during painting: never reach over your head. "You see guys out there on step ladders trying to paint the topsides as if they were painting a house," Gerry LaMarque says. "You can't do it on a boat topside. It's very important to address your work in a manner that's both safe, and gives you a chance to see what you're doing." Professionals use scaffolding. Borrow it for your job.

7. Finish a whole section of your boat in one session. Another sure sign of an amateur, comments Hans Gentsch of Minneford Yacht Yard in New York, is "the clear line of demarcation showing because he stopped work one afternoon and tried to paint into it the next." Just as the rings in a tree show its age, such lines on a boat show the inexperience of the painter.

8. Use paint retardant in a breeze or bright sun; use a dryer in damper conditions. Herman Quarnstrom of Z-Spar suggests adding up to 10 percent by volume of the company's thinner #10 or #11 for hot weather, or #8 for colder temperatures. Retardants keep paint from drying too fast, a problem causing lapping by preventing proper feathering-in. Dryers speed up the process. "Keep diddling with your paint," Bray suggests. "In spite of what the manufacturers say, paint just doesn't come ready for use. The amount of thinner depends on the conditions." But thinners, Al Merritt says, do take away from the life of the paint. The experts' consensus: don't be afraid to experiment to get the best consistency, but do it cautiously. Some pros point out that any departure from the thinning procedure recommended on the label would hinder chances of a refund in the event of the purchase of a bad batch of paint.

9. Plan your work so that the job is finished by the middle of the afternoon. Painting during the early evening dew may sound time-saving, but it can lead to spotting and mottling and loss of luster, the result of moisture condensing in the partly dried paint film. Most paints and varnishes should be allowed at least four hours' drying

the paint has a chance to sediment out.

4. Paint in sections about a foot wide, stroking into areas already painted. This is called "feathering in." If the paint is the right consistency, the technique eliminates the horizontal ridges, called "laps," or their vertical equivalent, called "curtains." Planning your work in sections also reduces the chance of "holidays," bare patches where your brush ran out of paint.

5. If you're right-handed, work clockwise

time before bombardment by tiny water particles. The best temperatures for painting, according to the International Paint Co. of New York are between 50° and 80° F, with a relative humidity not higher than 65 percent. Obviously the threat of rain should be enough to prevent you from opening a can. Hans Gentsch says that light offshore breezes provide preferable working conditions compared with an onshore blow and its resultant humidity. In an emergency, says Tom Errickson, a semi-retired yard foreman with 15 years' experience, you can remove moisture from the surface to be painted with an alcohol-soaked rag; a quart would be plenty for a 36' boat.

10. Use wet sanding on the bottom for a smoother racing hull. Special "wet-or-dry" paper is required; it comes with a waterproof backing and its grit is held together by an adhesive insoluble in water. Fineness generally runs from 180 to 500—but it can go as high as 800 for extra slick work. The secret, according to Gentsch, is using plenty of water. Keep dunking the paper in a bucket and spraying the surface with a hose, working in small patches. "The water does the cutting," he says.

11. Varnish everything you can indoors. "Take all your loose pieces home," Maynard Bray suggests. "Then you can put five or six coats on under ideal conditions. So many amateurs spend forever wooding down their work, sanding it, then hoping to make the varnish last with one or two coats. And the work always looks worse by August than it did before they started." Bray suggests using linseed oil mixed with pine tar and turpentine as a substitute for varnish on larger pieces. A gallon of oil mixed with a pint each of the pine tar and turps forms enough of a membrane to prevent rot and checks in the wood. Obviously, a pro never does varnishing or paint work in dusty conditions. And good finishers do not work out excess varnish from their brushes into their work pot of varnish. Instead, they scrape the frothy excess from their brush into a spare container. This trick prevents bubbles.

12. Buy the cheapest antifouling paint that works for your area and intended boat use. The list price of antifouling paints, says John Harken of Interlux paints in New York, is between $22 and $50 (some companies make extra-strong compounds costing up to $70). "If a boat is used only on weekends," Harken says, "a boatman might require a softer or faster-leaching paint. That's less expensive than the hard, racing type required if the boat is used frequently. The softer the paint, the faster the toxic ingredient is released."

Fitting out

When I launched this book, I promised myself that I would be the first writer about pleasure boating who did not refer to (1) what J. P. Morgan said about being able to afford a yacht (see February); (2) what Kenneth Grahame's Water Rat said about messing about in boats (see September); (3) the joke about the two happiest moments in boating (so far so good). I guess that some bits of nautical trivia are inevitable because they are applicable. Right now, for instance, it seems appropriate to introduce the ancient definition that a boat is a hole in the water surrounded by wood into which you pour money. You can substitute the material of your choice for wood, but the definition is still relevant, especially in the month of May, when fitting out is in full swing.

Fitting out means equipping a boat with what she needs. What a well-found vessel needs depends (after Coast Guard regulations are satisfied) on how you are going to use your boat and on your life style. For example, a dinghy is important both as an emergency exit and as a cruising convenience. But what kind should you get? Some possibilities are mulled over in the pages following.

And what about electronics? This is an open-ended department that can knock hell out of what is left of your budget. A VHF radio puts you in touch with the outside world (within a line-of-sight radius of 25 miles). An RDF can beam you in to a fogbound harbor. A depth finder can keep you from bending a prop in unmarked waters. Jack Kessler surveys a field that can be limited only by your cash flow (see page 62).

May is just about the right time for you to orient yourself in power boatmanship. I don't mean the kind of thing that's taught at the Power Squadron and Coast Guard Auxiliary classes: that's small boat *handling,* and it's a primary skill that won't prepare you for handling small boat conversation, the art of power boatmanship.

Since 50 percent of powerboating is talk, or maybe more, depending on the weather, this can be a serious deficiency. Here are a few tips on marine dialogue:

HOW TO TALK TO SAILBOAT PEOPLE

The best defense is a good offense. Before the owner of a sailboat has a chance to snarl something about "stinkpots" and wake, tell him you envy his boat. It's safer. (The majority of marine accidents do happen to powerboats.) It's less complicated. (No fuss about who has the right of way. It's always him.) It's more relaxing. (He can spend the weekend racing or just sailing about—while you really need to plan a destination. Will it be Mystic Seaport this weekend or Block Island? Cape May on your vacation, or Lake Champlain? Up through Canada to Lake Michigan, or down the Inland Waterway to Florida?) His eyes should start to bulge at this stage. Before he can answer, throw a line over your shoulder about how hard it is to replace a drive belt in six-foot swells, and walk away with a rolling gait.

HOW TO TALK TO POWERBOAT PEOPLE

Never ask another powerboat owner what he thinks of your boat. Veteran boatmen follow the unwritten law of motor boatmanship: Always knock the other man's boat. By knocking yours, they reassure themselves about theirs. Thus the unsuspecting lubber who asks someone what he thinks about a Whizcraft cruiser may get the following answers:

1. Whizcraft gelcoat cracks and crazes like an old teacup.
2. Whizcraft hulls have soft spots in the fiber glass.
3. Whizcraft has been bought by a pinball machine company which has worked a tilt into the hull.

If you want to respond to these comments, change the subject. Tell your friend that you heard somewhere that some Comfy-Cruze sedans (his boat) have been recalled because of an undetectable leak. That should give him something to think about.

HOW TO TALK TO FISHERMEN

Don't.

As for the rest of it, keep the following lines in mind, to use when appropriate: If you have a single engine, "twins are double trouble"; if you have twins, you "like the security of two engines"; if you don't have a depth finder, you "know of more boatmen who've piled up on the rocks with a depth finder"; if you have one, "gunkholing is the best part of boating." These should start you off. You have a few weeks yet to work up similar retorts for automatic pilot, radar, wet storage as opposed to dry, etc.

And be sure to develop a knowing smile. One knowing smile is worth a thousand words of boatmanship.

ABC's OF ELECTRONICS: A WORKING GUIDE

By Jack Kessler

may

Depthsounders/Sonar

What It Does

Measures depth of water beneath the boat. Sometimes can locate fish swimming between boat and bottom. Also helpful in coastal navigation for position-finding.

How It Works

Projects ultrasonic sound waves into the water through a hull-mounted transducer. The round-trip time of the sound waves reflected from the bottom and returning to the transducer is measured and translated to depth. Information can be displayed by a flashing light on circular dial, by meter needle, by illuminated numbers (digital readout) by inscription on a moving paper strip or by an inline display of flashing lights.

(Closely related to depthfinder is sonar, which projects sound waves in a full circle around boat and presents return echoes on a radar-like display. Expensive, but very effective in locating fish and underwater obstacles.)

Performance and Cost

Small-craft, lower-cost models measure depth to 60 to 120 feet. More elaborate equipment extends range to over 600 feet, with top-of-the-line chart recorders. Accuracy for all equipment is typically better than 5 percent of measured depth. Cost varies from under $100 to over $600.

Important Features

Rotating flasher is oldest and most popular type. Circular display easily locates fish and discloses nature of bottom by intensity and width of light flash. Display is hard to read in bright sunlight and relatively vulnerable to spurious but identifiable flashes from engine ignition noise.

Easiest to read and least affected by engine noise is digital display, which surrenders good fish-finding and bottom-identification ability. Much the same is true of meter displays.

Chart recorder is most expensive type and most vulnerable to water damage. Difficult to read from a distance. Chart display is best for fish finding and bottom identification, especially if equipped with "white-line" feature to "lift" bottom-feeding fish into view. Permanent record may be useful for navigation.

Many models, regardless of type, include multiple range scales and sensitivity controls, useful to adjust performance to various operating conditions. Some equipment, especially digital, adjusts automatically for best performance.

Adjustable depth alarms on some models are a mixed blessing subject to false alarms from engine interference or schools of fish. But may be helpful in fish finding or navigation.

Installation

Typical installation is through-hull mounting, though open boats may do better with removable transom mount. In powerboats, locate transducer in region of laminar water flow, as bubbles and turbulence degrade performance. Transducer in sailboats should be mounted to avoid sound reflections from keel. Off-center installation may require port and starboard transducers with automatic selector switch.

For best installation on any boat, check depthfinder handbook, boatbuilder or, most important, owners of similar boats.

In-hull water-box mounting is okay with thin-skinned fiberglass boats. Drag, fouling and leakage are avoided, but depth range is cut about 50 percent.

Route transducer cable away from engine to reduce interference.

WHO MAKES DEPTHFINDERS

Aqua Meter Instrument Corp., 465 Eagle Rock Ave., Rockland, N.J. 07068

Benmar, Div. of Cetec Corp., 3000 W. Warner Ave., Santa Ana, Cal. 92704

Bristol Electronics Inc., 651 Orchard St., New Bedford, Mass. 02744

Brocks Electronics USA, 12 Blanchard Rd., Burlington, Mass. 01803

Conlow Electronics (Garcia Corp.), 329 Alfred Ave., Teaneck, N.J. 07660

Danforth Div., The Eastern Co., 500 Riverside Pkwy., Portland, Maine 04103

Datamarine International Inc., 4 Commerce Park Rd., Pocasset, Mass. 02559

ITT Decca Marine Inc., 40 W. 57th St., New York, N.Y. 10019

GemTronics, 356 S. Blvd., Box 1408, Lake City, S.C. 29560

Heath Co., Benton Harbor, Mich. 49022

Lowrance Electronics, 12000 E. Skelly Dr., Tulsa, Okla. 74128

Morrow Electronics Inc., Box 7064, Salem, Oregon 97304

Pearce-Simpson Div., Gladding Corp. Box 520800, Biscayne Annex, Miami, Fla. 33152

Ray Jefferson, Main & Cotton Sts., Philadelphia, Pa. 19127

Raytheon/Apelco, 676 Island Pond Rd., Manchester, N.H. 03103

Ross Laboratories, 3138 Fairview Ave., Seattle, Wash. 98102

Simpson Electronics Inc., 2295 N.W. 14th St., Miami, Fla. 33129

Sonar Radio Corp., 73 Worth Ave., Brooklyn N.Y. 11207

Telisons International Corp., 7075 Vineland Ave., N. Hollywood, Cal. 91605

Unimetrics, 123 Jericho Tpk., Syosset, N.Y. 11791

Vexilar Inc., 9345 Penn Ave. S., Minneapolis, Minn. 55431

Western Marine Electronics, 905 Dexter Ave. N., Seattle, Wash. 98109

Radar

What It Does

Indicates presence of vessels, land masses and other objects within its range by electronic means. Obviously useful in conditions of poor visibility, but can be helpful in navigation and collision avoidance at any time.

How It Works

Radio waves at 10 MHz or other microwave frequency are radiated in a narrow beam by a rotating antenna. These waves travel in a straight line towards the horizon and are reflected back to the antenna by any large objects, especially metallic ones, that they encounter. Return echoes are displayed as bright spots on a TV-like screen. As the antenna rotates, it traces on the screen a rather complete picture of the terrain, traffic and obstacles around the boat on which it is mounted.

Performance and Price

Most small-craft radars have ranges of between 10 and 30 miles, depending on antenna height and power. More important than range is clarity of display, sensitivity to small objects and resolution of closely spaced objects, especially at moderate ranges.

Prices for full-size radars begin at about $2500, plus installation costs of at least several hundred dollars. Short-range radars and audio-display portable radars also are available at considerably lower cost.

Important Features

There are two approaches to designing a small-craft radar. The more popular, lower-power radars include the transmitter and the antenna in one package that is mounted aloft. This reduces electrical losses and cuts installation costs. Only the display and power supply are housed in the control unit at the bridge. The drawback to this approach is the need to go aloft for most trouble shooting.

With larger radars, the transmitter becomes too unwieldy for external mounting. Most of the electronics therefore are housed below decks. Radar signals are then piped to and from the antenna by rather expensive metallic waveguides or coaxial cables.

Some antennas are enclosed in a protective housing or radome. Others rotate in the open. Each design has its merits. The radome adds bulk, but offers some protection and cuts wind resistance. The open antenna costs less and looks impressive when rotating. Take your choice, but keep in mind that the wider the antenna, the more detail will be presented on the radar screen, all other things being equal.

Look for the largest display screen for a given

price. Magnifying covers are a makeshift approach. Low power consumption also is welcome. The more powerful radars have a rather enormous appetite for electricity. Review your boat's electrical system against the power requirements of any radars on your short list. A 32-V electrical system is almost mandatory for larger radars.

Control functions are similar for most radars. All units should have, at least, controls for range, pulse repetition frequency, sea clutter and rain clutter suppression, display brightness, local-oscillator control and sensitivity. If a radar seems lacking in control functions determine to your satisfaction why that is so.

Installation

Weight aloft, safety and a clear path for the radar signal should be considered in all installations. Sailboats and certain powerboats cannot tolerate much top hamper. Therefore, some sacrifice in range must be made by lowering the height of the antenna.

On the other hand, the antenna must be mounted well above eye level because of the health hazards entailed in microwave radiation. Deck mounted antennas not only sacrifice range, but can be biologically dangerous.

Metal masts and some rigging will not unduly block the radar signal, but avoid tuna towers, complex rigging and deck houses in the path of the radar unless you can tolerate a blind spot in the direction of the obstacle.

WHO MAKES RADAR SETS

Benmar, 3000 W. Warner, Santa Ana, Cal. 92704
Bonzer, Inc., 90th & Cody, Overland Par, Kan. 66214
Brock's Electronic Corp., 12 Blanchard Rd., Burlington, Mass. 01803
Epsco, 411 Providence Highway, Westwood, Mass. 02090
Konel, 271 Harbor Way, S. San Francisco, Cal. 94080
Kelvin Hughes, 9 Petersburg-Clearwater Airport, Box 5389, Clearwater, Fla. 33518
ITT Decca, 40 W. 57th St., New York, N.Y. 10019
Ray Jefferson, Main & Cotton Sts., Philadelphia, Pa. 19127
Raytheon Marine Co., 676 Island Pond Rd., Manchester, N.H. 03103
Ridge Electronics Corp., Rt. 6, Box 401A, Charlottesville, Va. 22901
Whistler Marine Inc., One Adams St., Littleton Common, Mass. 01460

Loran and Omega

What They Do

Determine position electronically by receiving specially broadcast signals from government-operated shore stations. Special charts are needed to convert the received signals to geographic position. Range varies, depending on the system, but can be world-wide.

How They Work

Principles of Loran and Omega are very similar. Shore stations at various locations broadcast synchronized signals. The time and/or phase difference between signal pairs arriving at the receiver locate it along a certain line of position as set forth on special charts. By selecting different pairs of stations in turn, the navigator can quickly cross two or more lines of position to locate the vessel with high accuracy.

Broadcast frequency of Loran C is 100 KHz; Omega operates at 10.2 and 13.6 KHz.

Performance and Cost

Automatic Loran-C equipment is accurate to better than ¼ mile. Manually adjusted receivers fare somewhat worse. The Loran-A system, which predates Loran-C, is still in use but will be phased out in the early 1980s. It is not nearly as accurate. To take advantage of both systems, with their different coverages, there are combination Loran A/C receivers. Purchase of a separate Loran-A receiver is not recommended because of its now-short useful life.

Loran-C coverage is concentrated in the northern hemisphere, especially in U.S. waters. Effective range is about 1000 miles offshore. Simple, manually operated receivers are available for less than $1000. Automatic tracking receivers needed to obtain the full inherent accuracy of the system cost between $2000 and $5000. Greatest accuracy is developed by units with built-in cycle-matching systems. Prices of all units are dropping significantly as sales volume increases in response to planned termination of Loran-A.

Omega receivers will offer world-wide coverage before 1980 as a planned chain of eight stations finally goes on the air. Present coverage is concentrated in the northern hemisphere and the South Atlantic Ocean.

Accuracy is better than one mile and range is over 5000 miles.

The nature of the Omega signal creates a position ambiguity that must be resolved by knowing initial position at the beginning of a voyage and constantly updating known position. Thus, the Omega receiver must be operated continuously throughout the voyage. Interruption by power failure or otherwise requires position to be recalculated by celestial navigation or dead reckoning. Therefore, many Omega receivers include built-in standby batteries, or a chart recorder to indicate position at all times.

The automatic receivers that must be used in Omega are more expensive than the manual Loran systems, but comparable to automatic Loran-C equipment. Figure $2000 to $7500 for an Omega receiver. The latter price is for a unit with a built-in computer to convert Omega readings to geographic position without the aid of special charts.

Antennas and sometimes-difficult installation would add several hundred dollars to the price of any navigation receivers.

Important Features

Manual Loran receivers measure the difference between signals by displaying them on an oscilloscope, which resembles a small TV screen. Some skill is required to extract the most accurate position, especially at extreme ranges. With practice, better accuracy is achieved.

In contrast, automatic equipment is much easier to use, and the cycle-matching feature built into the better units results in highest possible accuracy. A drawback to automatic equipment is its somewhat higher power drain.

Some units automatically generate and display two lines of position, thus providing a continuous fix for the navigator.

Installation

Omega and Loran systems are quite vulnerable to electrical interference from engines and other electrical equipment. Generators, power lines, inverters, etc. all should be carefully shielded and suppressed.

Antennas must be carefully installed for best reception. Given the constraints of a shipboard installation, this is often more of an art than a science. Several attempts may be needed to achieve a satisfactory installation.

WHO MAKES LORAN AND OMEGA

LORAN
ITT Decca Marine Inc., 40 W. 57th St., New York, N.Y. 10019
Digital Marine Electronics Corp., Civil Air Terminal, Bedford, Mass. 01730
Epsco Inc., 411 Providence Highway, Westwood, Mass. 02090
GemTronics, 356 S. Blvd., Box 1408, Lake City, S.C. 29560
Konel Corp., 271 Harbor Way, Box 2343, So. San Francisco, Cal. 94080
Litcom Div. of Amecom, 5115 Calvert Rd., College Park, Md. 20740
Micrologic Inc., 9436 Irondale Ave., Chatsworth, Cal. 91311
Mieco, Div., of Polarad Electronic Corp., 109 Beaver Ct. Cockeysville, Md. 21030
Morrow Electronics Inc., Box 7064, Salem, Oregon 97304
Nautical Electronics Co. Inc., 7095 Milford Ind. Rd., Baltimore, Md. 21208
Ray Jefferson, Main & Cotton Sts., Philadelphia, Pa. 19127
Raytheon Marine Co., 676 Island Pond Rd., Manchester, N.H. 03103
Simrad Inc., One Labriola Ct., Armonk, N.Y. 10504
Teledyne Systems Co., 19601 Nordhoff St., Northridge, Cal. 91324
Vexilar, Inc., 9345 Penn Ave. S., Minneapolis, Minn. 55431

OMEGA
Dynell Electronics, 75 Maxers Rd., Melville, N.Y. 11746
Epsco Inc., 411 Providence Highway, Westwood, Mass. 02090
Micro Instrument Co., Box 1565, Escondido, Cal. 92025
Mieco, Div. of Polarad Electronic Corp., 109 Beaver Ct. Cockeysville, Md. 21030
Raytheon Marine Co., 676 Island Pond Rd. Manchester, N.H. 03103
Tracor Industrial Instruments, 6500 Tracor Lane, Austin, Texas 78721

VHF Radio

What It Does

Broadcasts and receives voice signals over line-of-sight distances (about 20 miles) for ship-to-ship and ship-to-shore communication. Vital for emergencies and convenient for calling shore via marine-operator channels.

How It Works

FM signals are broadcast on frequencies in the 156-MHz band. Fifty-six transmitting channels available, but specific functions are assigned to each channel. For example: Channel 16 for emergencies, Channel 13 for harbor traffic and Channel 26 for marine operator. Two channels for receiving government weather broadcasts also available.

Signals are broadcast and received by a short whip antenna. Transmission is "Simplex"; unlike telephone, one cannot talk and listen at the same time.

Performance and Cost

Maximum power is legally limited to 25 watts, with one watt selectable for very short range operation. Walkie-talkie models offer 1 or 2 w. Maximum range more dependent on height of receiving and transmitting antennas than on transmitter power. Coast Guard receiving system designed to hear emergency communication to 30 miles offshore with only 1-w transmitter power. Reasonable range between boats is 15 miles. Marine operator range is somewhat better.

Cost of 12-channel set with crystal complement is between $400 and $700. Synthesized all-channel radios cost from $600 to $1500. Add typical cost of $50 to $100 for antenna and installation.

Important Features

Most receivers provide for 12 working channels with a few offering 18 or 24. Latest trend is to all-channel synthesized receivers. Expensive, but not that much more costly than 12-channel sets with all crystals installed. Better access to all channels is important with heavy radio traffic in popular boating areas.

Twenty-five-watt maximum power is now virtually standard among manufacturers. Lower-power units, except for portables, are hardly justified. All equipment on market is fully transistorized, but look for such desirable features as output stage protection to save transistors from damage if antenna or cabling become defective.

Performance specifications of "selectivity" and "sensitivity" are important. Sensitivity is given in microvolts; the smaller the number, the better (one is typical). Sensitivity and Spurious Signal Rejection are stated in dB; the larger these numbers, the better. 60 dB or better are good levels of performance.

Deluxe features, nice if you need them, include continuous monitoring of designated channels (especially 16), remote speakers and controls for boats with multiple steering stations and telephone ringers coded to actuate only your radio.

Operating convenience features also should be noted. Some radios are designed with hard-to-read dials, impossible-to-use controls, too-short microphone cords, clumsy mounting brackets, etc. Good audio quality promotes intelligibility, so try to listen and touch before you buy.

Installation

No radio is better than its antenna. Choose the best you can afford. A so-so radio and good antenna will perform better than the reverse combination. Mount the antenna as high as possible to increase range. That's easy on sailboats; on powerboats, a tall whip antenna is indicated. Such antennas often are designed to provide a certain amount of signal gain as compared to smaller antennas—a good idea.

Use good quality antenna cable to reduce losses. The heavy RG-8 cable is preferable to the thinner RG-58. Foam-insulated cable is best for the heavier sizes.

Electrical power requirements are moderate, but a separate battery dedicated to the radio is recommended. Leave enough slack in cable and power leads so that the radio can be removed from its bracket to a convenient location for on-board troubleshooting.

WHO MAKES VHF RADIOS

Benmar, Div. of Cetec Corp., 3000 W. Warner Ave., Santa Ana, Cal. 92704

Bristol Electronics, 651 Orchard St., New Bedford, Mass. 02774

Brocks Electronics, 12 Blanchard Rd., Burlingham, Mass. 01803

Emergency Beacon Corp., 15 River St., New Rochelle, N.Y. 10801

GemTronics, 356 S. Blvd., Box 1408, Lake City, S.C. 29560

General Aviation Electronics Inc., 4141 Kingman Dr., Indianapolis, Ind. 46226

Hy-Gain Electronics, 8601 N.E. Highway 6, Lincoln, Neb. 68505

ICOM East, Suite 307, 3331 Towerwood, Dallas, Texas 75234

Intech Inc., 1220 Coleman Ave., Santa Clara, Cal. 95050

ITT Decca Marine, Inc., 40 W. 57th St., New York, N.Y. 10019

Konel Corp., 271 Harbor Way, Box 2343, So. San Francisco, Cal. 94080

Linear Systems Inc., 220 Airport Blvd., Watsonville, Cal. 95076

Lowrance Electronics, 12000 E. Skelly Dr., Tulsa, Okla. 74128

Morrow Electronics Inc., Box 7064, Salem, Oregon 97304

Pathcom, 24049 S. Frampton Ave., Harbor City, Cal. 90710

Pearce-Simpson Div., Gladding Corp., Box 520800, Biscayne Annex, Miami, Fla. 33152

RF Communications, 1680 University Ave., Rochester, N.Y. 14610

Ray Jefferson, Main & Cotton Sts., Philadelphia, Pa. 19127

Raytheon/Apelco, 676 Island Pond Rd., Manchester, N.H. 03103

Sailor Radio A.S., 9000 Aalborg, Denmark

SBE Inc., 220 Airport Blvd., Watsonville, Cal. 95076

Simpson Electronics Inc., 2295 N.W. 14th St., Miami, Fla. 33125

Sonar Radio Corp., 73 Wortman Ave., Brooklyn, N.Y. 11207

Standard Communications, 639 N. Main. Wilmington, Cal. 90744

Swan Marine Electronics, 305 Airport Rd., Oceanside, Cal. 92054

Unimetrics Inc., 1534 Old Country Rd., Plainview, N.Y. 11803

Radio Direction Finders

What It Does

Aids navigation by measuring the compass bearing of a vessel from special radio beacons or AM commercial broadcast stations. Cross-bearings on more than one station, or successive bearings on the same station, let the skipper determine his position with reasonable accuracy. The beacons also can be used for homing. Used primarily for coastwise navigation.

How It Works

A cylindrical ferrite rod antenna is highly directional. Comparable in size and shape to a ball-point pen, it is a very sensitive antenna if oriented broadside to the radio transmitter, but a very poor antenna when it is pointing directly at the station. If such an antenna, connected to a receiver, is rotated about its axis in the horizontal plane, a sharp reduction in received signal strength indicates that the antenna is directly in line with the station. The bearing is read on a built-in compass or from a pelorus ring.

Signal strength can be measured by ear or by a meter. Accuracy is about equal with either method.

World-wide, the beacon band extends from 230 to 430 KHz. But in American waters, the more than 100 radio beacons operated by the Coast Guard operate between 286 and 325 KHz.

Performance and Price

Range is determined by the power of the beacon station and can be anywhere from 100 miles for major seaport approach beacons to less than one mile for some beacons on inland waters.

Accuracy with a properly calibrated unit can be ±1 degree in the hands of a skilled operator. The average boatman, with little practice in direction finding and with a unit that probably has not been calibrated for deviation, should not hope for more than ±5 deg. accuracy. Somewhat better results would be obtained with an automatic direction finder.

Most hand-held and table-top units cost between $100 and $300. A few imported direction finders built to rather high standards cost more than $1000. Automatic direction finders are available at prices from under $500 for table-top models to more than $1500 for commercial-grade equipment.

Important Features

The three basic types of RDF are the hand-held, the table-top and the automatic finder. The handheld RDF is convenient in that it can be used away from engine interference and deviations caused by lifelines, rigging and other metal masses. Because hand-held units include a compass, bearing of the station can be read directly without reference to ship's course. The finder also can be used as a hand-bearing compass.

A drawback to hand-held RDFs is absence of a separate "sense" antenna. Without this feature, a part of many table-top units, one cannot unequivocally know which end of the loop antenna points to the beacon. However, reasonable care in navigation or a group of successive readings on the same beacon should resolve this 180-degree ambiguity.

Table-top units usually include multiple operating bands and are as much designed to be entertainment receivers as for navigation. Their array of meters, dials, switches and scales adds a certain flexibility, but they are not inherently more accurate than simpler equipment.

Best of all, if correctly installed and calibrated, is the automatic direction finder. Signal direction is established without ambiguity by electronic circuits and displayed on a compass circle. Table-top ADFs require especially careful calibration because the antenna is not remotely lo-

Ray Jefferson Model "202" Depth Computer

Pearce-Simpson "Bimini 25A" VHF/FM Radio Telephone

Pearce-Simpson "Dolphin 360" Depth Finder

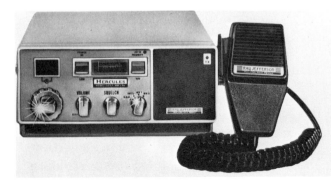

Ray Jefferson 71 Channel VHF/FM Radio Telephone

Ray Jefferson Automatic Radio Direction Finder, Model "6150"

cated for interference-free rejection. The more elaborate ADFs have large, remotely-mounted multiple-loop antennas that can be located for greater accuracy.

The major difficulty in using a non-automatic RDF is that the beacon stations broadcast in code and at staggered intervals. If one is slow in tuning the station and recognizing its code, the broadcast cycle is completed and the navigator must wait about 5 minutes for the station to resume broadcasting. As most RDF dials are not very precisely calibrated, many users have some difficulty.

Three improvements are offered for this problem. Some table-top units have several crystal-controlled channels for push-button tuning of selected beacon frequencies. One hand-held RDF has plug-in modules preset to the various beacons. Finally, there's a table-top RDF with a digital tuning indicator. Any of these tuning methods can be helpful.

For homing in on a beacon rather than measuring its bearing, some RDFs have a left-right course indicator.

Installation

The below-deck location of a table-top RDF is probably the worst place for its use in navigation. As a practical matter, the unit should be well removed from engine interference and should be held outside of error-inducing lifelines or rigging.

Since it is too heavy to be held and used in this fashion, the RDF must be calibrated for its position of use. Such calibration should be made at frequencies near the center of the beacon and broadcast bands. The boat is "swung" near a visible beacon or broadcast antenna and a deviation chart compiled in the same way that a compass deviation chart is generated. Automatic direction finders must be calibrated similarly.

WHO MAKES RADIO DIRECTION FINDERS

Apelco Marine Electronics, 676 Island Pond Rd., Manchester, N.H. 03103
Benmar, Div. of Cetec Corp., 3000 W. Warner Ave., Santa Ana, Cal. 92704
Brocks Electronics, 12 Blanchard Rd., Burlington, Mass. 01803
Brookes & Gatehouse, 154 E. Boston Post Rd., Mamaroneck, N.Y. 10543
GemTronics, 356 South Blvd., Lake City, S.C. 29560

Heath Co., Benton Harbor, Mi. 49022
Konel, 271 Harbor Way, So. San Francisco, Cal. 94080
Pearce-Simpson Div., Gladding Corp., Box 520800, Biscayne Annex, Miami, Fla. 33152
Ray Jefferson, Main & Cotton Sts., Philadelphia, Pa. 19127
Sailor Radio, 9000 Aalborg, Denmark
Sonar Radio Corp., 73 Wortman Ave., Brooklyn, N.Y. 11207
Unimetrics Inc., 1534 Old Country Rd., Plainview, N.Y. 11803
Vec/Trak Research & Development Corp., South Dixie Highway, Pompano Beach W., Fla. 33060

Fuel-Vapor Detectors

What It Does

Samples the atmosphere in boat for presence of explosive gases and sounds alarm before concentration of such gases becomes dangerous. Some detectors also respond to smoke, rising bilge water and carbon monoxide gas.

How It Works

Equipment consists of a sensing element and control circuitry. Sensors operating on various principles may be used. Electrical characteristics of the sensor change in presence of explosive mixture. These changes are measured by control circuit which displays the condition by audible alarm, flashing light or meter needle. Some devices may also automatically kill the engine.

Performance and Cost

All units on the market achieve their primary function of detecting explosive vapors without significant difference in performance. Sophistication of display, engine interlock, multiple sensors, etc., distinguish one unit from another.

Price range of $75 to $150 for most instruments is narrowest among all classes of marine electronic equipment. The 2-to-1 price ratio suggest a well-developed technology that has solved its basic problem.

Important Features

Two sensing methods are used, divided about 50-50 among manufacturers. First is the so-called "cold sensor." This is a solid-state, low-current device sensitive to a wide variety of combustible and non-combustible gases. Its drawbacks are susceptibility to water damage and longish recovery time after exposure to vapors. In practice, neither of these drawbacks is significant.

The other type of sensor uses a semiconductor that achieves a flameless reaction with explosive vapors. It is housed in a protective double-mesh cage which, if punctured, could create an explosive hazard. Like the cold sensor it has a long and reliable operating life. Of possible advantage is its use as a smoke detector.

A third method, still used by a few manufacturers, is the hotwire sensor, now obsolete because of its short life compared to other methods.

Display should always include an audible alarm. Additional visual display is helpful as a backup and to indicate the severity of the explosive hazard. Meters are the most common indicators, but flashing lights are also used.

All units have a self-test feature that should be exercised whenever the instrument is turned on. However, this usually tests only the electronic equipment, not the sensor. Therefore, the sensing element also should be inspected occasionally.

Installation

Explosive vapors, usually gasoline or cooking gas, are heavier than air and settle in the bilges. The sensor should be mounted as low as possible without danger of immersion and near the fuel system of the engine. Locate it so as to be visible and accessible for inspection and testing. Test the sensor by bathing it in a few drops of gasoline or the gas jet of an unlit propane torch.

The control box should be placed where visible from the helm and near the ignition switch to suggest its use before starting the engine.

WHO MAKES FUEL VAPOR DETECTORS

Aqua Meter, 465 Eagle Rock Rd., Roseland, N.J. 07068
D.C. Electronics, Box 15183, Seattle, Wash. 98115
Danforth, 500 Riverside Industrial Pkwy., Portland, Maine 04103
Heath Co., Benton Harbor, Mich. 49022
Ray Jefferson, Main and Cotton Sts., Philadelphia, Pa. 19127
JW Division of Bacharach Instrument, 2300 Leghorn St. Mountain View, Cal. 94043
Lucci Marine, Sarasota, Fla.
Koehler Mfg. Co., Box R, Marlborough, Mass. 01752
Seaboard Imports, 808 Devonshire Rd., Victoria, B.C. Canada
Selectromarine, Poole, Dorset, England

United Recording Electronics Industries, 11922 Valerio St., N. Hollywood, Cal. 91605
Vetus, W. H. Denouden (USA), Inc., 7170 Standard Dr., Parkway Industrial Center, Dorsey, Md. 21076
West Wind Products, 150 Tejon St., Denver, Col. 80223
Whistler Marine, 1 Adams St., Littleton Common, Mass. 01460

Single Sideband Radio

What It Does

Broadcasts and receives voice signals over extremely long distances. (Ranges of several thousand miles are routinely possible) for ship-to-ship, ship-to-shore and safety communications. SSB thus is a supplement to VHF short-range radio for the boatman.

How It Works

Operation is in various bands from 2 to 22 MHz. Each band has a different optimum range depending on time of day, season, sunspot activity, etc. Transmission is much more efficient than conventional AM or FM radio because nearly all the signal is concentrated into one information-carrying "sideband" frequency. Ordinary broadcasting divides and wastes power among a central "carrier" frequency and two adjacent sidebands above and below the carrier in frequency.

Range also is vastly increased because the frequencies used are reflected by an electrically charged layer of the atmosphere (the ionosphere) and can return to earth thousands of miles from their origin. Signal propagation within the first few hundred miles is by normal radiation along the earth's surface. Beyond that zone, ionospheric propagation is more significant.

An international network of hundreds of shore stations assures world-wide coverage with even moderately powered receivers.

Signals are broadcast and received by long wire or whip antennas. Lengths of 21 and 35 feet are common. The antennas, their requisite ground systems and associated electronic equipment are much more complex than VHF antennas.

Specially designed radios are needed for SSB operation. A hybrid "compatible" SSB mode that allows communication with previously accepted AM marine receivers is obsolete as of Jan. 1, 1977.

Performance and Cost

Contact with at least one shore station, regardless of where the vessel may be, is possible with an output power of 100 watts and, sometimes, with even less power. Most SSB radios of interest to the pleasure boatman are in the 50 to 200-watt power range. Frequency bands offered increase with equipment complexity and price. At least the 2- and 4-MHz bands are included in all units on the market. Capability in the 6-, 8- and 12-MHz bands also is fairly common. The 16- and 22-MHz bands are less frequently offered as their value is erratic, depending on the vagaries of the 11-year sun-spot cycle.

Basic units cost under $1000. More elaborate equipment can exceed $10,000, depending on the power, number of bands and channels offered. However, a very competent unit should not cost more than about $2000. Add to this anywhere from $200 to $2000 for antennas, couplers, grounding systems and installation.

Important Features

Within your budget, look for the most power and the largest coverage of bands and channels. All-transistorized design is almost universal under 200 watts. It is preferable for reliability and for lower power drain. Even so, a 100-w transistorized unit will draw nearly 15 amps at 12V when transmitting.

All-channel synthesis as available in CB and VHF radios also is offered in SSB equipment. Price is much higher because several hundred channels are possible among the various bands.

Installation

Antenna design for SSB can be troublesome. Many frequency bands must be handled by the same antenna. The length of the antennas also complicates installation, especially on power boats. Most sailboats can use insulated backstays as antennas.

Except for certain still-controversial units, all SSB antennas must be grounded. The ground cannot be simply a wire or Dynaplate immersed in water, but must present large areas of metal under the antenna. Decks and lockers lined with copper mesh, engine blocks, water tanks, etc., all may be pressed into service. Metal boats, particularly aluminum ones, avoid this problem.

Power requirements are severe. Heavy wiring, a rugged battery located well above the bilges and quality installation of the entire system are essential. More so than with VHF or CB radio, one's life when offshore may depend on performance of the SSB radio. For these, and other reasons, installation of an SSB radio is not a do-it-yourself proposition.

WHO MAKES SINGLE SIDEBAND RADIOS

Benmar, 3000 W. Warner, Santa Ana, Cal. 92704
Communication Associates, Inc., 200 McKay Rd., Huntington Station, N.Y. 11746
ITT Decca Marine, 40 W. 57th St., New York, N.Y. 10019
R. L. Drake Co., 540 Richard St., Miamisburg, Ohio, 45342
General Aviation Electronics (Genave), 4141 Kingman Dr., Indianapolis, Ind., 46226
Harris Corp, 1680 University Ave., Rochester, N.Y. 14610
Konel, 271 Harbor Way, So. San Francisco, Cal. 94080
Maritak, Inc. 1819 South Central, Kent, Wash. 98031
Modar Electronics, 2100 N. Meacham Rd., Schaumburg, Ill. 60172
Northern Radio Co., 4027 21st. Ave. West, Seattle, Wash. 98199
Raytheon Marine Co., 676 Island Pond Rd., Manchester, N.H. 03103
SGC, Inc., 13737 S.E. 26th St., Bellevue, Wash. 98005
SideBand Associates, Inc., 1133 Old Bayshore Highway, San Jose, Cal. 95112

CB Radio

What It Does

Broadcasts and receives voice signals over short ranges (about five to ten miles). Useful for informal boat-to-boat conversations, but is not monitored officially by the Coast Cuard or tied into the marine telephone operator system. CB is the only prevalent communication system on many inland waters and has definite value for certain marine applications.

How It Works

AM signals are broadcast on frequencies in the 27-MHz band. Twenty-three channels are available, with 46 additional channels open for non-compatible single-sideband transmission. Additional channels may be allocated in the near future, but these will supplement the existing 23 and will not obsolete existing equipment.

Antennas are whip types about six feet long, still convenient enough for boats. Grounding is usually not required. Note: conventional automobile CB antennas will not work afloat.

Performance and Cost

All equipment is legally limited to 4 watts output power. Accordingly, typical range is perhaps ten miles over open water in ship-to-ship communication. If one station is ashore and equipped with a tall, high-gain antenna, somewhat greater range can be expected.

Walkie-talkie units develop 1 or 2 watts, have shorter antennas and should not be relied upon for more than a few miles of range.

A basic 23-channel transceiver with minimum frills will cost about $100. More elaborate models may run to about $250 and single-sideband units to about $400.

Higher price does not buy more power or range, but can improve intelligibility by including noise limiters, power microphones, delta tuning and more precise frequency control. All such features are useful, but even the simplest CB works fairly well without them.

Twenty-three channel hand-held transceivers coat from $150 to $200. Because of space limitations, their design usually is rather basic.

Equipment with less than 23 channels, though available at lower prices, is not recommended. With the heavy radio traffic in most metropolitan areas, the more channels one can choose from, the better.

Antennas and installation hardware should cost about $50.

Important Features

Most CB radios, though designed for the booming automotive market, are perfectly suitable for marine service if they are protected from water and spray. The basic radios work well enough in most cases. However, a noise blanker (better than a noise limiter) is a very desirable extra feature.

All 23-channel units use a frequency synthesizer that generates all frequencies from only a few crystals. Phase-locked synthesizers available in premium equipment are more accurate and stable, but of interest only to those who desire the ultimate in performance. Single-level indicators, digital displays, microphone mounted controls and delta tuning also are nice to have but not essential. Some CB radios include a public-address system. This last feature could be valuable for some boatmen.

Single-sideband CB now accounts for about ten percent of the market. Somewhat better range is achieved, but only if both parties to a conversation use SSB. All SSB radios also can operate in the conventional AM mode.

Installation

Nothing could be simpler. Mount the bracket to a bulkhead, hook up the battery, plug in the antenna and you're on the air in reasonably fine fashion. There's lots of extra equipment available to test and tune the antennas and cabling, but that's for the technically minded user. The average boatman will be happy simply to know he can communicate, which is what America's CB party line is all about.

WHO MAKES CB RADIOS

Boman Astrosonix, 9300 Hall Rd., Downey, Cal. 90241
Browning Laboratories, Laconia, N.H. 03246
Cobra (Dynascan) 1801 W. Belleplaine, Chicago, Ill. 60613
Craig Corp., 921 W. Artesia Blvd., Compton, Cal. 90220
GemTronics, Box 1408, Lake City, S.C. 29560
General Aviation Electronics (Genave), 4141 Kingman Drive, Indianapolis, Ind. 46226
Grand Banks (Shakespeare), Box 246, Columbia, S.C. 29202
Handic of USA, Inc., 14560 N.W. 60th Ave., Miami Lakes, Fla. 33014
Hitachi, 401 W. Artesia Blvd., Compton, Cal. 90220
Hy-Gain Electronics Corp., 8601 N.E. Highway 6, Lincoln, Neb. 68505
Johnson, E. F., Waseca, Minn. 56093
Lafayette Radio, 111 Jericho Turnpike, Syosset, N.Y. 11791
Midland International Corp., Box 19032, Kansas City, Mo. 64141
Motorola, Inc., 1301 East Algonquin Rd., Schaumburg, Ill. 60172
Pace (Pathcom), 24049 S. Frampton Ave., Harbor City, Cal. 90710
Pearce-Simpson (Gladding), 4701 N.W. 77th Ave., Miami, Fla. 33166
Radio Shack (Tandy Corp.), Ft. Worth, Tex. 76107
Ray Jefferson, Main & Cotton Sts., Philadelphia, Pa. 19127
RCA, Special Products Div., Cherry Hill Offices, Camden, N.J. 08101
Regency Electronics, 7707 Records St., Indianapolis, Ind. 46226
Royce Electronics Corp., 1746 Levee Rd., N. Kansas City, Mo. 64116
Sanyo Electric, 1200 W. Artesia Blvd., Compton, Cal. 90220
SBE Inc., 220 Airport Blvd., Watsonville, Cal. 95076
Sharp Electronics, 10 Keystone Pl., Paramus, N.J. 07652
Siltronix, 330 Via El Centro Ave., Oceanside, Cal. 92054
Sonar Radio Corp., 73 Wortman Ave., Brooklyn, N.Y., N.Y. 11207

Standard Communications, 108 W. Victoria, Carson, Cal. 90746

Teaberry Electronics Corp., 4655 Mass. Ave., Indianapolis, Ind. 46218

Unimetrics, 123 Jericho Tpk., Syosset, N.Y. 11791

Vexilar, Inc., 9345 Penn Ave. S., Minneapolis, Minn. 55431

Zodiac Communications, Chrysler Bldg., New York, N.Y. 10017

Autopilots

What They Do

Automatically and continually steers boat along a preset compass course. In some sailboat models, steering is at a constant angle to the wind.

How They Work

The automatic pilot (autopilot) consists of a compass or other magnetic sensor, an electronic control unit and a steering motor, either electric or hydraulic, connected to the rudder. If the boat deviates from the desired course, an error sensor in the compass (usually a pair of photo cells) delivers an error signal to the control unit.

In turn, the control unit drives the steering motor so as to return the boat to its course. A sensor at the rudder informs the control unit how far the rudder has turned so as to reduce overcorrection. In some autopilots, the error signal also can be exercised by a small wind vane rather than by a compass. Such autopilots should not be confused with true self-steerers because an electric motor, rather than wind or water power, actuates the rudder to correct the course.

Performance and Cost

All automatic pilots are very accurate insofar as steering along the average course is concerned. Eventually, the boat should arrive within a degree or two of its objective.

Where some autopilots are better than others is in how straight or how smoothly the course is steered. If the boat zig-zags along the desired course, writing its name in the water, the comfort, economy of time and reduced fuel consumption promised by the unit are not achieved.

The sophisticated control systems that respond smoothly to an error signal and that are unaffected by pitch and roll of the vessel do not come cheaply. Neither do the heavy motors and hardware needed to swing the rudder of large,

high-speed pleasure boats. Fortunately, there's equipment for every purpose. Some boatmen want only a device to free them from the monotony of long hours at the wheel on those bright, calm days or cold, damp nights. For the pleasure boatman, $500 to $3000 spans most of the available or suitable equipment.

Important Features

Small-craft systems are invariably all-electric; in larger units hydraulic systems often are used. There is no special advantage to either method, but hydraulic systems can be more convenient in larger boats. In any event, power drain is considerable, ranging from a few amps continuous draw in small boats to a dozen or more for heavy-duty models.

Magnetic sensors rather than compasses tend to be found in premium equipment. Such devices are less affected by motion of the boat in a seaway. They also are more compatible with electronic control systems. The avoidance of moving parts in the sensor also can be an advantage.

Autopilots should have "dodger" control to override the system for immediate manual operation in emergencies. The dodger then allows the boat to resume its previous, automatically steered course.

In tiller-operated automatic pilots for small sailboats, the dodger may consist merely of lifting the tiller out of the control yoke.

Remote controls for flying bridge or tuna towers are available in some units.

Installation

Except for portable, tiller-mounted units, an automatic pilot is definitely *not* a do-it-yourself installation. The sensing unit must be located well away from magnetic influences, while the motors and other electronic equipment must be installed so as not to affect the boat's conventional steering compass. In any event, compass adjustment is highly desirable after installation of an automatic pilot.

Steering hardware must be precisely aligned and securely installed. The forces exerted by even a smallish steering motor can be substantial.

Equipment also must be installed for easy inspection and servicing. It is part of your steering system, like it or not, and its failure also could affect the manual part of the steering.

Automatic pilots have not yet been sold in large quantities and not every dealer or boatyard has the necessary experience in installing such equipment. Check around and talk to boatmen who already have autopilot installations.

WHO MAKES AUTOPILOTS

Benmar, Div. of Cetec Corp., 3000 W. Warner Ave., Santa Ana, Cal. 92704

Brocks Electronics, 12 Blanchard Rd., Burlington, Mass. 01803

Danforth Div., The Eastern Co., 500 Riverside Industrial Pkwy., Portland, Maine 04103

ITT Decca Marine Inc., 40 W. 57th St., New York, N.Y. 10019

Electro-Mechanical Products Inc., Box 330778, Miami, Fla. 33133

Helms-Mate Corp., 200 Terminal Dr., Plainview, N.Y. 11803

Isotack Co., 1409 Mimosa Lane, Silver Spring, Md. 20904

Metal Marine Pilot Inc., 2119 W. Mildred St., Tacoma, Wash. 98466

Neco Marine, Walton Rd., Cosham, Portsmouth, England

Orinda Control Systems, Box 203, Orinda, Cal. 94563

Ray Jefferson, Main & Cotton Sts., Philadelphia, Pa. 19127

Safe Flight Instrument Corp., Box 550, White Plains, N.Y. 10602

Signet Scientific, 129 E. Tujunga Ave., Burbank, Cal. 91510

Sky-Way Communications, 10833 E. Jefferson, Detroit, Mich. 48214

Tiller Master, Box 1901, Newport Beach, Cal. 92663

Unipas Inc., 1303 Jefferson Blvd., Warwick, R.I. 02886

Vec/Trak Research & Development Co., 1331 S. Dixie Hwy. W., Pompano Beach, Fla. 33060

A TENDER DECISION

By Michael Matza

Gone are the days when a boatbuilder would supply a specially-built tender, designed and fitted to your specific boat. In this age of stock boats and assembly-line production, the boat owner chooses his own yacht tender—one that meets the requirements of his crew, his larger boat's space possibilities, his cruising habits, and his pocketbook. Instead of brooding nostalgically on the grandeur and attention to detail of times gone by, today's boat-owner is faced with an important decision, a decision that's complicated by the sometimes opposing considerations of pleasure, convenience and safety.

First, who needs a tender? Certainly, the coastal motorboat owner, with no plans for overnighting in the wilderness or long offshore day cruises, will have little need for a small boat to accompany his big boat, although a case could be made for the purchase of one for the simple pleasure of rowing quietly around a harbor or favorite cove, admiring neighboring yachts, exploring new gunkholes, fishing, watching mer-

maids, or enjoying any of the numerous pleasures to be had in a little boat that's close to the water.

For the ocean cruisingman, a good, dependable tender is an absolute necessity. Beyond its obvious function as an alternative source of flotation in an emergency severe enough to render the mothership useless, a serviceable tender has many uses that contribute to safer and more pleasurable boating. On extended cruises to unfamiliar spots, the cruisingman may find himself far removed from the nearest marina or other shore facility. At times like these, a reliable tender will be the "taxi" that gets him and his crew ashore. Then, too, the tender-as-taxi can be invaluable for reaching a mooring—even in home port—on those crowded days when to wait for the launch after breakfast might not even assure you of a moonlight cruise. A note here on size. The most functional and convenient tender for weekend (coastal) cruising will be one of sufficient size to transport half the expected number of passengers ashore in one load. For extended, bluewater cruising, where a tender takes on the added role of a lifeboat, it should be of sufficient size, or a sufficient number of such little boats should be on hand, to accommodate all passengers, crew members, emergency rations, flares, anchors, etc. Let form follow function for safety at sea.

The taxi capabilities of a tender can be applied to equipment as well as people. When at anchor in an especially hard blow, a tender can be used to "taxi" and drop a spare anchor for additional holding power and extra security in those exotic but sometimes *too* secluded anchorages. A similar anchor drop-off arrangement can be accommodated by a dependable little boat when it becomes necessary to kedge off a shoal after suffering the ignominy of running aground.

For waterline inspections and quick repairs, a tender can give the do-it-yourself boatowner the maneuverability, stability and utility he requires.

What is the best means for powering a tender? It can be, of course, sail, oar, or outboard. Purists maintain, however, that oars are the only acceptable means for powering a tender. For those who don't relish the idea of rowing one of these stubby and sometimes clumsy hulls, small featherweight outboards are available to move them along at a respectable pace. Low-horsepower models available from British Seagull, Mercury, OMC, Gladding and other manufacturers are all good performers. Sailing rigs are available for many tenders although, unless both rig and hull are carefully designed, they can prove less than adequate. With all due regard to the mechanical wizardry of our leading engine companies, and with equal regard for the prowess of Mother Nature and her omnipotent West Wind, oars remain the surest means of dependable power for most tenders. The "rowability" of a tender should be an important factor in its choice. Besides, it's good exercise.

Today's tenders can be divided into two major types: rigid-hulled designs and inflatables. Each type has design features that the other lacks and the ultimate decision as to which to stake your life and pleasure on will result in an inevitable trade-off.

For "row-ability," rigid hulls (wood or fiberglass) have generallly proven superior in terms of maintaining a heading in a seaway, and in ease of propulsion. Inflatables lie much flatter on the water than rigid tenders and are often blown from pillar to post by the same wind and sea that rigids can ride more easily. The recognized leaders in inflatable technology with distributorships in the U.S. (Avon and Zodiac) have added inflatable keels to their boats to give them more grip on the water. These innovations notwithstanding, inflatables still take a stern seat to the more stable rigids in the area of "row-ability." This initial disadvantage can be even further complicated by the addition to the tender of the dead weight of a spare anchor to be rowed out and set under adverse weather condtions, or several passengers, or a full load of groceries and supplies.

Moving from the area of rowing to stowing, inflatables gain considerable ground. Stowing a rigid hull on most of today's creatively cramped motorboats is a problem. Rigid tenders have been lugged aboard, hung from stern davits, stowed against the transom on swimming/boarding platforms and towed on painters. Regardless of how they are taken to sea, rigid tenders cannot compete with the ease and versatility of stowage methods available to the inflatable. Inflatables can be easily hauled aboard and either entirely deflated or partially deflated, allowing an owner to custom size his dinghy to fit available space. Most inflatables can be fully inflated

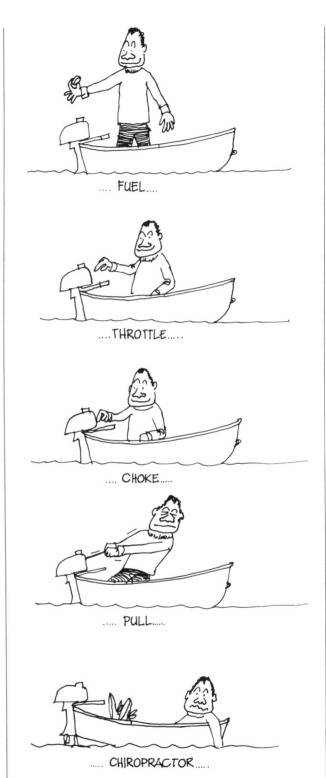

.... FUEL....

....THROTTLE.....

.... CHOKE.....

..... PULL......

..... CHIROPRACTOR.....

and outfitted with optional wood floorboards (for a more stable ride) in under 30 minutes. Owners who keep their tenders partially inflated, with floorboards permanently installed, can be ready to launch in anywhere from 5 to 10 minutes. Indeed, they can complete the inflation process after launching the partially inflated boat. The boats are easily inflated by means of a foot bellows that is, in the case of Avon boats, constructed of the same durable Du Pont Hypalon-impregnated nylon as the boats themselves. The rough treatment these bellows stand up to is testimony to the resilience and strength of the hull fabric. A note here on comparative strength and ease of repair. A popular misconception is that inflatable boats run the risk of bursting like a balloon when contacted by sharp rocks, a rough shoreline, or other abrasives. The fact is that inflatables are generally pressured to between two and three pounds per square inch, and buoyancy is provided by multiple, independent air chambers that are highly puncture resistant. In the unlikely event of a puncture, the uninjured air chambers continue to float the tender admirably. At two to three pounds per square inch, the ruptured chamber would leak rather than burst. Punctures can be patched to a degree of strength and integrity equivalent to undamaged hull fabric. In addition, the bounce inherent in an inflatable may cause it to glance off potentially damaging objects that would punch a hole in a rigid hull. Damage to rigid tenders can be repaired in the same way that damage to wood and fiberglass motherships is repaired. Overall, the patching procedure for an inflatable might be roughly equaled to patching a spare tire. For the uninitiated, repairs on a rigid hull may prove more difficult. Remember, however, that rigid tenders, with good hardwood skids capped with brass strips, should prove resistant to the toughest scrapes and abrasions.

Inflatables have a tremendous load-carrying capacity and are virtually uncapsizable, except when towed. For this reason they have been chosen for use as lifeboats and for use by scuba and spearfishing enthusiasts who are constantly moving into and out of these boats. Since they are highly shock absorbent, they will not damage the topsides of a yacht when shipped or lying alongside. Indeed, an inflatable, properly positioned between two rafted ships, can serve as a huge and very protective fender. Inflatables with extended buoyancy tubes and integral heavy-duty wood transoms can, as a rule, take larger outboards. They are capable of surprising speeds when planing. Indeed, a middle-range inflatable tender can, outfitted with the proper outboard, serve as a fine waterski boat. It should be noted, however, that the ride of a low-freeboard inflatable is quite a bit wetter than the ride in a comparable rigid tender.

In the area of towing, both rigids and inflatables may experience some difficulty with this often tricky operation. The key to towing is remembering that both boats (the mothership and the tender) should be kept in step by adjusting the length of the painter so that the lead boat and her tow are both on the crest or in the trough of seas at the same time. This is more easily described than done in constantly changing seas, where a towed dinghy may find itself straining against the direction of tow by slipping into unmatched seas. This will put an unusual strain on the towing eye of the tender and may even tear it loose. The lightness of inflatable tenders tends to make them float off the crest of a sea and flip over. As Antilles cruisingman Donald M. Street reports, "They don't tow particularly well right side up, but they don't tow worth a damn upside down." Rigid tenders can be taken in tow more easily.

Weight and one-man launchability are additional factors in evaluating what type of tender will be right for your needs. Tenders in the 9' to 15' class will generally run between 80 and 175 pounds and, contrary to many advertising claims, inflatables are not always significantly lighter and easier to manage in their inflated state than rigid tenders.

Prices of the inflatable sportboat models are generally higher than comparable rigid hulls. For a given 12' tender, the two leading inflatable companies charge slightly under $900. A comparable rigid boat could cost $300 to $800 for fiberglass. Companies building more traditional wood tenders are few and far between. Wood tenders are often home-built, or they may be custom ordered and built to owner specifications for anywhere from $700 to $1800 depending on the fluctuating prices of wood and local hourly rates for labor.

For an interesting little boat that can add immeasurably to your cruising enjoyment and safety, investigate today's assortment of versatile tenders. As capable and comfortable as your big boat may be, the little boat can often improve its possibilities and serve as everything from a water toy to a taxi to a life raft.

ANYONE CAN SPLICE

By Hervey Garrett Smith

may

So much has been written on the subject of splicing in recent years that to toss in my ha'penny's worth might seem to be useless repetition. My only defense is that newcomers who want to learn are constantly being added to the ranks of yachtsmen, and their inquiries seem to justify this effort.

For the sake of clarity the following instructions are numbered to correspond with the illustrations. So we will start with Diagram 1. Take a length of ⅜ inch manila rope and clap a seizing on about 6 inches from the end. This will be known as the working end. Unlay the three strands to the seizing and whip the end of each strand. These strands are labeled A, B and C. Note that B is the uppermost strand. Now grasp the rope as shown and twist it so the strands are opened up a bit. You now have three strands exposed which are labeled a, b and c. It is here that the first tucks are made, and since all beginners seem to go wrong right at the start you should stop at this point and study the procedure. A, B and C are the left hand, the center and the right hand strands of the working end. a, b and c are the left hand, center and right hand strands of the standing part of the rope. Strand A is tucked under strand a, B under b, and C under c. Just remember how the strands are paired up, left under left, center under center, and right under right.

Diagram 2 shows the first tuck. Center strand B is tucked under center strand b, across the standing part of the rope to the left. Remember here that you always tuck the center strand first.

Diagram 3 shows the second tuck. Left hand strand A is tucked under left hand strand a. Notice that it passes over center strand b. You are now ready to tuck strand C, but in order to do so it is necessary to turn the whole works over as shown in Diagram 4. Right hand strand c is now easy to get at. Strand C, although it now appears on the left side, is still the right hand strand as in Diagram 1.

Diagram 5. Strand C is now passed around to the right of and tucked under strand c to the left. Note that all tucks are made against the lay of the rope, or to the left. Your first row of tucks has now been made and if you have mastered the sequence the worst part is over. Before you go any further you should take out the tucks and try to do it again without looking at the diagrams. Draw all three strands up until they lie snugly, each having equal tension.

Diagram 6 shows the second row of tucks started, with strand B passed over strand a and tucked under the next strand to the left. Continue by tucking strands A and C over one and under one to the left. All three strands will now have been tucked twice. Tuck each strand once more in turn and the splice is completed.

Diagram 7. Your finished splice should look like this. Do not cut the strands off too close. Leave at least ⅜ of an inch protruding. Notice that all three strands have been tucked three times, and all emerge opposite one another. Lay the splice on the floor and roll it back and forth under your foot. This will even up the strands a bit and make the splice symmetrical.

These drawings and directions are as clear and simple as I know how to make them. They are directed to the beginner, and for that reason I have not mentioned the finer points such as tapering, etc. In splicing, as in everything else, practice makes perfect and in the doing you will learn more than from reading any ten books on rope work.

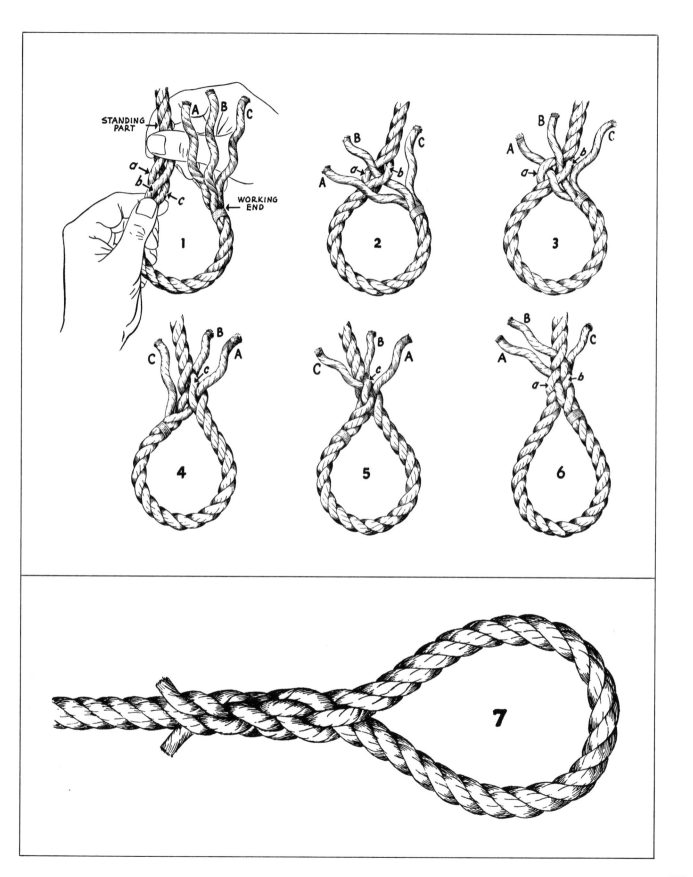

Brush up on
your boat handling
and piloting

After commissioning and fitting out, the next logical move is to turn on the engine and go somewhere. Which brings us to (1) boat handling and (2) piloting. Boat handling involves driving your boat efficiently and safely by taking into account action of the wind, tides, currents, and other craft. Piloting is the art of getting to go where you want to go by means of reference to fixed geographic points, and without incident. An example of incident is piling up on a reef because you zigged where you should have zagged. Obviously, boat handling and piloting require instructions, information, and practice. If this seems obvious to you, there are horror stories about skippers who hopped into their brand new boats as if they were U-Drives, and barreled off toward the horizon. Every summer I hear of boats piling up on Stepping Stones, rocks at the Western end of Long Island Sound. Since the rocks are prominently guarded by a lighthouse that hasn't moved since Victorian times, they can't be blamed for what happens when someone goes inside the nun buoys when the chart tells him to go outside.

Marine engines and automobile engines work on the same principles, but they have different drive systems. (This shouldn't come as a surprise.) Someone has compared steering a medium-sized boat to driving a truck on ice with no brakes. That's a good analogy as far as it goes, but it could go farther. Ice has no tide or current. And boats don't have wheels—not your run-of-the-mill boat, anyway. This is brought dramatically home to you when docking a single screw inboard for the first time. It does not respond to the controls like a Volkswagen, especially in reverse, when it has a tendency to veer to the left no matter how the rudder is positioned. You will find some inside stuff on handling both single and twin screws in the pages following.

I said that piloting is an art, but I didn't say it first. Nathaniel Bowditch said it back in 1802, in the first edition of the *American Practical Navigator.* Part of the art lies in knowing what you are looking for and at. Theory is not enough. You can plot a safe course with a pair of parallel rulers and a chart. But there is a knack to translating what is on paper into what is on (and under) the water. It's a knack that can be cultivated by careful study of the chart and course, by visualizing beforehand landmarks and navigational aids and hazards. And by familiarity. On the water, familiarity breeds respect.

Two publications to aid the navigator are *Coast Pilots* in four volumes, published by the U.S. Coast & Geodetic Survey and Eldridge's *Tide & Pilot Book,* published by Robert Eldridge White, 178 Atlantic Avenue, Boston, Mass. 02110. These references contain information about the weather, coast, harbors port facilities, and sailing directions.

Both piloting and boat handling are allied to a knowledge of the rules of the road. You can't get from here to there if you can't make up your mind how to pass a speedboat approaching at two points abaft on your starboard beam. Know the rules of the road and paste an abridged version next to the wheel. But use your common sense even if you have the right of way and the other boat doesn't seem to know it.

> *Here lies the body of Jonathan Day*
> *Who died maintaining his right of way.*
> *He was right, dead right. He was right all along.*
> *But he's just as dead as if he was wrong.*

The handiest way to pick up instruction in piloting, boat handling and seamanship is to enroll in one of the free courses of instuction given all over the United States by either the U.S. Power Squadrons or the U.S. Coast Guard Auxiliary.

SINGLE-SCREW THEORY AND HOW TO USE IT

By the Editors of <u>Rudder</u> in Cooperation with the Annapolis Marine School

june

The new skipper, faced with the problem of taking out his inboard-powered single-screw vessel, cannot simply drive the boat away from the dock or slip as he would take his new car out of the garage. Nor can he return it to its berth without first understanding some of the forces that work for and against his boat. Single-screw boat handling is a learned art that comes with practice, experience and knowing one's own boat thoroughly. It is, in some ways, more difficult to accomplish well than handling a twin-screw craft where the force of counter-rotating props used in various combinations can help to maneuver the vessel.

The purpose of this series is to first explain the forces that help the boatman maneuver his boat, then show how these forces can be used in typical undocking, docking and man-overboard situations. In teaching single-screw boat handling, instructor Doug Hoogs uses the "backing and filling" exercise.

Backing and filling is the procedure used when it becomes necessary to turn the single-screw vessel in its own length. It also is a very good exercise for the new skipper—one that he should practice first in open water where there is no danger of collision and then in more confined waters such as a turning basin or a relatively narrow channel.

By maintaining constant right rudder throughout the exercise, the boat will turn its bow to starboard and the stern to port while going ahead. Exceptions to this would be in the case of a prop turning left (counter-clockwise when viewed astern) or unique hull configurations.

It is obvious that a vessel going ahead with starboard rudder and a normal right-hand turning screw will turn to starboard. It is not obvious why the stern turns to port when the boat is backing down and the prop is turning *counter-clockwise*. The phenonmenon is called the "paddle-wheel effect" and is explained below. As in all powerboat maneuvering in close quarters, the skipper should use just enough rpm to counter wind and current. Ideally, the skipper should work with his engine, moving his gearshift from forward to neutral to reverse. In the backing-and-filling exercise, for instance, the engine stays in reverse just long enough to allow the stern to swing to port slightly before kicking it into forward again. The effect of stern "walking" can be skillfully utilized in a number of ways.

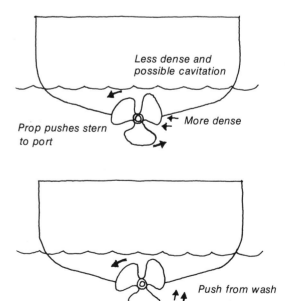

Less dense and possible cavitation

Prop pushes stern to port

More dense

Push from wash

The paddle wheel effect

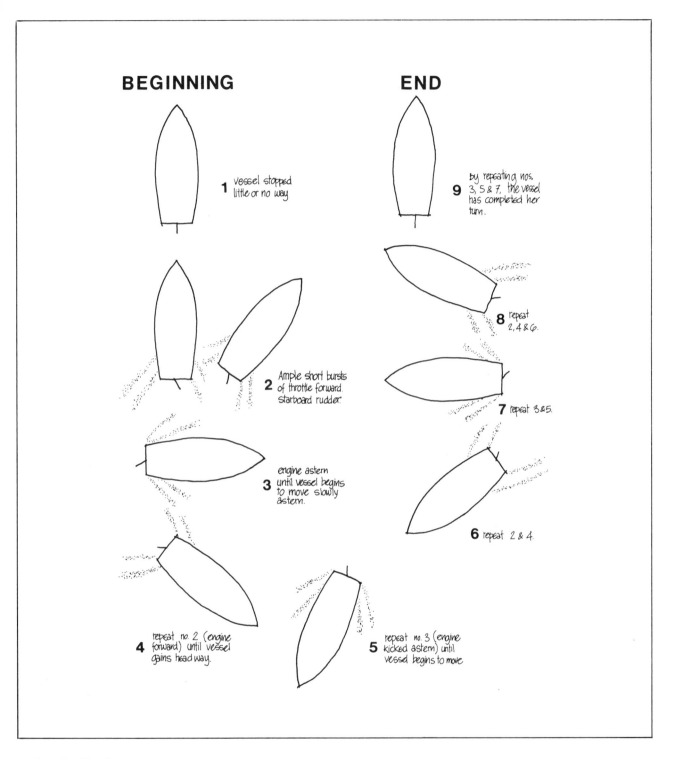

BEGINNING

END

1 vessel stopped little or no way

9 by repeating nos. 3, 5 & 7, the vessel has completed her turn.

2 Ample short bursts of throttle forward starboard rudder.

8 repeat 2, 4 & 6.

3 engine astern until vessel begins to move slowly astern.

7 repeat 3 & 5.

6 repeat 2 & 4.

4 repeat no. 2 (engine forward) until vessel gains head way.

5 repeat no. 3 (engine kicked astern) until vessel begins to move

Boat Backing Down

1. The paddle wheel effect is caused by the propeller turning through two different densities of water. The deep blade, in the more dense water, meets more resistance than the shallow blade in the less dense water. The illustration shows how this resistance moves the stern.

2. The wash from the prop as the blade ascends pushes

water forward and up to starboard side of the keel and also pushes the vessel.

3. The rudder has no effect when the engine is going astern but the vessel has no way on because the prop is not sending any wash in the direction in which the rudder is turned (to starboard).

MAKING TWIN SCREWS WORK FOR YOU

By the Editors of
<u>Rudder</u> in Cooperation
with the Annapolis
Marine School

june

Leaving a Dock

Clearing a dock or slip becomes relatively easy with twin screws as the boat has the power and the turning ability to counter most problems, including those of wind and current. In this article, some common situations are discussed; the skipper may encounter others which are more complicated, but the same general rules apply—the use of minimum power (speed) to get the job done, the use of the counter-rotating force of the twin screws with little application of the rudders, the use of spring lines and fenders in tight situations and, as in all boat handling, pre-planning.

Of all of the situations that the skipper encounters, getting underway allows him the most time to carefully plan his moves. Obviously, if his boat is kept at a permanent dock or slip, getting underway becomes second nature to him and all of the moves are generally the same. But there is always the first time—and of course, when cruising, undocking situations differ.

Start-up and Fueling

Much has been taught about the dangers of gasoline fumes. Yet despite the fact that start-up and fueling safety procedures should be assumed to be mandatory by the skipper, the most frequent cause of accidents listed by the Coast Guard is explosion and fire. The procedures, therefore, cannot be overemphasized.

If you plan to get underway without fueling, you must: (1) Lift up engine hatch and sniff for gasoline fumes. If there is a smell of raw gasoline, then check the source very carefully and make sure it is fixed before starting. (2) Open all doors, cabin hatches, etc. (3) Turn on exhaust blowers for at least five minutes. (4) Start engines. Prolonged periods of warm-up are not essential.

When fueling: (1) Everyone off the boat other than the person doing the fueling. (2) Extinguish all stoves, cigarettes, etc. (3) Stop engines, motors, fans capable of producing a spark. (4) Close all doors, hatches, ports. (5) Make sure fire extinguisher is at hand. (6) Measure fuel in tank so that you will not overfill. (7) When filling, keep nozzle tight against side of vent to prevent static spark. (8) Close vent immediately after filling. (9) Wipe up spilled gasoline immediately and dispose of rags *on shore.* (10) Open all doors, hatches, ports. (11) Turn on blowers for five minutes minimum. (12) Check engine compartment and bilges for fumes and do not start until fumes disappear. (13) Start engines and get underway as quickly as possible.

Leaving A Slip

One of the most common methods of storage of the larger cruiser is the U-shaped slip. It may either take the form of a finger pier with docks and mooring bollards or pilings on one or both sides of the boat, or simply be pilings at right angles to a dock with just enough room between sets of pilings for the boat. For easy access the cruiser usually lies with its bow facing toward the stream, held by crossed stern lines (to minimize sideways motion), two bow lines to the outside pilings, plus spring lines as necessary. If there are no current or wind problems, the boat can literally be "driven" out of the slip. Take in all lines (remembering to take them through chocks). *ahead* on both engines at *minimum* speed. If there is enough room in the chan-

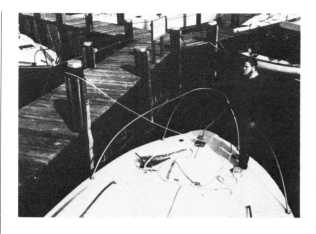

Undocking with the help of a spring line (above). Bow line is used to help boat pivot on port bow quarter. One turn is taken around bit to allow crewman to ease line slowly (top). As strain is taken on line (center) inboard screw is backed, outboard screw ahead. Boat pivots against mooring bollard as stern swings to starboard in twisting turn. Then line is slackened and cast off.

nel or marina to turn, then continue straight ahead until there is sufficient room to clear the stern of the dock end or pilings before doing so. One common beginner's fault is to neglect watching the stern quarters. As the stern swings in a wider arc than the bow, be careful not to turn too quickly, especially if there are outside pilings near the slip, otherwise the stern is bound to collide with the piling. This rule, of course, applies to boat handling in any situation and to all boats. Once the external pilings are cleared, then the turn can be made—either by holding both engines ahead and applying appropriate rudder (turn the wheel in the direction you want to go) or, in a narrow channel or marina, by going ahead on one engine, holding the other in neutral or reverse and twisting into the turn, then when the desired course has been reached, going ahead on both. Judicious use of the rudders will help the turn as needed.

When there is a current set against your boat's beam, the bow line on that side of the boat from the foremost piling can be walked aft from chock to chock to help control it. Fenders and rub-rails will help protect the boat if it slides along the pilings.

The use of a spring line (a line used to maneuver the boat around its pivot point) will work in easing the boat out into a narrow channel (see Fig. 5). In this case the boat had been moored bow in and a spring line from the port stern quarter was used to pivot the boat around the piling with the starboard engine backed, the port engine ahead and some right rudder applied.

Leaving a Dock

Because of the larger arc swung by the stern of the boat, it is customary in most instances to leave a side-to berth stern first. The reason for this is easy to understand. Simply turning the boat away from the dock once the lines are cast off will throw a stern quarter into the dock with resultant damage to dock, boat and possibly the propeller and shaft on that side. This is especially true if the boat has been berthed between other boats and the maneuvering space is minimal.

If the current set is off the dock, then the maneuver is relatively simple. Cast off the stern line, or take it in and the stern will drift out, then take in the bow line and back straight out.

If the set is against the pier, or there is a boat

berthed directly aft of yours, follow the same procedure but use the twin screws to help. The stern line is taken in and the bow line used as a spring to pivot the boat out. As the bow line is held, the inboard screw is backed, the outboard screw is ahead, twisting the boat's stern out. To help maneuver, full rudder can be used in the direction of the twist, and power applied as needed to counter the current. Use a fender between bow quarter and dock so that there is no damage to either. Once the boat has been twisted sufficiently into the stream, then both engines go into reverse and the boat is backed out, after the bow line has been taken in. Remember to bring the rudder amidships before backing, otherwise the boat will back into the pier.

When the boat is clear and into the channel, then the skipper can either (1) stop engines, then come ahead on both and steer into the desired course or (2) come ahead on the inboard engine and back the outboard one, twisting into the desired position before going ahead on course.

A variation of the wind or current on the dock situation is shown in Fig. 4B, where a stern spring line is used as a method of helping you ease your boat away from the pier. This method is useful where it is not possible to back clear, but the skipper must be careful not to pivot on the pier, but on the line itself, for fear of damaging steering gear or propeller on the dock. In any case, a fender should be used between boat and dock. The lines are singled to a stern line which is eased out with the port engine ahead, starboard screw stopped or reversed. The port stern quarter then pivots on the line, which is taken in when the boat is clear forward. Then, both engines ahead and into the channel.

This maneuver is also useful when the wind or current set is ahead of the boat as in Fig. 1. The bow line is taken in, allowing the bow to swing away from the pier. Using the stern line as a pivot, with the port engine ahead, the boat will twist out. As the sternline is released, with screw stopped, the boat will drift clear at enough of an

Undocking from slip (shown on facing page). Held by crossed stern lines and port forward quarter spring, with engines at idle, port engine is reversed to bring port bow closer to piling so that line can be cast off (1). One stern line having been taken in, (2) spring line is cast off. Remaining stern line is taken in (3) as skipper helps by backing starboard engine. Both engines ahead, then, (4,5) as boat moves straight out of slip. Note fouling danger in spring line not coiled.

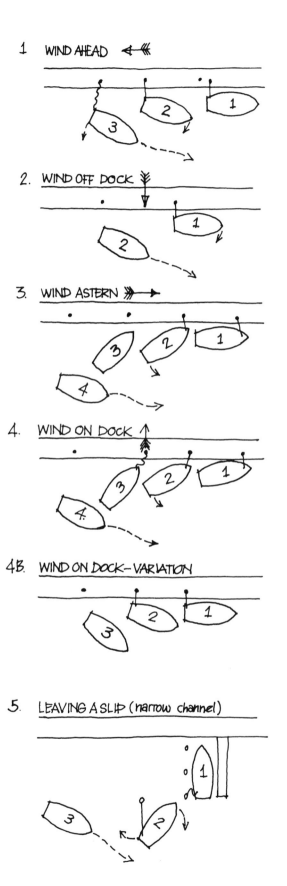

1. WIND AHEAD

2. WIND OFF DOCK

3. WIND ASTERN

4. WIND ON DOCK

4B. WIND ON DOCK—VARIATION

5. LEAVING A SLIP (narrow channel)

angle to put both engines in forward and move away.

Sometimes, the wind may be astern—in which case a bow spring can be used. (Fig. 3). The stern line is released, allowing the stern to swing clear as the bow pivots on its line, which can be used as a bight on a piling further aft to give more pivoting momentum as the port engine is backed. As the line is eased, the boat drifts clear and then proper engines and rudders are applied to put the boat on course.

When leaving a dock or slip it is good form—and absolutely required if the channel is crowded—to give the proper signal. According to the Inland Rules of the Road, one long blast should be sounded. If there is a danger of collision while backing—then three short blasts should be sounded. Some other tips:

When preparing to leave a berth make sure that the boat carries all of the proper safety equipment specified by Coast Guard regulations—including the appropriate number of life jackets and fire extinguishers.

Lines and fenders have an annoying way of becoming fouled, either on the dock, pilings, or props. Check before getting underway and be sure the crew is aware of what is happening to the lines at all times. Dock lines should be pulled through their chocks and stowed, ready for use when docking again. Fenders are stowed out of the way after clearing the docking area. If a line is to be used as a spring then taken on board, it is easier to use it as a bight—cleat one end, take one or two turns around the piling then ease off from on board. The line can be pulled on board after the maneuver is completed.

Familiarity with your boat, of course, will help in all maneuvers. And be loud and clear and understandable in your instructions to the crew. It'll save your temper and theirs.

Docking with Ease

Of the basic maneuvers that a twin-screw boat owner must accomplish, probably the one that creates the most tension for the skipper is bringing the boat into a slip or dock. For the novice it is the moment of truth—more than five tons of shiny new hull coming in at far too much speed. This is when many docks get rearranged along with the hull paint, guard rails and what-have-you on the new boat.

This need not be the case. Docking is not always easy to accomplish. But, remembering the lessons that were taught in the first two articles in this series, the operation can be simplified and the tension reduced. Some points to keep in mind: (1) Use the minimum power necessary to do the job. In most cases, this means idling engines. Powerboats, not having keels, are less affected by current than by wind pressure on superstructure, although the combination of a fast-moving tide and wind can create problems. (2) With engines just ticking over, use gears and let the twin screws work for you in maneuvering the boat.

Now that you are not concerned with the throttles, it's also possible to dock in most instances with the rudder amidships, using the screws for direction. This again reduces the number of things that the skipper must worry about. If the rudder setting is a little off, it can be compensated for by giving one engine slightly more power than the other. (3) The name of the game, according to instructor Bob Pringle of the Annapolis Marine School, is *control*—the ability to keep the boat in check at all times. This includes, as the reader will see in the accompanying illustrations, the use of a spring line to warp the boat around its pivot point—a handy device whether backing into a slip or docking side-to, especially in a strong offsetting wind/current situation.

Docking in A Slip

Most larger cruisers are docked in a slip stern-to for easier access to the cockpit area. In essence, the skipper is "aiming" his boat into a small area stern-first. In quiet waters, the procedure is relatively simple. The boat is lined up by the bow on its heading into the docking area. With engines in idle, gears in neutral, as taught by Pringle, the skipper then faces aft and with his hands behind him (works well if the gear levers are spaced wide apart) shifts into reverse. This technique has the advantage of letting the new skipper literally point his hands, like a boxer, in the direction he wants to go. Now he can control direction in reverse with the use of either engine, both or none at all (or in forward to control momentum once in the dock, if needed). As the boat enters the slip, the bow lines, which have been taken aft, are slipped over the leading pilings and then used as a brake on boat mo-

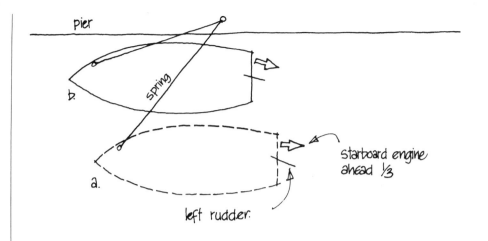

pier

spring

b.

a.

starboard engine
ahead ⅓

left rudder.

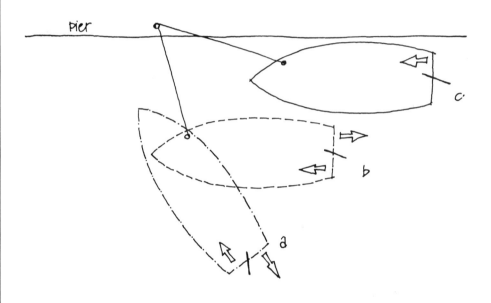

pier

c.

b

a

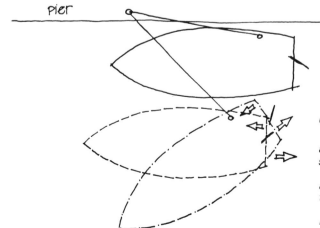

pier

Use of Mooring Lines for Docking

1. Bow spring is used to bring boat alongside by going ahead on starboard screw with left rudder. (Arrows show screw wash.)

2. Twisting against a bow line with starboard engine ahead, port backing and left rudder. Once alongside, stop twist and back starboard engine.

3. Twisting against a quarter spring is not efficient since it moves pivot point aft.

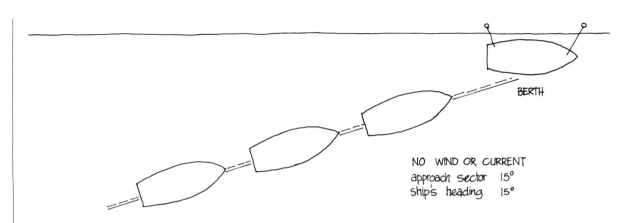

NO WIND OR CURRENT
approach sector   15°
ship's heading   15°

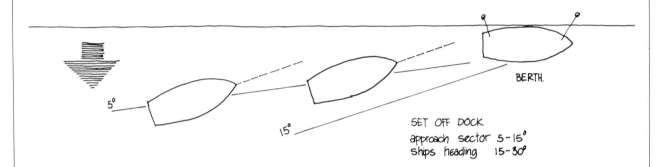

SET OFF DOCK
approach sector 5-15°
ships heading   15-30°

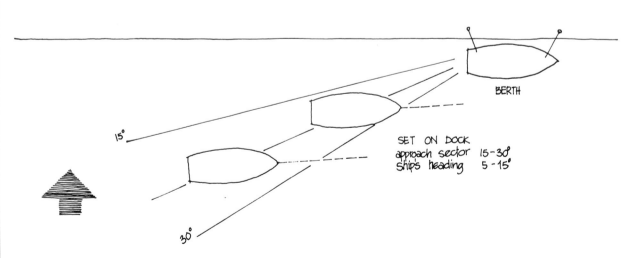

SET ON DOCK
approach sector 15-30°
ships heading   5-15°

Docking in Typical Wind/Current Conditions

Diagrams show docking patterns when (top) wind or current are not factors and (center and bottom) when they are. Angles represent the track of the boat's pivot point when coming into a berth.

mentum—taken in as the boat moves into the slip area.

Another method, for use in a tight channel or in a strong wind/current set, is to lay the boat against an outer piling and then pivot the boat around the piling into the slip. A spring line can be used to help maneuver the boat; *engines only,* again, is the key. And the skipper still faces aft.

Docking Side-to

Docking alongside a pier, especially when there are boats fore and aft of yours, involves more intricate maneuvering. But again, the principles are the same: slow speed and use of engines and enough rudder to twist the stern of the boat into the dock. No matter what the approach angle, another principle applies—get the bow into position, use the bow line as a spring and pivot in on it with the help of the appropriate engine. Again the pivot point is considered to be ⅓ aft of the bow.

Approach angles differ with the wind and current set. If there is a strong wind *on* the pier, the approach angle can be as much as 90 degrees to the dock. Then the bow line is used as a spring and the appropriate engines and rudder are applied to swing the stern into the dock. More usual is an approach sector of 15 to 30 degrees with the boat maneuvered so as to lay the boat off the dock and allow the leeway caused by wind and current to bring it into the docking space. One warning here: the boat needs to be laid fairly close to the dock and stopped, otherwise the effect of too much leeway caused by wind, plus the boat's own momentum, may cause a collision. Fenders are a must.

Under quiet conditions, it is recommended that the angle be relatively flat (about 15 degrees) with a course directly for the berth. If the set is *off* the pier, two procedures are possible. The "book" suggests that as flat an approach as possible be made with the boat heading to a point that seems almost inboard of the berth, thereby cheating the wind and not allowing it to push the bow away from the dock. Another procedure is similar to the 90-degree approach for wind on the dock: take the bow in, use the spring line and, with the help of engines and rudder, warp the boat into its berth.

TOOLS FOR PILOTAGE AND NAVIGATION

By W. S. Kals

june

We all think we know the difference between pilotage and navigation. But try to give a definition of pilotage, and some nasty sea lawyer will make a monkey out of you.

Use shallow water in the definition, and he'll invite you to show your methods for piloting on the Bahama Banks, where in two to three fathoms of water you can be out of sight of land and without lighthouses or buoys for fifty miles or more. Use the term "out of sight of land" in a definition of navigation, and he'll trip you again. He'll put you in the Erie Canal in fog, fog so tarnal thick you couldn't spy the land. Then you hear a dog bark on shore, and change course. That is navigation?

Pilotage or navigation, their purpose is to get your little ship from the place you've been to the place you want to be—or at least some other pleasant place—keeping water under her keel all the time.

From basic pilotage—learned from a book or a course you've taken—you know about the three L's of pilotage: Lead, Log, and Lookout. Perhaps we can add a little to that.

Whoever made the phrase "swinging the lead" mean to loaf, had never swung a lead. It's stinking hard work, skilled work, right under the eyes of the mate, while the old man anxiously waits for results. The deep-sea lead ("deep-sea" pronounced to rhyme with "gypsy") weighs anywhere between thirty and one hundred pounds. You have to heave it far enough ahead so that it has time to sink to the bottom before the moving ship brings the line up and down. Much too hard for yachtsmen. We use 7–14 pound leads to measure the depth of water in an anchorage, perhaps as a shot line in skin diving, or as a drag indicator. On the rare occasions when you use the lead as a navigational tool, you might as well slow down, stop the engines, or heave to. For normal navigation the echo depth finder has taken over.

To feel your way into a sandy cove, there is a simpler tool: the sounding pole. A bamboo pole, perhaps twelve feet long, is popular. You can make your work easier by drilling a hole in the business end of the pole, filling the cavity with shot, and plugging the hole. That'll make the pole seek the bottom. Then mark the depth in feet by wrapping the pole with tape. If you draw four feet, make the first wrap at four feet. A pole is not only easier to use than the lead, it also saves the sing-song between foredeck and bridge; the skipper at the wheel can read the depth while someone in the bows works the pole. If you don't find it convenient to carry this bamboo pole, which on a sailboat can hang from a shroud when not in use, you can mark your boat hook to make it into a sounding pole.

Log, as a navigational tool, means as you know a device to measure speed, not the book that records your trips. The old chip log, dear to all writers on nautical lore, is a bit obsolete. The most interesting part of the device is that it has given us the worldwide measure of speed through the water, one knot meaning one nautical mile per hour. To get to this measure the knots in the chip log line were spaced 47 feet 3 inches apart, with five smaller knots in between for two-tenths of a knot. The number of knots that ran out while the sandglass emptied—28 seconds—gave directly the speed of the vessel in knots. Why 47¼ feet (or similar length), why 28 seconds? Why 437½ grains to the ounce avoirdupois?

The taffrail log—a spinner towed astern that drives a counter and measures the distance run through the water—was a great improvement and is still a useful tool for the small-boat sailor on a long overwater hop. It has a few drawbacks. It sometimes catches floating weed and then stops or slows down enough to make its reading useless. To guard against being misled by such false readings, you can mount the register right in sight of the helmsman, where supposedly he'd notice when it acts up. Have him read the register every half hour, on the dot, and write the figure read in the margin of the chart. When the reading suddenly drops, he'll notice, and clear the weed from the spinner. You can later allow for the underrecorded distance by using an estimated half-hour run.

When a sailboat gets becalmed, the spinner she tows sinks to the bottom where it may anchor the boat. When she starts sailing again, the line may part. To save the register, the most expensive part of the rig, secure it with a lashing much heavier than the log line. And, of course, carry a spare spinner, line, sinker, and hook.

Sharks are supposed to be attracted to the whirligig, and some skippers paint theirs black, dull black. I've towed one over hundreds of miles—it lets a single-hander get some sleep without losing track of his dead reckoning—in waters where sharks must have lurked (where don't they?), but never lost a spinner that way.

But once I almost lost my boat to the log line. I gently ran aground under power; the line wrapped itself around the propeller and stopped the engine. Before I could throw out an anchor, a wicked surf bore us ashore.

Even with all these shortcomings a patent log is a very useful gadget, especially on a sailboat. It lets you calibrate your senses for speed. After you have measured runs at a few typical speeds on different points of sailing, you can guess your speed to a few tenths of a knot from the feel of the tiller, the angle of heel, the gurgling at the bow, and the fuss she makes in the water.

Under power, engine revolutions, adjusted for sea conditions, give a good indication of a boat's speed, as long as her bottom is clean. Ideally rpm's times propeller pitch (converted to feet) gives the boat's advance through the water in one minute (in feet), from which you can calculate speed or distance run. But there is always slip.

On a freighter, over breakfast one morning, the chief engineer announced that, as far as his department was concerned, we had arrived at New York. "And where are you fellows?" he asked with a stern look at the watch-keeping officers who placed her only three-fourths across the Atlantic.

Knowing the percentage of slip under various conditions of sea and foulness of bottom, you can estimate your speed very accurately. Even without tachometer or revolution counter, you can gauge it pretty well by throttle setting.

An interisland freightboat skipper let me in on his personal speed-indicator secret. He opened the throttle one notch above its cruising setting. Soon you could feel the whole vessel vibrating. "See, one notch back from that, we make exactly nine knots."

"What about bad weather?"

"In bad weather, one notch past. The vibration stops and we still make our nine knots."

Then there are the magic wands you hold over the side, and speedometers and odometers that show speed, or distance run, right in the cockpit. We have come a long way since the chip and the sandglass. But a knot is still a nautical mile per hour, and when your chrome-plated gadget reads in statute miles, you must not forget to deduct about fifteen percent to convert to nautical miles, or from miles per hour to knots.

The third "L" stands for Lookout. Most of the time the helmsman on a yacht will also be the lookout, and perhaps he'll also be the navigator. And you'll be all three. So make life easy for yourself—get a pair of binoculars. Other authors seem bashful about recommending sizes. I'm not. I find glasses of more than 7-power difficult to hold still on a moving boat. So I'd get 7 × glasses.

The second number on binoculars indicates the diameter of the far lenses in millimeters. Never mind about millimeters, but the greater the number, the better you'll see at night. A 35mm glass will show no more than you can see without glasses. A 50 mm glass will bring out unlighted buoys and daymarks you can't see with the naked eye. Even if you don't plan to run at night, ever, someday you may come in late; then you'll be glad you got 7 × 50's. All good glasses now are coated to cut down reflections and improve night vision. You'll see that coating as a colored film when you look at the lenses sideways.

You have a choice of center-focus or individual-focus binoculars. The word focus is misleading: you don't have to focus for distance, unless you want to watch the girl on the boat in the next slip. You focus to adjust for your own eyes. In center-focus glasses you adjust until the image for the left eye is sharpest for you, then you adjust the right eyepiece to make up for any difference in power between your two eyes.

In individual-focus glasses you adjust each eyepiece separately. If you always sail alone, it doesn't matter much whether you get CF or IF binoculars. But if your crew and guests occasionally use the glasses, by all means get the individually focused kind. Shipboard etiquette requires that you reset the glasses to how you found them. But only you can adjust CF glasses for the captain's setting. On individually focused glasses resetting is simple: You just have to remember the original setting—and yours, so you can adjust them quickly the next time.

When I want to look through my glasses I want them right away. So I put triangular bits of tape where they adjust for me. Even if some clown has screwed them all up, I can set them for myself in seconds, even in the dark.

Individual-focus glasses, having no sliding tubes, also happen to keep spray out of the works. They are simpler to make, and so are usually less expensive than center-focus glasses of the same quality and make.

So I strongly recommend 7 × 50 IF's. Make sure everyone who uses them also uses the neck trap. Even so, you may lose a pair overboard someday. That's why I'd get Japanese glasses. A good pair will cost about thirty dollars. A few small bubbles in the lenses don't matter, but make sure that looking through them is comfortable. One pair I once tried, after a few minutes made my eyes feel as if they wanted to come out of their sockets, sideways.

Back to lookouts, including yourself. Naturally a lookout looks forward; if he has been drilled in the Rules of the Road, he concentrates his watchfulness in the right quadrant where a vessel approaching from starboard has the right of way over his own vessel. Of course he also looks forward to port. But that is not enough. An overtaking craft has to keep clear of you. But if some fast big craft barrels down on you from astern, unseen and unheard over the noise of your own power plant, you might unthinkingly put the wheel hard over when you first become aware of her, and get right in the way. Even escaping that, you'd like to have taken evasive action before

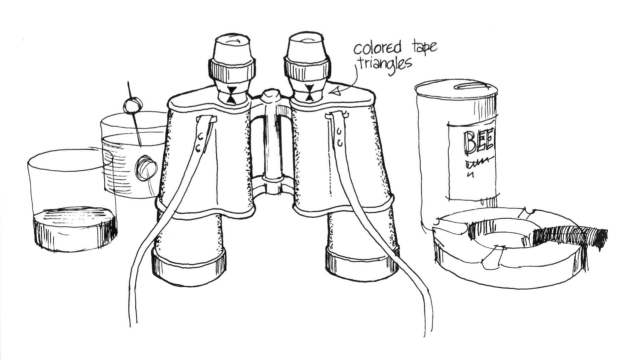

colored tape triangles

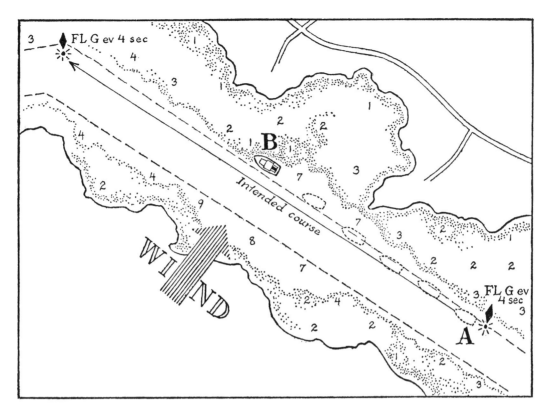

Leeway—the boat that started from "A," although steering correct course, and pointing straight at the next marker, will run aground at "B."

her wake hits you. How can you, if you never look aft and don't know what's on your tail?

There is another reason for the helmsman to look aft frequently. Wind, current, compass deviation, and helmsman's error all combine to set you off course. The compass gives no indication of these effects, often called "current" as the universal alibi for any difference between the course planned and the course made good.

Here is a simple rule of thumb that lets you evaluate the amount of set from such a mythical current:

> *In a run of one nautical mile*
> *a current of one degree*
> *will set you off one hundred feet.*

This rule works for any small angle and for any distance. Without much error you can use statute miles in place of nautical miles. Here are examples of the use of this simple formula. A three-degree error, in a run of one nautical mile, will set you off three hundred feet. Or, on a five-mile

run, a one-degree error will set you off five hundred feet.

That last example is just to illustrate the working of the rule; I know that yachts with their usual compasses can hardly be steered to one degree close.

This rule also lets you estimate how accurately you'll have to navigate. On a run from sea buoy to sea buoy along shore in deep water for ten miles, a three-degree error will probably not get you into trouble in clear weather. You'll be three thousand feet, about half a mile, from the buoy at the end of the run; but you'll see the buoy in ample time to correct your course.

On the other hand, if you are starting in the middle of a two-hundred-foot-wide dredged channel, the same three-degree error will have you on the spoil bank in one-third of mile. That's probably the cause of many of the groundings of shallow-draft pleasure boats in the Inland Waterway, where tugs with much deeper draft don't even stir up the mud.

How does the tugboat skipper do it? He knows that merely pointing the bow toward the next marker, or steering by compass, isn't enough. He looks over the stern. If the last marker he passed stays dead astern while he aims for the next one, he knows he'll stay in the channel. If the mark astern drifts off to one side, he knows he's being set toward the bank. If he can, the skipper will try to line up the mark astern with some object ashore, a tree perhaps, to give him a range astern. As long as marker and tree stay in line, he is on course; when the range opens, he'll correct to bring the marker and tree again into transit. That method is equally useful when leaving port for a long dash across a sound or across a lake. Teach it to your helmsman-lookout, and you'll make better landfalls.

We have strayed from basic tools of navigation and pilotage. Some of them need little discussion. Obviously you'll need pencils; equally obviously the hexagonal kind doesn't roll off the chart table as easily as the round kind. Don't hesitate to do your chart work on the chart. It's printed on paper meant to be written and drawn on with soft pencil—HB or No. 2—and to be erased later. An art eraser works well. If around your home port the chart gets a bit smeared after a season, all the better; you should get an up-to-date chart next year anyway.

For measuring distances, a piece of paper, transparent or other, will do. Small-craft charts have scales printed on them to which you can transfer your marks made at the edge of your paper. On *all* charts one minute of latitude (on left and right margins, unless the chart is tilted with north not being uppermost) equals one nautical mile (1.15 statute miles), regardless of the scale of the chart. Dividers are perhaps more elegant for measuring distances. I like the one-hand model that looks as though Admiral Columbus might have used it; press near the top and they open, press near the points and they close.

I also prefer dividers to calculators in speed problems. The trick is simply to open the dividers to some convenient setting. Say you steam at twelve knots. How long will it take to cover seven nautical miles? I'd open the dividers to two miles, the distance made good in ten minutes (about two inches on 1:80,000-scale charts), and step off the dividers along the course, count-

ing ten, twenty, thirty, and coming to thirty-five minutes.

Next, one needs some way for picking up a compass course from the chart. Some *Coast Pilots* and lake and river charts give courses to follow. Most charts don't. And sometimes at the meeting of two channels you'll encounter too many buoys. Which ones lead to where you want to go? The chart will tell.

When I first came to the Bahamas native skippers in the Out Islands were always surprised how I'd found their harbor. "Who gave you the course?" An old man who used to go to sea would offer to give me the course to the next destination. He and other skippers had memorized the courses for everywhere. If they ever had to go to a strange place, they'd go ashore and from some second cousin by marriage get the next course.

About the same time, *Sailing Directions for the West Indies* dropped the warning to ship masters not to follow native craft into harbor. These craft, so earlier editions stated, were likely to mislead the unwary skipper and plunder his wreck as soon as she'd piled up on the hidden reef.

Even where the wreckers have found other steady sources of revenue, don't navigate by proxy. It's so easy to get your own course from the compass roses printed on your charts. If your compass has been adjusted—we'll talk about that later—you can use the inner rose on the chart without any arithmetic.

All you need is some mechanical device to transfer a line (say from one buoy to the next one) to the nearest compass rose on the chart. Here you can let yourself go. If you have a proper chart table you can use parallel rules, sliding rules, a hexagonal pencil, a pair of triangles, any of several types of course protractors (with or without movable arm), and if you have room for it, a drafting-machine-type plotter.

For on-the-lap navigation as practiced in the cockpit of a sailboat, a courser—a piece of plastic with parallel lines drawn on it—is about as simple and reliable as you can get. You can improvise this gadget in a few minutes on a sheet of tracing paper.

Whatever gadget you use to transfer courses (and plot bearings), try not to become too attached to it. Or secure it firmly. I once dropped my favorite, an English number called Douglas,

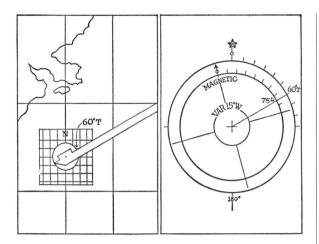

Finding magnetic course—proceed in two steps: (1) Move arm of protractor over intended course, say from one buoy to the next; align protractor grid with grid of chart, then read off the true course on scale of protractor (e.g. 60°T.). (2) Draw a line from true course (e.g. 60°) on outer scale of nearest compass rose on chart toward its center; read off magnetic course on inner compass rose (e.g. 75°M.).

behind the ceiling and into the bilge where I couldn't retrieve it without removing a whole mess of iron ballast. Yes, you're right: I removed the ballast and restowed it . . . all to get back a square 360-degree protractor that had cost me all of fifty cents.

For cockpit and by-the-wheel navigation I like a protractor that lines up with the meridians of the chart. Then I convert this true course into a magnetic one by laying a straightedge from the outer rose to the center and then reading the course on the inner rose, in degrees. If you prefer to steer by points and quarter-points, you'll find those by the same method on the innermost compass rose on the chart.

After chart weights have dropped a few times on your bare toes, or made dents in your deck sole, you'll consider replacing them by shock cord over the chart table to hold the chart flat and more or less in place.

There is one navigation tool I would like to carry, but I've not found the right one yet. Perhaps one is made, but I've not come across it. The gadget I want is a rangefinder. How often have we all steered wide around a headland,

fighting current and popple, when we could have shortened the misery by knowing exactly how far off we were? How many times haven't we bucked a midstream current not trusting our own distance estimate enough to run close to shore? How often does a sailboat go off the winning tack too soon rather than stand on, with nothing but the skipper's eyes to guide her around some hidden hazard?

I know how to take a vertical sextant angle on an object of known height, I know how to calculate the height of tide at any time, and I can find Tables 9 and 22 in Bowditch as well as the next guy. But often I don't know which hill to measure. I also know how refraction makes all angles near the horizon extremely doubtful. And it's far too much trouble all around. And who'd carry a sextant just for distance finding? So please design me a rangefinder, or let me know if you have found one that's reliable and that every small craft skipper can afford.

Although I like to do most of my chart work right on the chart, I always keep a clipboard with a spray-proof cover handy. On that I scribble fuel aboard, and taken on; time of departure, of starting and stopping engine (to keep oil changes and other maintenance chores scientific), of sail or wind changes; readings of the log, estimates of speed, and other figures that often don't belong on the chart but are soon forgotten unless one jots them down somewhere.

Unless I ran a very hungry ship, I wouldn't want to be without a hand bearing-compass. It lets you take bearings accurate to one degree all around the horizon, by day and by night, something that most yacht compasses won't do. Squinting over the steering compass is all right for deciding whether to take this channel or that. But on most yachts the main compass won't let you take bearings in all directions. How about yours? Can you take a bearing dead astern on the last marker to check your leeway? Can you take a bearing on a star with your compass? Can you without leaving the wheel tell when you are exactly abeam of a lighthouse?

I use my bearing compass not just for taking bearings, but for adjusting the main compass, and seeing that it's still in adjustment.

RULES OF THE ROAD: Meeting, Passing, Danger Zone

june

These are the "traffic laws" of the nation's waterways. Complete detailed instructions are contained in three Coast Guard publications entitled "Rules of the Road, International—Inland, (CG-169); Rules of the Road, Great Lakes, (CG-172); Rules of the Road, Western Rivers, (CG-184)." The particular pamphlet applicable to your area should be at hand. They are free from your local Coast Guard District Office. In brief, these rules provide:

1. *Meeting head-on*—pass to the right.

2. *Meeting at right angles* (or nearly so)—vessel on your starboard (right) bow has the right-of-way.

3. *Overtaking*—keep clear of the overtaken vessel and signal your intention.

These are explained in detail below:

Meeting Head-on

When meeting a boat coming head-on, keep to the right. Show that you intend to do so by swinging the bow of your boat in that direction—even more than necessary. The proper signal is one short blast from either boat, to be answered by one blast from the other. A "short" blast is 1 second.

Maintaining Course

When meeting a boat coming toward you, but at a safe distance to your right, here is how to avoid collision by showing that you intend to stay on the same course: Either boat gives two short blasts; the other boat answers with two blasts. Both maintain course.

A boat coming toward you from within the Danger Zone area—shown on the diagram—has the right of way. He may sound 1 blast on his horn or whistle. You should reply with 1 blast, then slow down and pass behind him.

Overtaking

The *overtaken* boat has the right of way and holds her course and speed. The overtaking boat must stand out of the way until well forward and no danger of collision exists.

When is a boat *overtaking?* When she approaches from within the angle formed by lines 2 points abaft the beam (22½ degrees) of the overtaken vessel.

Does the Overtaken Vessel Always Have the Right of Way?

Yes, even if she is a motor boat and her follower is a sailboat who would normally have the right of way over her.

Departing

When leaving a slip, float or pier, always give one long blast on your horn or whistle, regardless of whether you are backing out or running ahead. This is the warning signal for any nearby boats that you are coming out.

An old Sea Dog we knew used to say "You never have the right of way *through* another boat." This is stated formally in both the Inland and the International Rules and is called the "General Prudential Rule." It reads . . . "In obeying and construing these rules due regard shall be had to all dangers of navigation and

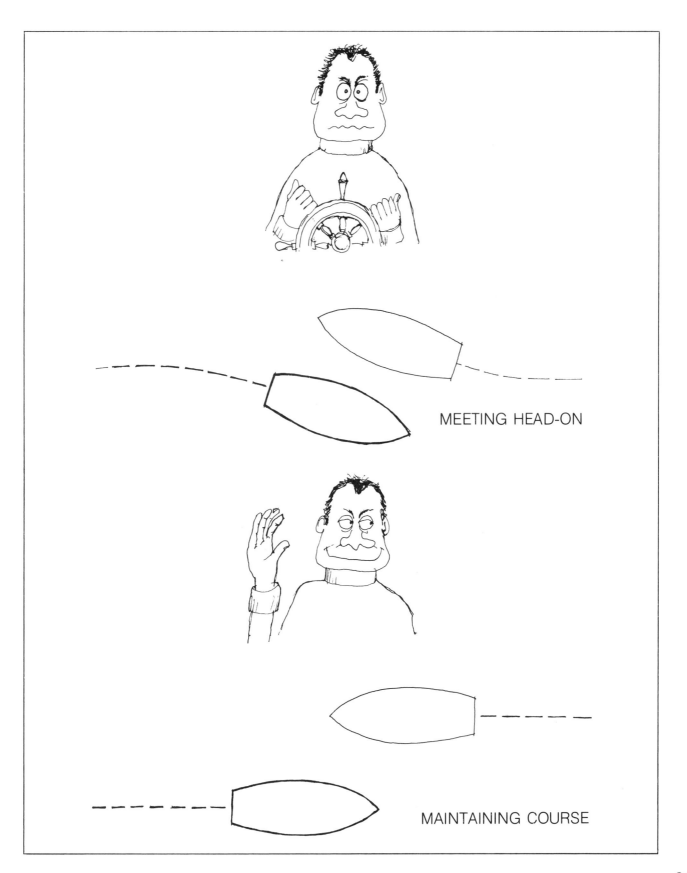

MEETING HEAD-ON

MAINTAINING COURSE

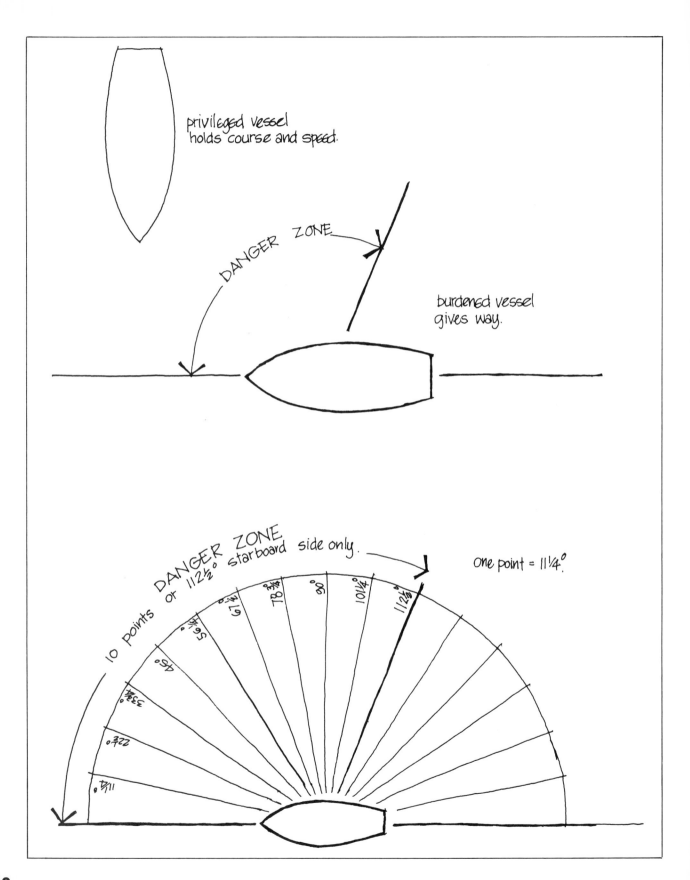

privileged vessel
holds course and speed.

DANGER ZONE

burdened vessel
gives way.

DANGER ZONE
10 points or 112½° starboard side only.

One point = 11¼°

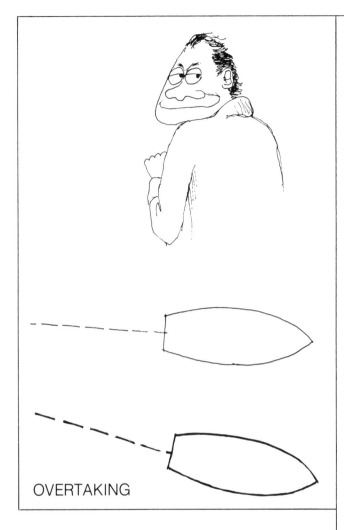

OVERTAKING

collision, *and to any special circumstance* which may render a departure from the above rules necessary in order to avoid immediate danger." (Emphasis supplied by us. Article 27, Inland Rules; Rule 27—International Rules; 33 U.S.C.A. sections 146, 212.)

So, if you have the right of way, hold your course and speed (Art. 21, Rule 21)—but don't do so blindly. It may be necessary for you to consider some "special circumstance"—maybe the other boat can't physically maneuver to avoid you, which, among other "special circumstances", may render a departure from the Rules necessary.

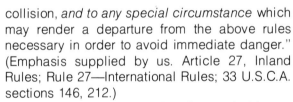

DEPARTING

AIDS TO NAVIGATION: Buoys, Waterway Markers

june

These are your water highway sign posts. Learn them, learn what they mean.

When entering a harbor keep the red buoys on your right and the black ones on your left. The red buoys will be even-numbered and the black odd-numbered. This is summed up in the words, "red right returning."

"Returning," in this case, means entering the harbor from seaward. When a harbor has two entrances "entering" means coming in from the north or east.

Intracoastal Beacons

On the intracoastal waterway, the buoyage system is somewhat different, and the markers may be on land.

Uniform State Waterway Marking System

This is a system of marking the waterways located entirely within the boundaries of a state, such as lakes or rivers. The navigation signals are similar to the Federal ones (red and black buoys in pairs). The "Regulatory Markers" may be signs or painted buoys, international orange on a white background.

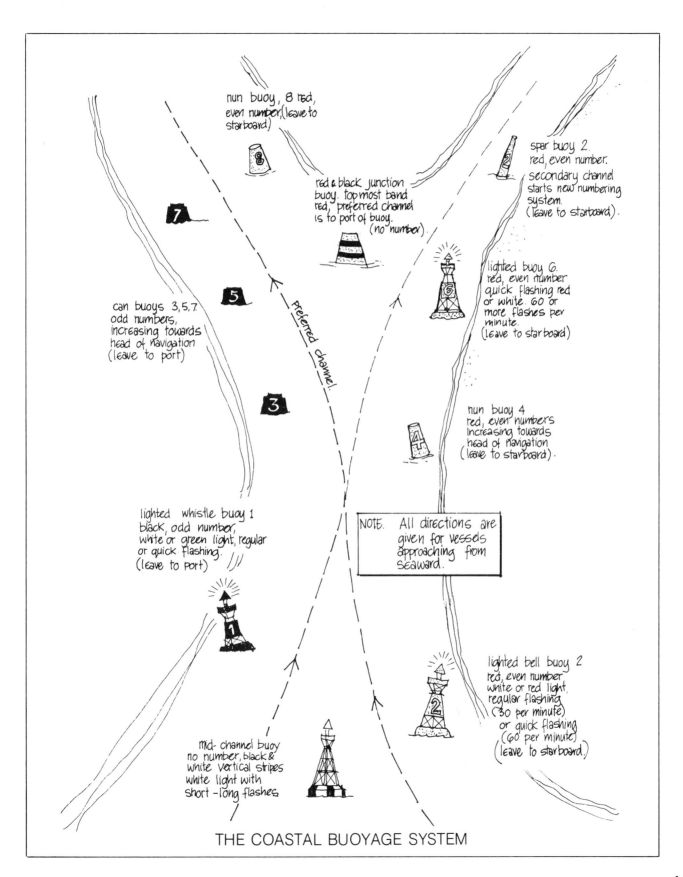

nun buoy, 8 red,
even number (leave to
starboard)

spar buoy 2.
red, even number.
secondary channel
starts new numbering
system.
(leave to starboard).

red & black junction
buoy. topmost band
red, preferred channel
is to port of buoy.
(no number)

lighted buoy 6.
red, even number
quick flashing red
or white. 60 or
more flashes per
minute.
(leave to starboard)

can buoys 3, 5, 7.
odd numbers,
increasing towards
head of navigation
(leave to port)

Preferred channel

nun buoy 4
red, even numbers
increasing towards
head of navigation
(leave to starboard).

lighted whistle buoy 1
black, odd number,
white or green light, regular
or quick flashing.
(leave to port)

NOTE. All directions are
given for vessels
approaching from
seaward.

lighted bell buoy 2
red, even number
white or red light,
regular flashing
(30 per minute)
or quick flashing
(60 per minute)
(leave to starboard.)

mid-channel buoy
no number, black &
white vertical stripes
white light with
short-long flashes

THE COASTAL BUOYAGE SYSTEM

HOW TO SUCCEED IN THE GALLEY

By B. B. Williams

june

A 25- or 30-footer's cooking facilities are simple: two-burner alcohol stove, icebox, and possibly a second refrigerator box, either one that cools itself electrically in port and uses block ice during the cruise, or else a simple picnic cooler.

Success in the galley boils down to: 1) pre-planning, 2) simplicity of preparation, 3) tastiness of meals, and 4) wise provisioning. (Most items should not need refrigeration; they should be canned, in jars, or dry.)

Incidentally, although "cruising cookbooks" flood the market today, I find most useless to the small-boat chef because they count on large quantities of fresh or frozen foods, an electric or gas stove with at least four burners, and a chef with lots of preparation time.

Pre-planning

Few remarks of a seagoing cook annoy a careful skipper as quickly as: "We really *have* to get to some port with a grocery store tonight. I have nothing left for dinner."

If you pre-plan your menus for the cruise and stock enough food on board in the beginning so that you *could* eat during the complete cruise without going ashore, you'll never have to utter that remark. You'll also be at ease knowing you won't have to run off to the grocery store at every port—while the rest of the crew sits watching the sunset with drinks in hand. Naturally, when the opportunity arises to buy fresh fruits, vegetables, meats, and fish, you'll probably want to buy some, then relegate some of your canned and dried foods to the next cruise.

Pre-planning also means that when it's time to prepare the next meal, you (who are already weary from handling sheets or winches or helm) won't have to stand hovering over the stowage hatch wondering what to cook. You simply consult your handy "menu for the day" and start cooking. You chose the menu with imagination when you were rested and alert, something you rarely are at the end of a cruising day.

Finally, should you opt out of the galley for an evening, how simple to hand your delegate a menu and know he'll find whatever he needs on board, and that he won't be messing up the rest of your week's menus by dashing together bits of three different day's foods.

Tastiness

Using primarily canned foods doesn't necessarily mean that all your meals must be of the hot-dog-and-beans variety. Almost everything edible comes canned (or dried)—from corned beef to pudding—some as good as it would be fresh, some not as good. And any canned food can be enlivened with certain additions. Spices, for instance, spark up dishes and take up very little space on board. I generally take along minced garlic (dried), minced onion (dried), freeze-dried chives, whole celery seed, dry mustard, sweet basil leaves, dehydrated mint leaves (a dash added to peas tastes great, or try some in iced tea), curry power, poultry seasoning, and, of course, salt and pepper. I also use Worcestershire Sauce and A-1 Steak Sauce a lot, but clearly each chef must decide what he likes best to work with.

Try heating canned fruit as a side dish with meat. Cranberry sauce and applesauce are especially good garnishes. I find that if everything else is canned, a fresh salad can make the whole meal seem fresh.

Canned foods come in all sorts of textures and colors as well as tastes—with some thinking ahead you can avoid serving three mushy white foods at one meal. Basically, the same rules of cooking that apply on land apply on water; you just need a little more imagination.

Simplicity

If you've never spent time in a galley, take my word: You do not ever want to spend more than 30-45 minutes preparing a meal, and the less time the better. Here's why: 1) the boat's motion. If you stay below too long you're liable to get seasick, and there's nothing more awful than cooking when suffering from *mal de mer*. And even if the water is calm, there's always the chance of exhaust fumes or heat doing you in. If you do start to feel a little funny, by the way, the best cure is a fast turn about the deck, up in the bow in the wind and the spray; 2) Everyone is usually ravenous, and if you don't feed them quickly the crew is likely to pester you until you do feed them, or else get roaring drunk before

dinner; and 3) Who wants to spend a lot of time cooking? You could be enjoying the scenery, acquiring a tan, conversing, reading, taking photographs.

One easy way to start off meals on any cruise is to bring aboard some large piece of meat you cooked at home, like a ham, a corned beef, a turkey, a stew. Then your first dinner will be a snap, and you'll have leftovers for sandwiches. Also in the name of simplicity, I usually bake a large pound cake as a versatile base for desserts (add fruit, a sauce, toast it, etc.).

Wise Stowage

Bearing in mind that a 25-pound block of ice is pretty far gone after two or three days, especially in summer, and especially if it is being chipped away to furnish ice for drinks, don't take aboard more fresh food than you can eat up in that time. It's horrible to watch $20 worth of fresh meat, butter, milk, and eggs, all spoiling swiftly, as the ice melts down the drain and the sails go slack (or the motor gives out), and the captain announces that he needs the gas he has left to negotiate the entrance to Cuttyhunk, so "we won't motor, we'll just have to sit here. . . ."

Dried foods won't spoil. I haven't stressed using dried foods because for a one- to three-week cruise they are rather expensive and harder to obtain than the canned items. They *are* lighter and take up less space, so if you're planning to be at sea a long time, you'll want to use them more extensively.

Foods such as crackers, bread, potatoes, carrots, hard squashes, turnips, onions, and fresh fruit (especially if purchased unripe or only partially ripe) will hold up without ice pretty well: at least a week.

Canned foods: They can really be pretty good, perhaps not up to French *haute cuisine* standards, but who needs *haute cuisine* on a cruise? The crew is usually so hungry that even a minor effort in the galley produces raves. Besides, they'll all think you're so great to stay below in the haze of heat, cooking odors, and pitching seas long enough to cook a meal, that they'll be effusively grateful for anything edible. There are great psychological/emotional rewards for the galley chef which are never proffered the same cook on land!

MEALS FOR ONE-WEEK CRUISE, EASTHAMPTON TO NANTUCKET, FOUR PEOPLE

Day No.	Breakfast	Lunch	Dinner
1	*Orange juice Boiled eggs *Toast with butter & *jam	Lettuce & *fruit salad *Crackers *Beer	*Corned beef, with *onions, carrots & potatoes *Coffee *Homemade pound cake
2	*Orange juice Fried eggs *Toast with butter & *jam *Coffee	Swiss cheese, lettuce, mayonnaise sandwiches *Pickle tray Fresh fruit *Beer	*Ham steak with *pineapple rings *Candied yams Salad (lettuce & tomato) *Fruit cocktail & *cookies *Coffee
3	*Cereal with *sugar, milk, sliced bananas Melon *Coffee	*Corned beef, *mustard, rye *bread sandwiches *Vegetable relish tray *Pound cake *with fruit sauce *Beer	*Tuna, boiled egg, sliced tomato salad platter *Rolls & butter *Chocolate pudding *Coffee
4	*Heated rolls *Orange juice Scrambled eggs *Bacon *Coffee	*Cheese spread, tomato & lettuce sandwiches *Chicken noodle soup *Beer *Cookies	*Chicken noodle soup, grated cheese "casserole" Salad (fresh) *Coffee *Pound cake with canned chocolate frosting
5	*French toast *with syrup *Orange juice *Coffee	Fresh vegetable salad plate *Crackers *Tomato soup *Beer	*Shrimp, crab, chicken, *stewed tomato, *saffron rice skillet *Sweet pickles *Canned peaches *Coffee
6	*Apple juice *Cereal with *milk & sugar & dried *strawberries *Coffee	*Ham spread, lettuce, sliced cheese sandwiches *Dill pickles *Canned pears *& cookies *Coffee	*Bacon, baked beans, hot dog skillet *Brown bread *Coffee Fresh fruit
7	Melon *Pancakes with *syrup *Bacon *Coffee	*Tunafish, *celery seed, mayonnaise sandwiches *Vegetable soup *Beer *Tapioca pudding	*Chicken chow mein *with rice & noodles *Canned apricots with cookies *Coffee

Note: All coffee served with sugar and/or "dry creamer."
Starred items (*) canned or in jars or dry, i.e., not refrigerated.

Keep all cold drinks in one ice chest or cooler, the food in another. Thirsty people will be in and out of the drink cooler all day long and its contents will warm up faster, but you'll probably need to open the food cooler only three times a day.

Wrap carefully foods to be kept cool. Celery, lettuce, and other vegetables will become limp and water-logged if they are not tightly encased in plastic wrap. Butter stays best in a small aluminum box with screw-on lid, neater too. Even though not in the cooler, other foods need to be wrapped tightly to stay crisp: crackers, bread, chips, pretzels, rolls.

Stow cans anywhere you can find room so long as they don't get *wet*. Bilges are great unless your boat leaks; at worst salt water will corrode away the cans, and at best it will soak off the labels so you'll have to play open-the-can roulette. Campbell's Soup does offer a code list for identifying label-less cans—that's worth investigation. The type of galley-ware you'll need, incidentally, depends on what you plan to serve on the cruise. I consider the following as basic:

For Cooking

Two no-stick (Teflon) coated frying pans; one large stew pot with lid; no-stick saucepans with lids, one medium, one small; coffeepot (I prefer drip pots); whistling tea kettle (for all water heating).

For Serving and Stowing

Stainless steel bowls (large for salad, one small and one medium for everything else); wicker baskets (for crackers, rolls, fruit); plastic bottles with tops (1 qt, 1½ qt, 2 qt); plastic bowls, plates, mugs (for when you run out of paper).

Utensils

Stainless steel forks, knives, spoons; no-stick spatulas (one large, one small); pot holders; serrated spoon, cooking fork, ladle; two large, extra-sharp carving knives (one serrated, one plain); one wire whisk; several extra-sharp paring knives; can opener, potato peeler, several beer-can openers (they seem to get dropped overboard).

Other Items

Scissors; wooden cutting board; tray; ice picks (two, in case one breaks); stove-top toasting rack.

There are no items more useful to the galley chief than aluminum foil, paper towels, paper napkins, plastic wrap, plastic garbage bags (regular and large, "trash-bag" sized), plastic food storage bags, paper plates, paper cups (hot and cold), and paper bowls. Paper plates, cups, bowls, etc. are all made in myriad patterns, weights, textures, and sizes these days. The best plates are heavy and coated with plastic, and they successfully serve wet food; paper plates can be made even stronger by putting them inside reusable wicker holders. And you can get click-in disposable paper cups that fit reusable cup holders (these worked out best for me), cold drink cups in various sizes, and sturdy foam cups, as well as the standard hot drink cups. You might wish to carry regular plastic dishes in case the paper ones run out, but I'd plan on using them only in such an emergency. They're just unnecessary work!

Plastic garbage bags are the only way to go to sea. They don't leak, they don't soak open (one session of cleaning wet garbage off the sole should cure you of using paper ones). Best of all, a single large trash-sized garbage bag will serve for two or three days, and can be kept all neatly contained, odorless, and stowed out of sight until you reach port.

Aluminum foil is another infinitely helpful and versatile product. It can line a pan, serve as a lid, be fashioned into an extra cooking pot when needed, wrap up heavy items, make a top-of-the-stove "oven" for heating rolls and bread. Also aluminum foil can be used in pouch form for cooking several types of vegetables in the same pot. Put the vegetables, a little butter, salt, and pepper and other seasonings in the foil, seal tightly, and pop into a pot of boiling water. The pouches of vegetables cook beautifully and there is only one pan going on the stove—it won't even need washing.

Lastly, consider paper towels. Their uses are limited only by your imagination: cleaning up spills, draining cooked foods, serving as a disposable dishcloth, drying off wet vegetables, catching fruit and vegetable parings when you are in the midst of preparation, lining shelves, washing windows, drying dishes. I could leave behind several complete changes of clothing if it came to a choice between aluminum foil and paper towels or the clothes!

You'll undoubtedly prefer to devise your own menus, so I've included here one meal plan which might serve as a model. It was worked out for a one-week cruise for four people, with two stops for ice and groceries.

Bon appetit and happy cruising.

Cruising and coping

It's hard to tell where July ends and August begins. For boating purposes, you could really consider them one month: Jaugust, or maybe Auguly. It is a time of great pleasure and miscellaneous perils. I am being cautious because July and August can mean anything from 14 days of unremitting rain during your vacation to engine problems that may give you an extended stay at a port that is not of your choice. The weather we can do nothing about (though Manfred Meisels starting on page 138 tries). As for engines, they have a way of conking out far away from professional help. Preventive maintenance can minimize that nasty possibility, and Mort Schultz starting on page 129 tells you how to cope with that sinking feeling.

   The pleasures of cruising may or may not involve guests. I find that guests of the right kind can enhance a cruise. Guests of the wrong kind are not bad people; they are just not boat people. They don't lend a hand. They are always underfoot. They want lemon peel in their martinis. They don't understand that the best laid plans depend on the weather. ("Gale warnings? It looks calm out there to me.") Boat people seem to have been born with webbed feet (or topsiders) and shipboard manners. They will heave a line when required, come aboard carrying a hero sandwich for all hands, and are blessed with the patience necessary to accommodate the unexpected.

Part of the joy of cruising is knowing what you can anticipate at your next port. Word of mouth is rarely enough. Ask one of your shipmates where to go, and he gives you the name of a waterfront beanery. (But you've already had lunch.) Ask another grease-stained salt and he recommends a seaside hostelry that burned down two years ago. (He has been working on the engines for two years without leaving the dock.) Ask a weatherbeaten skipper who is just docking and he will tout sundry rocks, reefs, and wrecks. (He is a fisherman and his rendezvous are with porgies in season.) Boating is different things to different people. So, if you are a purist as a cruising yachtsman, read Morten Lund's advice on cruising starting on page 111—and fortify your nautical library with the cruising guides. Standard among these are the (updated) guides pioneered by the late Fessenden S. Blanchard, who began to set down his impressions of the Atlantic coast some thirty years ago, covering everything from New Brunswick, Canada, to Key West in four volumes. There are also the Waterway Guides and Boatman's Almanacs. But your best bet is to keep a constant eye on the output of nautical books in your bookstore or shipstore, or in catalogues, yachting magazines, etc. If you're lucky, your area is covered by a spectacular cruising guide like Julius Wilensky's *Where to Go, What to Do, and How to Do It on L.I. Sound* and *Where to Go, (etc.) on Cape Cod*.

Also, keep in mind that some of your best cruising guides are not really cruising guides, but logs of cruises in the form of books like Morton Hunt's incandescent account of circumnavigating the Long Island Sound (*The Inland Sea*), Marjorie Cahn Brazer's magical account of cruising *en famille* from the Great Lakes, via Canada, into New England, and ending up in Flushing, N.Y. (*Wind off the Dock*). Not only do you gain in cruising information, but suddenly each mini-cruise takes on the significance of one lap in a grand cruise . . . that somebody else made, but you could take . . . and will! Someday.

THE ART AND JOYS OF CRUISING

By Morten Lund

july & august

The cruising man is an entirely different creature from the sport fisherman, the marina sailor, or the racing skipper. He, the cruising fellow, has no yen for the hunting of slippery fish or for the exquisite agonies of the hard-nosed racer or for the devout socializing of the dry-sneakered marina mariner; the cruising man cannot bring himself to strain his patience by endless trolling or his temper by unremitting competition or his goodwill by relentless fraternization. And he hates to let his seamanship get rusty by inaction. His love is to sail, or power, in a given direction at no given speed. The getting there and enjoying it there are in themselves his reward.

For most of us cruising men, all begins with the hull.

We've got it and, at least for a while, we are stuck with it, for better or worse, sickness or health. However, assume we are thinking of a change, or even of buying our first cruising hull, what are the choices for getting the most out of cruising? The most general thing you can say is that your choice is between planing or displacement if you are a powerboat man. If you sail, the choice is between light (typically centerboard) and heavy (typically keel) displacement.

All too often, the choice is made on the basis of "What's up, Doc?"

We buy what's "in" at the moment, and think not about our real needs. Sit down. Decide how much you are willing to pay for either speed or real ocean-crossing capability. Thousands of cruising men today have paid heavily for one or the other; they don't really use what they've paid for, and never will.

The sagacious cruising man doesn't cruise very far, very much of the time. He likes to take it easy, to get in well before the sun is below the deck line, and to enjoy the fruits of his labor. Your hard-driving cruising man is really a misplaced racer. Those of us are at fault who feel guilty when we fail to match his speed, distance, and endurance.

Therefore, I say, the powerboat man who plans on no more than 20 to 40 miles per day of cruising is doing a very sensible thing. Most of the planing hulls, the high-powered, flat-bottom motor cruisers, won't plane in any kind of sea without shaking loose every denture aboard, and maybe a few gold inlays. Even if the chop is low enough for reasonably comfortable planing, going fast over anything but dead calm water is fatiguing. After a couple of hours of it, you have a reasonable right and need to come to rest, tie up, call the office, mix a Bloody Mary, and see what's going on at the other piers, or row a dinghy ashore to a beach if you've come to an anchorage rather than a tie-to.

If you don't approach power cruising this way now, you should. It will change your life. Further, unless you have special needs, like reaching a fishing ground 50 miles off and coming back the same day to escape weather, you might well take a cold look and see if a planing hull really makes sense. A trawler type, or displacement hull, which goes only half as fast as your planing hull at top speed, will really go just as fast as the planing hull in 60 percent of the sea conditions when the faster boat cannot utilize all that expensive horsepower without terrible pounding discomfort to everyone aboard. So, try to curb your ego and think about what your real desire is. A displacement hull is considerably more comfortable in most conditions.

On the sail side, you can stand a great deal more time on the water under sail than in a powerboat without fatiguing, since, normally, a sailboat, though slower, rides better than a powerboat. On the other hand, there is a limit to how much time you want to spend under sail each day, or on any given day. If you find this idea surprising, you have probably been sailing too far each day. Try cutting down the length of your hops. An average sailboat day's cruise of over 20 miles, except in ideal conditions, is often tiring enough to put the crew on edge, make the skipper prone to errors of judgment, and bring the yacht into strange harbors after dark. This may be fun as an exception, but do it four or five days in a row and I guarantee you a bad cruise.

If this be true, and I take it that it is, the case for light displacement becomes much stronger than it usually is seen, certainly as strong as the case for the keel boat.

The keel boat (and the heavy keel-boat-like centerboarder built to imitate) can take you across the ocean at reasonable risk. More to the point, it can slug it out with heavy crests coastwise and come off creditably. Your light displacement centerboarder will not. It will get knocked around and give you a bad day.

However, if you plan a cruise properly, you can lay over a day or so whenever heavy weather hits (it isn't all that much fun in a heavy displacement boat, either) and you can sail when it's calmer. What you gain in a heavy boat is time . . . but if you've planned your cruise well, you should have time to burn.

Moreover, a heavy sailboat has to carry a lot of sail to move that weight. And she has to have expensive gear to handle the strain of that sail. And the gear wears and damages more quickly. It is a cumulatively expensive situation.

This is not to say that I don't like keel boats. I like expensively-turned-out women, too, but keeping up with one will be costly. So you have to be sure it is worth it to you.

Light displacement boats have less draft. If there is one plus in cruising that is more of a blessing when it comes to interesting places than shallow draft, I don't know it.

The glory of shallow draft, the ability to go into or nearly into the beach and to get into that gunkhole, is a glamour trait for a real cruising man, on a par with the glamour of slugging it out in a head sea with a hundred-and-fifty-percent genny.

As an added attraction, the light displacement boat is likely to be beamier, and have a good deal more room inside at and above the waterline.

And that brings us to the cabin.

The Cabin

Next to the desirable properties the hull has when going to sea, the convenience, comfort, and coziness of the cabin is the single most important item in a cruising man's world. The cabin is going to be home, after all, during the cruise, and that is 100 percent true when the weather is foul, which it will be quite often.

A yacht that has been around as a type for a long time is likely to have a better-arranged cabin than that of a fairly newly developed design. The builder of the more mellow design has had time to get feedback from his customers and has undoubtedly improved his cabin layout a great deal. I am thinking now of a Hinckley, say, which, for its type, is about as neatly put-together in the cabin as you could want. It is hard to think of a thing to add or move.

This is not so on the newer, lighter boats, because they are new. It is particularly not true on multihulls, which are very new, relatively, and often have atrocious cabin layouts. However, if you know what you want, everything can be improved a good deal with time.

We will get into the crew question in depth later on, but in relation to cabin comfort, a most dramatic way to improve a cabin's livability is to have one bunk empty during the whole cruise. This gives you extra stowage, a place to put things and leave them, and in general lightens the whole cabin problem about 50 percent. If you want to take on a full crew overnight, that is not a crucial decision. But a longer voyage, with every bunk full, is likely to call for everyone to be brimful of good humor all the time. Who is?

The single most important item in the cabin is the stove. If it works, things are good, and if not, things are bad. You burn up an awful lot of energy in a day's cruising: You need something to replace it, and tunafish sandwiches are not the whole answer.

Therefore, whether you are a mechanic or not, you should have the necessary tools and be able to take the stove apart, replace the burner elements (you have them, of course, in your spare parts kit), and put things back together again. If it is a pressure stove, as most are, you should certainly have spare leathers to go in the piston to pump up the pressure. They tend to wear out the second day at sea, as a rule, and it's cold hash until you replace them.

Another must to save the day, and for use as an auxiliary in making a more elaborate meal: Carry a small spare stove, a light back-packing stove, or a gimbaled frame that takes canned heat or charcoal and can be stowed or hung out of the way until needed.

I dwell on these galley details because the psychological value of food is so high that a cruise with poor food is usually seen as a poor cruise.

One more consideration where cabin comfort and the question of cooking meet: One good way to make the cabin work well is to let the cook get out of it in good weather by having on-deck cooking capabilities. There are a number of inexpensive charcoal grills that can be hung over the side, or you can simply set up an outdoor stand for the stove.

I won't venture too far into the food question, but the truth is, you should plan to be independent of grocery stores, or else you cruise from one A&P to another.

There is nothing wrong with fresh food, but take enough cans and storables so that you could get by if you had to without going ashore once. It takes a little planning but it is more than worth it. One secret of the art of cruising is to recognize the interdependent variables. If your meals are dependent on shore, you are not going to get away from it all very much.

We are going to deal with one final galley parameter, as the engineers would say: the problem of garbage. About half the yachts I've looked into treat the subject as if it were something that didn't happen to people. But it does. And if there is one thing that makes a cabin unbearable it is the whiff of inedible leavings. Unless you have ample space to slip in a plastic garbage bag and keep it sealed, or a plastic can with lid, you are going to have a smelly cabin. If you have an ample supply of garbage bags, you can even stow garbage on deck for a while without bad results, until it can be appropriately dumped. And that is so much more esthetic than sinking

it. Some even let it float—and a pox on their cruising!

The way the cabin works, in summation, is so important, that I can make a strong case for spending the money to charter a type of boat you think you would like to buy, or imitate in layout, in order to test cabin layout under way. If the refrigerator is across the chart table, and the toilet can't be used while the cook is at the stove, don't buy.

Charts

When a well-versed cruising man begins his cruise, he begins with charts, goes by charts, and ends with his last chart. That goes even if he just daysails. Hardly a cruising man of any experience hasn't come across a very nervous crew in a light sea haze or at dusk who come beelining up in their yacht to ask where they are, please. Chart? Oh no, they are just out for the day.

We won't talk about navigating because, with all due respect, what most of us do is simply coastwise piloting. A good pilot is a very simple-minded man, who knows that he is very easily confused. So he takes elaborate precautions to do things as clearly and as simply as he can, and keeps track of what he expects to see next at what time. Anticipation is really the big secret. Almost every normal piloting error arises because the pilot, all right, let's call him the navigator, started meditating at the last navigational mark and just as he passed this one saw it was the wrong one.

Unless you have the time to get really sharp at piloting and navigation, do it the easy way: Rule Number One is to keep track of the numbers. That means go from one buoy to the next, buoy-to-buoy it's called, and check off the numbers even if it isn't the short-cut way to the anchorage, and even if it means motoring instead of sailing in your approach. Number Two is don't necessarily believe that the buoy is there because the chart says it is. Buoys get misplaced, swept off, or founder. The way to work with buoys is to spot their pattern so that you have two or three or four of them in sight if possible, and know which should be which. Then, if one is missing, it will be apparent quite soon.

Three is, don't sail at night in strange waters. This may sound chicken, and it is, but it is also the result of a lot of experience as skipper and crew. Sailing at night by lighted navigational aids lacks the most important aid of all: depth of field. It is almost impossible to see how far off a given light is in relation to another. What looks so logical on the chart turns out to be a can of worms in practice. Lights that are not navigational aids (and thus are not on the charts) will mess up your perceptions. Unless you are very sharp, one try out of three attempts at night landfalls will find you darting around like a dragonfly inside a black bowler hat.

Four is, have a lead line or a depth sounder: Have a lead line anyway, in case the depth sounder goes whack. You can get good, accurate results, and more important, tell whether you are in the channel or outside, by heaving a weight on the end of a marked line and reading off the depth, like on a Mississippi riverboat ("By the mark, twain!"). As a child you must have learned that's how Sam Clemens took his pen name, didn't you?

Not only is a lead line a good sturdy instrument for channel finding, but when you want to anchor it will let you know when your depth is just right so you can let out your 50 feet of anchor line for proper scope for average conditions so the anchor will hold (the answer is ten feet).

Five: Have a radio direction finder and know how to use it. There are a couple of tricky things about RDF. One of them is having it work. Test before you take off.

Another is, what side of the station are you on? I've gone past the station on one occasion without knowing it and been ever so confused when I turned the set on. However, your radio direction-finding pamphlet offers you a way out of this dilemma. So read about "sensing" before the crisis strikes. If you are caught out in a fog (you aren't a cruising man until you have been), then your RDF is the very best way to cure that sick headache.

Six, have some idea how fast you are traveling. That necessitates a log or knotmeter. You don't have to have an expensive through-hull fitting. You can trail an elegantly accurate log from time to time. Then, when you know your speed and tidal current, you can figure how soon you should be seeing what, one of the main points to concentrate on. Oh yes, the tidal currents are published in handy chart form by the U.S. Coast Guard for most cruising grounds. Note: A current

going with you makes you approach a shoal at an increment twice as large as the current going against you.

Tides

They wait for no man, but they can give you a lot of help. The depth figure numbers on your chart (make sure whether they are in feet or fathoms) are, of course, mean low water. Mean, because they won't let you into an approaching marvelous anchorage. You draw four, and the sand bar is three. But, aha, it is one hour before high tide and the tide is four feet. (You have the other Coast Guard publication, the tide tables, of course for the current year.) No problem, then, and you go in to a starbright evening where no other boat had dared to venture. This night, at least, you are a hero to your crew for finding such a place. And you feel secure, knowing that the tide in that region inexorably reverses every six-and-a-quarter hours: You can safely sail back over the bar in eleven, twelve hours, or thereabouts. (Ninety percent of the tide will be in at the end of the fifth hour or so.)

A word of caution, however: Don't call it too close. I live on a tide cove and know that the rise and fall often vary up to two feet from one tide to the next. Check your tide tables for the variation that can be expected locally.

The last thing I will mention in connection with navigation is the compass.

This is not because the compass is unimportant, but because it has been overemphasized, and made a point of pain for countless cruising novices.

If you want to drive a learner crazy, have him steer by compass for a while, and make sure the compass is between his knees, that there is nothing he can steer by on the water, and make sure there's no lubberline for him to use.

The truth is, the only time you should be turning the helm over to someone who doesn't have much time behind the compass needle is when there is something on the water or on the shore to point at. Otherwise you are going to alienate him or her and lose valuable help. Steering by compass should be like learning to walk tightrope, a little at a time. And for everyone concerned, the salt as well as the beginner, the compass should be as high as possible. You should insist on one that has a lubberline to mark the place the needle should be held—it eliminates so much fatigue.

The Ship's Company

Now we are down to it: the skipper and crew.

The first thing is that there has to be a skipper. It may not be democratic, but you can't run a vessel by vote. If you have to pick a skipper by lot, do it. But someone has to have the deciding voice or surely calamity will ensue in the wake of rhetoric.

The second thing is, the skipper should be a damn nice guy except when he has to make split-second decisions. That is, just because one man is the owner, charterer, or chosen captain, it doesn't mean he has been given leave to write his own little Red Book and have everyone memorize it.

I have been a member of one crew where the captain all but frothed at the mouth because I refused to flemish the sheets after every change of trim. The only relief I had, beside leaving as soon as I could get ashore, was to thoroughly enjoy the skipper's running aground as he tried to steer with one hand and flemish the sheets with the other.

Some people may want to participate fully in working the yacht and others may want to be left out as much as possible. It is really up to the captain not only to make the ship go but to make sure his crew (who are after all guests of his) have a good time. Easy does it, especially with the captain's own family. A guest can always get called back to the office if he hates the whole thing, but the captain's family is stuck with the captain and vice versa.

The successful skipper not only is a diplomat with regard to passengers, but to make a cruise work he also has to cleverly pick people who will fit in well together and form a combination of fun and hardworking types, graciousness and salt-of-the-earth.

Beware of bringing on people you don't know, especially women, for an extended cruise. To be a male chauvinist skipper for a minute, let me say that women inexperienced in sailing tend to be highly imaginative when it comes to the word "cruise". They may picture a swimming pool and waiters with mint juleps on the foredeck. I have seen parasols brought aboard a small sail yacht. No kidding. Unless you have a large power cruiser, make sure the girls who come are really good sports. A girl may be an awful lot of fun being crazy and kooky, the life of the party in her super pants suit; she may be the bitch of all time at sea when she doesn't have her own vanity in front of her for an hour before appearing in public. It's not that women are worse people than males, but their conditioning is different.

Seamanship

The successful cruise doesn't necessarily demand a great sailing hand at the helm at all times, or even a part of the time, assuming you have some kind of adequate power aboard; nor, in a powerboat, do you need to have the head of the local Power Squadron aboard in order to make a four-hour crossing, assuming some kind of common sense and acknowledgement of the foregoing principles on the part of the skipper. But for a good cruise, you do need rudiments.

When it comes to sailing, as in sex, most people I have talked to have gotten their knowledge by hearsay. I doubt one in ten cruising skippers has sat down with a book, or raced small craft, either one. I have sat around on deck while a cruising skipper has solemnly assured me that the farther the sails were trimmed inboard, the faster the boat would go (we were on a reaching wind). The hull underfoot was not worth less than $50,000.

I have watched skippers of powerboats who had not the remotest idea of how to maneuver, not the least idea of which way the stern swung in most readily.

I know of very few successful cruising skippers who are not bright and inventive in addition to being well-read in theory. Cruising teaches what is so easy to forget: That man survives supremely because he's a unique combination of action and invention, of reflection and reflex, decision and compromise. Cruising is a way of sharpening the proper balance of traits. There isn't a sport where man's contradictory qualities are called upon and exercised as an ensemble so compellingly as in cruising.

Cruising is also a process of relating to our surroundings.

This is the age of saving ourselves from ourselves. And by that I mean from over-extending the resources of the environment. There is nothing like a cruise week to make you more aware of the thin but precious and nurturing envelope of nature that covers us. The sea will not continue to nurture if we render it sterile by neglect. Cruising inculcates a certain awareness that we seem to have lost, vis-a-vis creation.

Cruising is a personal resource.

The compulsions and frustrations of modern industrial society are the unfortunate consequences of the artifice.

Cruising is a counterweight, an antidote to the society of mass man. I once debated the question of whether it was better to be a middle-aged corporation executive or a middle-aged pre-Columbian Plains Indian. The middle-aged Indian to my mind had a better time of it. He was not bored or stymied, and he was preoccupied by survival, and to some extent with maintaining his position in the tribe. His world was, in his terms, comprehensible and satisfying. His kids didn't grow up doing something radically different and his world wasn't shaped by some great blind power thousands of miles off whose actions were completely absurd. He had a world that worked according to definite principles and that would continue to do so, and that would reward him amply for very specific and direct acts.

The sailor has a chance to be very like that when he cruises. He knows what storm and tide can do, and takes his risks with respect to them. He is not going to be faced with a world where the rules suddenly change. The wind is going to blow or not blow across the water. The waves are going to continue to run. The tide will rise. The vagaries are visible. Cruising is the re-creation of a direct, satisfying world.

Finally, there is, above all, the pure joy of cruising.

Every youngster is on a continual sensational trip. He can sit in the wind and feel the sun and have a fantastic time. This is what we can so easily lose when we grow older in our complex, artificial society. We have to maintain periodic contact with these natural things or we simply lose the spirit. Wind becomes annoying and sun irritating. Sounds of water lapping at the hull don't carry to our inner selves. If we wait too long to get back to such things we risk losing them forever, trapped inside ourselves.

If there is great joy in cruising, and to most of us who cruise, there is, the ultimate goal consists of re-capturing the wonderment and enchantment of sounds and light and movement of the rhythms of the sea where once we had our home.

CRUISING WITH TEEN-AGERS

By Bill Robinson

july & august

Doesn't anyone ever cruise with teen-agers?

Over the years I have noted the existence of a vast literature on how to handle children under ten in a boat, but there has been silence about the next decade in a family's growth. We are heir to reams of advice on how to rig a kiddie coop in the cabin and the best way to clear zwieback from the bilge pump, but what of the terrible teens?

How to cruise successfully with, in our case at the moment, a boy 17 and girls 15 and 12, or any combination thereof? They like to cruise, we like them with us. No longer, though, does a walk from the harbor to the drugstore for an ice cream cone rate as the big treat of an evening in port, and we can't get away any more with having them chase mallards round the anchorage in the dinghy as a cocktail hour dodge.

Do the mothers who write articles in starry-eyed confidence about life afloat with toddlers get fed up with togetherness and subside, punch-drunk, into silence when the dreaded teen years approach? When we entered that era, we found we were on our own. With the Dr. Spock years astern, no ready reference was available, yet I know parents do take teen-agers along. We have even seen Dr. Spock cruising with his. To fill the gap, then, and to warn parents who think they have it made when there are no longer diapers drying in the rigging and plastic toys underfoot, here is a father's report on the strangely neglected subject.

As I see it, a cruise with teen-agers is possible, and can be successful, if it is planned to go from movie to movie via restaurants, with rock-and-roll music (I guess that's what it is) available on the radio at all times. Each passage should start in mid-morning (or later), end in early afternoon, and include a stop for swimming and snorkeling. At least every third day should be spent in port.

To show how their minds run, here is a typical afternoon conversation between one of the girls and me as we are lazing comfortably along in, say, Nantucket Sound. She has been reading—a novel or underwater adventure book, perhaps; a comic book more likely. The other one is doing her hair curled up on the forward bunk and strange wails and slurping sounds issue from the radio, which she has cradled next to her tummy. Mother is reading drowsily.

"Where are we going in tonight, Dad?" Alice asks.

"Vineyard Haven, maybe." (I would have preferred Hadley's Harbor and its quiet, uncivilized isolation, but I know better.)

"What's it like?"

"Well, it's a little old town at the head of a big harbor with lots of boats. It's where the ferry from Woods Hole comes in."

"Have you ever been there?"

"Yes."

"When?"

"Oh, a long time ago."

"How big is it?"

"Maybe a couple of thousand."

"Has it got stores and things?"

"I think so."

"What kind of stores?"

"Drugstore, grocery, gift shop, you know."

And this game can go on for hours, but at this point I usually break down and end it by saying, ". . . and I don't know whether it has a movie."

"Do you think it might?"

"Yes, it might."

Meanwhile, Martha has stopped doing her hair for a moment and has turned down the volume on the radio. She takes my wallet down from the bunk shelf, pulls out the Diner's Club booklet and starts to leaf through it.

"Massachusetts, Massachusetts—we're not back to Rhode Island, are we?" she asks. "What place did you say?"

"Vineyard Haven."

"I don't see it anywhere."

"Guess we eat aboard then," I say.

"Oh, gee," the girls sigh.

The conventional cruising guides do not have all the vital information for this kind of operation. They do not give radio schedules (I mean disc jockeys, not navigation beacons), or the location of movie theaters, bowling alleys, and amusement parks. Never mind about the type of holding ground or the availability of ice and fuel. How near the waterfront is the cinema palace?

Your idea of a perfect cruising harbor may be a snug cove with not another boat in sight and a shoreline unmarred by signs of human habitation, but don't go there on this kind of voyage. You'll want to see signs, preferably neon, as you move into the harbor entrance, and one of them had better read "Pizza," come to think of it. Also, as the cruise progresses and the wallet grows thinner, that chaste little Diner's Club sign on the door of a restaurant becomes an increasingly important one. Eventually, it always ends up as the only way we can eat ashore.

Scenery is "nice" to teen-agers, but they can take it in very quickly, and then they want to get ashore and do some exploring. The psychology is akin to liberty in the navy. Each new port is a challenge. Even after a passage of a few miles there is a great itch to get ashore there. If it only offers sand dunes and empty beaches, it passes as a lunch stop, but once the sun goes down and the lights come on, there had better be some sort of lights on shore.

A cruising boat must be big, and have excellent reading lights for each individual, to keep teen-agers happy aboard in the evening. We have cruised on everything from 24 to 80 feet with ours, and even after a couple of nights in an 80-footer in the Exumas, they were ready to get back to some sort of activity ashore. Hours of skin diving and snorkeling made them sleepy enough to cut down the restlessness for a few evenings, but then that "liberty port" psychology began to set in.

While under way, teen-agers take care of entertaining themselves pretty well. The stratagems for keeping tiny tots happy need not be employed. Gone are the coloring books, the stuffed animals, and the plastic toys. They enjoy most ship's business, including wheel tricks, and can be fed a modicum of practical navigation. If properly instructed, they can be as good as most adults and better than some in line handling, anchoring, sail handling, and other such maneuvers. When things are quiet, they can be kept happy with a supply of soft drinks, books, and cards. Our girls can play one or two games of cards, chess or checkers before the hair-pulling starts, and our son is one of the more accomplished sack artists in America. And then there is the radio.

Don't think you can avoid rock-and-roll music just because you're getting away from that station that drives you nuts at home. When we trailed to Miami to cruise in the Keys a couple of years ago I smiled smugly when the New York stations faded from the dial. At last I would be rid of "that" station and its pack of idiot announcers. Miami, however, had not one but several that sounded just like it, only worse. The kids have shown a remarkable knack for locating such outlets in places like Providence, R.I., Cleveland, Ohio, and Kingston, Ont. Even in the far reaches of the Exumas they exhibited a second sense that could tell when ZedNS in Nassau was going to play American music that sounded as though we'd never left home. And Miami came through at night, of course.

Housekeeping afloat with teen-agers is difficult, especially in something as small as our 24-footer. The jumble that can develop in a few minutes in the cabin of a small boat has to be seen to be believed, and it is enough to keep a mother in a constant state of helpless defeat. The kids seem content to live like trader rats for the whole time they are aboard, burrowing into their own little pile of supplies for whatever is needed at the moment, but adults have to keep this sort of thing under control if they want to hold on to their sanity.

We provide one bunk-net for each person. They are always organized with the greatest of care when the cruise starts. But as each day goes by and more objects have been stuffed into them hastily when Mother says "all right, let's pick it up," they become great bristling, bulging lumps. The clothes are balled up into odd shapes, with books, magazines, towels, hair curlers, foul weather gear, souvenir postcards, sea shells, fishing lines, make-up kits, diaries, sta-

tionery boxes, and many more mysterious objects jammed together. Each search for an object produces a more complicated jumble, and a deepening of the crisis. By the last couple of days it is impossible to lie on the bunk when the net is rigged, and the nets are therefore placed on the floorboards next to the bunks, making the cabin sole at bedtime resemble the back room of a Salvation Army depot. Sometimes it gets so bad the nets have to be completely reorganized.

Starting out in the morning, when the cabin is a solid mass of bulging bunk nets, can present its problems. I have been known to slip up on deck at daybreak, make sail by myself, and have several hours of quiet sailing before the others wake up. If I get up with the others and wait to get under way until they have everything organized, it can mean that we never do get going. Of course, the weather has to be good for this solo stuff, but I enjoy it, everyone else appreciates the sleep, and I don't have to help pick up the cabin. Sometimes we even anchor for a late breakfast after several hours of sailing.

Cruising with female hairdos is one of the biggest problems a skipper has to contend with, and when the females are in their teens the situation is at its most serious. Fresh water is a must at frequent intervals, curlers and bobby pins turn up in every corner of the boat, and almost every maneuver calling for help from the crew is ill-timed because someone is putting her hair up or down. For this reason, one of our most successful cruises was on Lake Ontario, where the girls spent a good part of the trip in the lake washing their hair. We didn't get much sailing in, but we sure used a lot of soap.

As can be seen, most of the teen-age problems we have had have been feminine ones. When everyone was younger, we all cruised together, but a 17-year-old boy has plans of his own, as well as summer employment. When he did cruise with us, he objected mildly to being a "sailing babysitter" and having to go to the movies with his sisters. He was much happier on nights when he could go exploring on his own. Now he uses the boat by himself with schoolmates for crew, and I sometimes join them for a stag operation. They make a raffishly effective racing crew, and there is no problem about entertaining them afloat or ashore. They have their own world, and all they need an adult for is a bit of cash now and then.

When we were all on board together, we not only had the problem of hitting a port where there was something to do on shore. Sometimes we also had a hard time getting away from one. After two days at Ocean Reef Club on Key Largo, for instance, the children had made so many friends ashore there that it was difficult to tear them away. The young man had found himself a lady love and was seldom to be seen, and the girls entered into the group of youngsters there as though they were staying for life. For a couple of days, in order to use the boat at all, we had to just go day sailing out to the reefs, inviting new-found friends along and come back in at night. The girls were just as loath to leave Nantucket after a few days there on another cruise, but we finally were able to tear them away when the Dreamland Movie Theater had to shut down because the films failed to arrive on the steamer.

Each family has its own systems and operational methods, and teen-agers can vary as much as adults. There may be some who love to go off for two weeks of isolated cruising with nothing but seashell collecting on empty beaches to keep them happy, but I have yet to meet them. It might seem, from some of the problems outlined here, that it is hardly worth it at all to cruise with kids during the difficult years. Strangely enough, we have enjoyed each expedition and keep planning on more.

As I plan, though, I am engaging in a secret search. I am looking for a cruising area out of range of disc jockeys.

THE POWERBOAT IN ROUGH SEAS

By Dag Pike

july & august

In spite of good weather forecasts, there is always the chance of bad weather arriving unexpectedly, literally out of the blue.

A freshening wind need not be such a frightening thing provided you are prepared for it. A well prepared boat should be able to withstand most of the bad conditions you are likely to meet, provided it is carefully handled. Preparation should begin long before you go to sea and should result in your having a boat which will stand up to bad weather. Many of the accidents which occur during bad weather are caused by some part of the boat failing. Once this has happened, attention is distracted from the job in hand, giving the sea the chance it is looking for.

Handling any boat in bad weather demands concentration since the sea is very rarely regular. If you are lucky, all of the waves will come from the same direction making the job easier, but more often than not there are two or more wave trains superimposed. This makes the sea unpredictable and can lead to waves of differing heights and characteristics coming at you.

The statistics are frightening. One wave in 23 will, on average, be twice the average height, one in 1175 will be three times the average height and one in 300,000 will be four times higher than the average. The last are the so-called freak waves; they may occur once a week in any given place and then they are usually very transient.

You may have seen what looks like a large wave approaching, only to find that it is no bigger than the rest when it reaches you. It is the truly larger than normal waves that you have to watch for. It is a simple matter to adjust the speed and direction of the boat to the normal pattern of the waves, but don't leave it at that, because it will be all wrong when the larger wave arrives. So the rule must be to maintain good concentration, watch the sea closely at all times. Big waves may not give much warning.

The two controls which you have at your command are the wheel and the throttle. The wheel is not usually responsive enough to be used for evasive action with respect to waves except on fast boats, and even then, at slower rough-weather speeds, steering is usually sluggish. However, the wheel can be used to advantage in avoiding the larger wave crests, provided they are well anticipated.

If you watch a rough sea for a time, you will notice that waves rarely break along a continuous front. Rather they break in patches along short lengths of the crest. The breaking wave is dangerous since the water in the wave is moving forward and can hit the boat with considerable force, so the object is to try to steer the boat through the areas where waves are not actually breaking. (The safest place is where a wave has just broken as it is unlikely to break again in the same place.) Wave crest dodging must be done with caution. In your enthusiasm to avoid breaking crests you may find yourself putting the boat beam on to the sea, which is not a very healthy position unless the boat has good acceleration.

The time will come when you cannot avoid a larger wave and this is when the throttle comes into play. To many people, the throttle is not to be used at sea more than necessary. To be sure, a large diesel engine does not like continual acceleration and deceleration, but if it gets you out of trouble in bad weather, then by all means do it. I think that much of the reluctance to use the throttles comes from bad positioning which makes them difficult to reach easily.

Apart from making the boat go faster or slower, the use of the throttles has a secondary effect, in that the bow of the boat will lift when the throttle is advanced and will drop when the throttle is retarded. The response is usually fairly quick, particularly with a planing hull, and can be used to good effect when running a boat in rough seas.

If you are driving your boat into a head sea, and this is the normal direction since the hull is designed to take impact from ahead, it should be possible to find a reasonable speed for the prevailing conditions. This must not be so slow as to lose steerage—that can quickly lead to disaster if the bow is knocked round by a wave. Minimum speed will depend on the boat and the size of the rudder—four or five knots should be about right.

The object is to prevent seas from breaking on board and causing damage, so ideally the bow should lift over the wave, and then plunge gently down the other side and not bury into the next wave. To lift the bow, the throttles should be advanced as the wave approaches. This will put the boat in the right attitude, and as the bow lifts, close the throttles so that the boat will cut through the top of the wave. This will reduce the drop on the far side, and as the bow starts to drop speed up again to get the bow lifting for the next wave.

By continually working the throttles, the thrust of the propellers is used to lift the bow without imparting too much headway. Since the rudder is usually behind the propeller, increased thrust will also help steering. A displacement boat will not have the quick reactions of the planing boat, for the displacement boat is usually more heavily built. Planing boats, being lighter, are much more responsive to the controls.

Planing boats often have trim tabs for use in controlling the attitude of the boat, but they are effective only when the boat is traveling fairly fast. Still, in a head sea the tabs should be kept down, because most planing boats have full bow sections which lift readily to a head sea, and with weight concentrated fairly well aft, the bow is likely to fly. But the tabs will help to prevent this.

In bad weather, the wind always seems to be against you, so you are normally faced with heading into the sea. However, the main object if you are overtaken by bad weather is to get into some sort of shelter. Shelter may be downwind, in which case you are faced with the prospect of running before the sea. This is what sailors dread, with the constant fear of broaching.

Running before the sea can be dangerous and is not to be undertaken lightly, particularly in a displacement boat being overtaken by the waves so that it has little control over its position in relation to them. When a breaking crest comes along, it is moving forward quicker than the boat, so steering is lost and the boat becomes uncontrollable and broaches. A boat with a flat transom will be more vulnerable as the water hitting the transom will accelerate the boat and take charge. A double ender will part the moving water and the wave will have less effect.

The best answer to this situation is either to stream a drogue, or turn and head into the sea. (A deep drafted boat will react better as most of the moving crest is near the surface.) A drogue which exercises a strong pull keeps the boat stern to the sea and makes steering much easier. Before you rush out and buy a drogue, remember that a boat has to be suitably constructed for it. It should be double-ended, have a strong, closed fairlead right aft, and a very strong samson post to take the drogue line.

If wave crests are breaking heavily, don't run before the sea in a displacement boat unless she is very maneuverable. With a planing boat you have a much greater choice of speeds, and provided you can do better than 20 knots you should be able to outrun the sea. It can be done, but it requires skill and concentration. The safest place in a following sea is on the back of a wave. In that position, the wave behind cannot catch you up. But it's not as simple as that. Waves have a habit of changing, particularly where there are crossing wave trains, and unless you concentrate very hard you may find the wave astern catching you, a potentially dangerous situation. If you adopt this course and you are in doubt, open the throttle.

Overtaking waves can be dangerous because you cannot tell until you are on top of the wave whether it is going to break. Also your arrival there may help the wave to make up its mind and it will break prematurely. This will give it a very steep forward face, and your bow will drop rapidly, to bury in the next wave. Opening the throttles at this stage may not be the answer, as the boat will be accelerating anyway.

A planing boat has another advantage over the

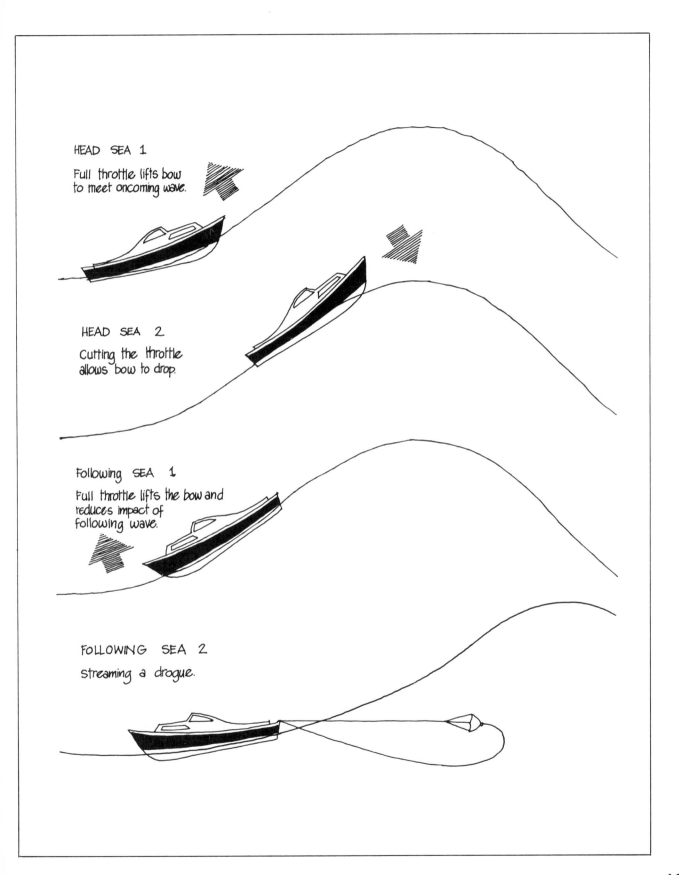

HEAD SEA 1

Full throttle lifts bow to meet oncoming wave.

HEAD SEA 2

Cutting the throttle allows bow to drop.

Following SEA 1

Full throttle lifts the bow and reduces impact of following wave.

FOLLOWING SEA 2

streaming a drogue.

displacement boat, and this is the ability to proceed with the sea on the beam. This sounds unseamanlike but bearing in mind that waves break only along short fronts it is possible by careful use of the throttle to dodge breaking sections, either by slowing or accelerating. Bear in mind that in this situation if you do make a mistake you may be traveling quite quickly and the consequences could be serious.

You will notice I have stressed the use of the throttle. It is speed, or lack of it, that is most important in rough seas. Steering is obviously important, but it is not usually very effective when trying to avoid trouble. If you are to use the throttle effectively it must be positioned where it comes readily to hand.

First, you only have two hands and if one is on the throttle you cannot steer properly. Secondly, if you are standing up and the boat lurches, you can neither steer nor work the throttles properly. Some people say that you cannot get the feel of a boat if you are sitting, but which would you rather do, stand or be able to control the boat properly?

If you are in a strong seat which gives good support, you have both hands free to control the boat. Nowadays, throttle levers are often combined with the gears, which makes handling so easy and logical in harbor. The single lever is not so good for rough sea use, though, because when you pull the lever back you are liable to disengage it which is good neither for control of the boat nor for the gearbox. It is difficult to get the delicate control required for rough-weather operation with a single lever because of the short throttle range.

Next in importance to being in a position to control the boat properly, is the ability to see what is going on outside. Only when you can see the advancing waves will you be in a position to do something about them. Visibility obviously demands efficient means of clearing water from the windows.

Internal reflections can be a great nighttime problem when your ability to see oncoming waves is greatly reduced. Operating at night in rough seas considerably increases the risks, and should not be undertaken lightly. Avoid it if possible and have some form of strategy in mind if you are caught outside.

Always have a refuge selected when planning your passages, so that you can be safely in a harbor when bad weather comes along. Since this is not always possible, consider the advisability of continuing on or looking for shelter.

Before making up your mind you will need some idea of what the wind might do. It is no use heading for shelter if by the time you get there the wind will have swung round exposing the shelter. It is difficult to cite hard and fast rules since there are too many variables, and only you as skipper are in a position to assess them.

One of the biggest variables in writing about rough weather is the tremendous variety of boats. Each has its weak points and characteristics which will affect behavior at sea. It's up to the skipper to look at his boat from the point of view of operating in rough seas so that before he gets caught out, he has some idea of what is or is not possible.

The sea is a very variable medium and should never be underestimated, but don't let this put you off. The sea is there to be enjoyed, and even rough seas can be enjoyable if you have confidence in yourself and your boat. Good preparation and maintenance is half the battle in surviving. Coast Guard rules and recommendations insist that you carry safety equipment, but this is to help you once you're in trouble. The aim is not to get into trouble in the first place.

FIFTEEN WAYS TO PREVENT ENGINE TROUBLE

By Eileen Holm Matthew

july & august

Leafing back through your log book, are there any entries that look like either of the following?

Time: Four hours after high water at the Battery.
Position: Hell Gate, East River, New York.
Weather: Heavy rain, gusty winds, current SW at four knots.
Situation: Engine stops suddenly.

OR

Time: Early morning, first day of vacation.
Position: Home port, tied to dock.
Weather: Sky clear, sea calm, air temperature 75 degrees.
Situation: Nothing happens when you press the starter switch.

Either way it's an unwanted situation; but then, there is never a right time to have trouble with your engine. Fortunately, most engine problems result from simple causes. With due care ahead of time, they can be prevented.

1. *Learn how your engine and its various systems operate.* Engines are really not as complicated as they seem to most of us at times. We've

found it helps to read the owner's manual that comes with a new boat or ask the dealer for one if it's missing.

Owners of older boats can usually obtain a manual for the engine by writing to its manufacturer. If a service manual is available, this is worth ordering, too. The owner's manual is likely to give basic get-acquainted material on the engine, while the service manual goes into greater detail concerning performance, specifications, maintenance, and repairs.

If you need information on basic marine engine operation, read a book on the subject. A good one, for example, is *Small Boat Engines, Inboard and Outboard* by Conrad Miller (Sheridan House, P.O. Box 254, Yonkers, N.Y. 10705; 316 p., Illus., $7.50). It covers both gasoline and diesel engines.

Besides reading a book, we took the course in Engine Maintenance given by the U.S. Power Squadrons.

A handy pamphlet to have aboard is given free by the U.S. Coast Guard. Called *Emergency Repairs Afloat,* it's available from district offices or Commandant (CAS), U.S. Coast Guard, 400 Seventh St. SW, Washington, D.C. 20591.

To become familiar with a particular engine, we look it over carefully with the owner's manual in hand. We trace the systems one by one, and learn where the various accessories are mounted. By knowing how the "healthy" engine appears, we have a better chance of spotting irregularities later on—corroded battery terminals or a loose fuel line, for instance.

2. *Keep the ignition system in tune.* The ignition system needs to be tuned up at regular intervals. This includes replacing the breaker assembly (points) in the distributor; checking and, if necessary, re-setting the timing; changing the spark plugs. We inspect our plugs between changes for burning or fouling, and to be sure the gaps are properly set. Burned plugs can be the result of operating under a heavy load or of running at high speeds for a long period of time. The remedy may be to switch to a "colder" (short insulator) plug. Fouled plugs can result from low-speed operation, or from long periods of idling. Such operation may require a "hot" (long insulator) plug. Follow the engine maker's recommendations on plugs, bearing in mind that the higher the plug's code number the hotter the plug.

3. *Watch out for poor electrical connections.* The most important factor in preventing electrical system failure is a simple one: Keep all connections tight, clean, and dry. Grease and oil act as insulators and interfere with the flow of electricity. These materials also tend to deteriorate rubber, which is still used to insulate some wires. Water, of course, promotes corrosion and causes increased resistance or even short circuits.

4. *Keep your fuel free of dirt and water.* Obviously, no engine can continue running after the fuel stops flowing. Breakdowns do result from mechanical failures or carburetor or fuel pump parts, but the more usual cause is dirt particles that clog tiny passages in the fuel system or cause equally tiny check valves to stick.

Most engines have several fuel strainers and filters. If yours doesn't, it's worth adding at least one strainer to your fuel tank filling line. All strainers and filter sediment bowls must be cleaned periodically—more often when you have been using fuel supplied in foreign ports. We recently added a second heavy duty filter in our fuel line for cruising in foreign areas. It removes water as well as dirt from the fuel. Now when an engine falters, the first thing we look for is foreign material in a sediment bowl.

Before starting up your engine after a long period of disuse, inspect the fuel pump inlet and outlet check valves. Stale gasoline can form gum deposits which cause these valves to stick.

Carburetor problems are generally caused by dirt. If you have installed and regularly maintained fuel strainers and filters where needed, the carburetor shouldn't be the cause of engine trouble. Yet professional mechanics say it's the engine part most-tampered-with unsuccessfully by boat owners. We've learned the hard way that it's best to leave it alone. When a carburetor needs adjusting, it should be done by an expert.

5. *Follow the factory-recommended schedule for lubrication of engine and replacement of filters.* A neglected lubrication schedule leads to excessive wear of engine parts and the likely need for an early engine overhaul or replacement. Recommended lubricants must be supplied to the various engine parts in the proper amounts, at the proper temperature, at specified time intervals. Filter elements should be changed regularly to continue removing impurities which enter the lubrication system. We in-

spect the oil lines for leaks, and check the oil level in the crankcase before every period of operation.

Oil changes, usually recommended every 100 operating hours, should be performed after the engine is warmed up. The oil filter element should be replaced, and the flame arrester removed and cleaned by rinsing in gasoline at every oil change. The various grease and oil cap fittings must be lubricated regularly. It's easy to forget the generator and the distributor, by the way. We carry extra grease and oil on board, and stow these in a cool place in closed containers which prevent oxidation and contamination.

6. *Keep batteries clean and fully charged.* Battery terminals should be kept clean. To prevent corrosion, we lightly coat the outside of the battery posts with petroleum jelly *after* the cables are connected. The water level in the cells should be checked frequently, especially during hot weather, and the cells kept filled to about ⅜ inch above the plates with distilled water or rain water stowed in a nonmetallic container. We use a hydrometer at least once a month to test the specific gravity of the electrolyte. When the reading is below 1.275 we trickle-charge the battery. It's important to keep in mind that banks of batteries are no more dependable than the individual batteries in them.

7. *Avoid damaging your power-generating system.* The system which generates electrical power for your engine can be built around a generator or an alternator. Learn how your particular system works and follow factory instructions on maintenance, including lubrication. If you have an alternator, be certain not to disconnect the battery or hook up a charger to the battery while the engine is running—the diodes in the alternator circuit are likely to be destroyed by the resulting high-voltage surge. Be certain, too, not to connect the battery cables to the wrong battery terminals, thereby reversing polarity. Similarly, watch polarity when you clamp on battery charger clips.

8. *Choose an engine oil suited to your operating conditions.* Engine oils are classified by the Society of Automotive Engineers (SAE) and by the American Petroleum Institute (API). SAE numbers refer to viscosity—the higher the number, the thicker the oil. Numbers followed by the letter "W" are winter oils. Multi-viscosity oils,

How to Read Spark Plugs

You can often diagnose an engine's ills by unscrewing and examining the spark plugs for symptoms of malfunction. The plugs shown here came from marine powerplants with typical afflictions indicated.

Tan to gray—normal

Dry, black—cold fouling

Wet, black—wet fouling

Eroded—overheating

Gap bridged—excess carbon

Core bridged—excess carbon

Throw-off—pre-ignition

such as SAE 20W-40, cover a wide range of temperature conditions. Use the viscosity suggested by your engine's manufacturer for the atmospheric temperature conditions under which you operate.

In addition to the SAE number, oils are given an API service classification. The former three-category system was replaced in January, 1971, by a system with five categories. Three of the new categories correspond to the old ones: The new SA replaces ML (light service), SB replaces MM (moderate service), and SC replaces MS (severe service). Two additional categories go beyond these first three in providing lubricating protection against extremes in operating temperatures. They are SD and, at the top of the list, SE. It's always safe to use a *higher* grade of lubricant than an engine requires, though it will cost more.

9. *Don't neglect the starter.* The starting motor should be checked regularly for tight cable connections and mounting bolts. Inspect the brushes, commutator, and drive assembly. The commutator, incidentally, should *never* be cleaned with emery cloth. Emery dust conducts electricity, and if it accumulates between the commutator segments and shorts across them it could burn out the whole armature of the motor. Regular lubrication of the motor and drive are

essential, along with any other regular maintenance recommended by the manufacturer.

10. *Keep your engine clean and painted, and all connections tight.* A neglected engine, like an unloved boat, is likely to deteriorate rapidly. The engine surface should be kept as free of grease and oil as possible, to help circulating air remove its share of the heat produced by combustion. To fight corrosion, the engine block should be kept painted with a special heat-resistant paint. Blistered paint can be a warning sign of overheating. We've formed the habit of inspecting our engine regularly for loose mechanical connections—nuts, bolts, and fittings—and for oil and fuel leaks.

11. *Consider adding a closed (freshwater) cooling system.* Most marine engines come equipped with an open cooling system that circulates whatever water the boat is floating in directly through the cooling passages in the engine and then discharges it overboard. Although this system is simple and inexpensive, it exposes the engine's interior passages to scale formation, and to marine growth and dirt deposits in the piping.

A closed cooling system, consisting of freshwater and saltwater systems separated by a heat exchanger, is often available as an extra. Since the salt water circulates through the heat exchanger only, the closed cooling system protects the inside of the engine. The engine will operate at slightly higher temperatures, insuring maximum efficiency, lower operating costs, and longer engine life.

12. *Keep the cooling system in good working order.* When you realize that the heat of combustion can reach 5000° F, and that aluminum alloys lose strength above 500° F, the importance of an effective cooling system becomes apparent.

A cooling system is generally trouble-free with a minimum of maintenance. Pumps should be checked for wear and parts replaced as necessary. At least once a season we clean the surface of the zinc plates and plugs which counteract the electrolytic action between dissimilar metals in the cooling system. These need replacing when they have disintegrated about halfway.

We've found that it helps retard the formation of scale and corrosion to use a freshwater treatment in a closed system, and to keep the temperature of the discharged seawater below 130° F. Jackets and heat exchangers should be cleaned in accordance with factory instructions. A closed cooling system, like a car's radiator, should be protected with anti-freeze when the boat is operated in cold climates. During winter lay-up, all water jackets must be drained to prevent damage from freezing. Neoprene impellers should be removed from water pumps or they may stick to the pump casing.

13. *Carry tools that fit your engine.* It's better to select a few tools of top quality than to buy a large assortment of inferior make. Any particular engine will have only a few sizes of nuts, bolts, and fittings. There's no need to carry tools that don't fit anything on board.

Be sure, however, that your selected minimum includes a tool to reach and fit every nut, bolt, and screw that might need turning. We carry several special tools, each of which handles a single fitting. Having exactly the right tool aboard has at times allowed us to make an otherwise impossible adjustment. Special tools of this type are usually listed on the engine's parts list or in the repair manual. We ordered ours directly from the factory.

14. *Carry spare parts on board.* A spare parts inventory, you hope, will work in the same way that carrying an umbrella prevents rain. And if a minor problem does occur while you are underway, you'll be equipped to fix it before it develops into something more serious.

Several engine manufacturers have spare parts kits which can be purchased from the factory. These are usually good buys, but you can assemble your own if a factory kit isn't available. Your on-board parts kit might include a set of points, condenser, distributor rotor and cap, water pump seal and impeller, generator drive belt, fuel pump diaphragm kit, ignition coil, assorted gaskets, and extra spark plugs. These should be stowed in a readily accessible waterproof box or ditty bag.

15. *Be alert for warning signals.* Keep all your senses alert for any symptom which might indicate that all is not well. One of the first warning signals is usually a change in the engine's sound. A missing cylinder may be quickly spotted, as may a high-pitched fuel knock or a lower-pitched bearing knock.

Watch the instrument panel for indications of a sudden reduction in rpm, an increase in engine temperature, loss of oil pressure, or the battery being charged or discharged when it shouldn't be. Look for leaking fuel lines, contamination in the fuel filter bowl(s), and shorted or broken wires. Check the appearance of exhaust smoke for signs of poor combustion. Black or dark gray smoke means that timing is off or not enough air is getting mixed with the fuel, for example.

Use your sense of smell to detect an overheated engine or a slipping clutch. You can feel abnormal vibration, such as that associated with a bent propeller shaft or blade. Even when you cannot correct the problem yourself, you may be able to keep minor conditions from becoming serious just by knowing that a problem exists, and operating accordingly while you seek immediate help.

An engine treated with timely care and understanding, chances are, won't fail just as you are entering a breaking inlet, or trying to claw off a lee shore.

THE INS AND OUTS OF I/O MAINTENANCE

By Mort Schultz

july & august

There's a right way and a wrong way to keep your inboard/outboard operating smoothly for the entire boating season. The wrong way is to do necessary services here and there, off-and-on in a helter-skelter manner. Disorganization leads to missing some important points.

The right way is to set aside an hour or two every month or so throughout the boating season to the upkeep of your sterndrive and inboard, then follow a sensible and organized procedure.

Here is the right way to do the job, point-by-point:

1. Start the engine, putting fuel and cooling system under pressure, and examine fuel lines and cooling system hoses for leaks. Tighten up all clamps. If a leak persists, replace the hose and clamp.

2. Squeeze cooling system hoses. If they feel mushy or show cracks—even hairline cracks—replace them now before they split wide apart while you're on the water. If you're undecided whether a hose is faulty or not, shut off the engine, disconnect the hose and run your fingers around the inside. If you get flakes of rubber, the hose is shot. Get rid of it.

3. Warm the engine to operating temperature and drain engine oil. If you can get to the drain plug in the bottom of the crankcase, okay—that's the easy way. If you can't, you will have to pump oil out through the dipstick tube with an oil sump pump.

4. Add fresh oil of the kind designated by your engine's manufacturer. He probably recommends a high-quality 10W-30 or 10W-40 grade designated for service SE.

Before adding oil, though, replace the oil filter. There's no sense mixing fresh oil with the quart of dirty oil left in a used filter.

5. Remove the carburetor flame arrestor(s) and wash in mineral spirits. Let dry completely before reinstalling. If gaskets have been botched up, replace them with new ones.

Don't overtighten a flame arrestor, which will cause the element to compress and act as a choke to the carburetor, leading to upsetting of the fuel:air ratio. Your engine will be forced to run on an over-rich mixture.

6. Shut off the fuel line valve to prevent gas from leaking, then clean or replace the fuel filter. Some engines have a sediment bowl filter. The bowl must be unscrewed, the filter removed and all parts washed in kerosene. If your engine has this setup, keep gas from spilling out when you drop the bowl by slipping a plastic bag over the bowl. Remove the bowl and bag together.

The other kind of fuel filter in common use is a paper element that's installed inline between fuel pump and carburetor. The element is contained inside a chamber. This filter can't be serviced. It has to be replaced with a new one.

After servicing or replacing a fuel filter, start and idle the engine for a few minutes, looking for gas leaks around filter connections. Tighten up on connections if a leak is apparent.

7. If your engine has a positive crankcase ventilation (PCV) system, like the one your car possesses, it should be tested. A clogged system allows blowby to remain in the crankcase where it mixes with oil to form sludge and shoddy engine operation may result.

Pull the PCV valve from the engine's valve cover. You can find the PCV valve by tracing the hose coming off the carburetor to the spot in the cover where the valve sits. Start the engine and hold your thumb tightly over the valve's end. You should feel a strong pull. If you don't, turn off the engine and pull the valve from the hose. Shake it. If it doesn't click, the valve is shot. Replace it.

There's a chance, too, that a blockage in the hose or carburetor passage is fouling up the PCV system. Clear out the carburetor passage or nipple to which the PCV hose connects by carefully twirling a ¼-inch drill bit inside it. If the hose is clogged, run a swab through it using a suitable size rod. If the hose is mushy or split, replace it.

8. If you have an older engine that has a DC generator and starter motor that require lubrication, put three or four drops of SAE 10W engine oil into the oil cups provided in each of these parts.

9. Take off the distributor cap and rotor. Put a drop or two of SAE 10W oil on the felt wick on top of breaker cam, but be careful not to get oil on breaker points. If there is no oil wick, put a drop of distributor cam lubricant equal to the size of a match's head on one lobe of the distributor cam.

10. Examine distributor breaker points. If they are badly burned or pitted, replace points and condensor. This, of course, assumes that your engine isn't equipped with electronic ignition.

11. Examine the rotor and distributor cap. Look for cracked or broken segments and corroded terminals. Any carbon track along the distributor cap indicates a hairline crack which might not be visible. Replace a rotor or distributor cap showing any signs of damage, no matter how insignificant.

12. Reinstall distributor parts. If the distributor has an oil cup, apply five drops of SAE 10W oil to it.

13. Inspect spark plug cables and boots, flexing cables back and forth along their length. Replace all cables and boots if any is cracked or has brittle insulation.

14. Remove spark plugs and examine their tips. If plugs are light tan or gray in color with insignificant electrode wear, they can be kept in service. Make sure, however, that they are gapped to specification provided in your owner's manual.

If spark plugs are badly fouled, show excessive electrode wear or have cracked or broken insulators, replace the set.

15. Examine drive belts for splits, fraying and tension. Replace a damaged belt. Belt tension should be no more than ½ of an inch when you press the belt midway between pulleys. Tighten a loose belt by loosening the bracket of the part the belt is servicing (usually the alternator), pulling back against the belt and tightening the bracket.

To service the outdrive, the unit has to come out of the water. But before doing this, run it to warm it up and get dirt suspended in the oil. You will need the lubrication chart for your particular unit. This should be contained in the owner's manual. Here's what to do:

16. Drain oil. Some outdrives have a single oil drain plug, but others have as many as three—one in the lower section, one in the intermediate area, and one on the upper case.

17. Replenish with fresh oil. Most outdrives use an SAE 90 hypoid gear oil, but not all. Other manufacturers require SAE 10W-30 or SAE 10W-40 engine oil. The lubrication chart should spell this out.

18. Check the sacrificial anodes attached to the outdrive to protect the unit from electrolytic action in salt water. If anodes are corroded to 50 percent or less of their original size, replace them.

19. Examine the propeller. If it has minor nicks and burrs, take it off and file it until it's smooth, but be careful. Don't remove any more metal than is necessary. If the propeller is cracked or bent, replace it.

20. Before reinstalling the prop, lubricate the propeller shaft with an antiseize compound or waterproof grease.

21. Give the engine outdrive a close inspection for chipped paint and corrosion. Sand or wire brush a damaged area to bare metal and repaint with an anti-fouling paint that contains no copper or mercury. You can usually find a matching color in an aerosol spray can at your marine parts supplier.

HOW TO TROUBLESHOOT YOUR OUTBOARD'S LOWER UNIT

By Mort Schultz

july & august

Like an I.R.S. audit or a trip to the dentist, the thought of an outboard motor not shifting into gear properly can send shivers up a boatman's spine. And with good reason—having a lower unit (gear case) disassembled and overhauled is both bothersome and expensive. Specific costs vary with make and model, but a ballpark figure would be $75 to $100.

Unfortunately, lower unit failure is not as remote as some novice outboard owners might think. In fact, a recent survey of five outboard repair shops revealed that lower unit repairs ranked second in frequency behind ignition problems. All of the mechanics that were consulted, however, agreed that most failures resulted from owner neglect and abuse.

Obviously, it is much more practical to prevent a breakdown than to make repairs. You may be able to use an outboard for its entire lifetime without having trouble just by following two basic procedures:

• *Lubricate the lower unit as often as the manufacturer of your equipment specifies in the lu-*brication instructions printed in your owner's manual, using only the recommended lubricant. Most are SAE 90, but gear lubes can vary, even between one manufacturer's models. The best bet is to stick to the manual's recommendations, since failure to use the proper lube can damage a gear case faster than all the underwater obstacles it bumps against.

Chrysler and OMC (Johnson and Evinrude) recommend that their gear cases be drained and refilled every 100 hours of operation or once each season—whichever comes first. Mercury advises replenishing the lubricant in the lower unit every 30 days. Between lubes, check lubricant levels frequently and add lubricant if necessary.

On most outboards, you drain the gear case by putting the motor in its vertical position, then removing both the oil drain/fill (lower) and oil level (upper) plugs, which allows the lubricant to drain completely.

The old lubricant should be drained in a sealable container such as an old Clorox bottle, then labeled and put out with the trash or taken to a gas station for disposal.

To refill the gear case, insert new lubricant with a grease gun into the drain/fill hole, gradually forcing any air trapped in the gear case through the oil level hole until lubricant itself reaches the upper hole. Reinstall the upper plug before you remove the grease gun from the drain/fill hole—once the upper plug is in place, you can withdraw the gun and replace the lower plug without losing lubricant.

Finally, check the old lubricant for signs of water or metal particles. If the lubricant appears milky or globules of water are evident, the gear case seals must be replaced. Metal particles are a symptom of gear case problems—worn gears or bearings—indicating that an overhaul may be needed.

• To prevent damage to your gears, shift correctly. This means shifting at a speed recommended by the manufacturer in your owner's manual. This speed is about 600 revolutions per minute, give or take 100 rpm.

And shift smoothly whether you have a remote shifting mechanism or you sit in the stern and shift gears manually by means of the motor's twist grip. Do not ease the motor into gear. Use a quick motion on the control, snapping gears into engagement.

Suppose, though, that despite your efforts, a gear case problem develops. What has to be done?

First of all, don't automatically conclude that the malfunction is in the lower unit if you have a remote control shifting device. Although the remote-control system is practically trouble-free, problems can arise. Troubleshooting the system to pinpoint the offending area is not particularly difficult. You know something is wrong, of course, when (1) you engage gears and nothing happens or (2) movement is a crawl when you open the throttle.

Failure to shift can signify trouble with either the remote control unit itself or the motor's lower unit. To find out where the problem lies, disconnect the remote control cable at the motor and try to shift the engine manually.

If the engine won't shift into gear manually, then your trouble is inside the lower unit (more on that later). If it does shift manually, the trouble is with the remote control system.

Suppose that gears engage, but the engine fails to respond when you try to accelerate. You can assume that the trouble most likely lies with the throttle control of the remote box. To make a positive diagnosis, disconnect the throttle control cable at the engine and operate the throttle by hand. If the engine responds, the remote control needs repair. If the engine does not respond, there is a malfunction with the throttle control on the engine or with the throttle linkage.

Most often a remote-control failure can be traced to trouble with the cables and not with the box itself. There are all kinds of remote control setups, but let's discuss the simplest one—a single cable control which operates gear shifting and throttle speed only.

Although one cable usually leads from the remote-control box to the engine, be aware that it is actually two cables, one inside the outer. cable. One controls shifting, and the other operates the throttle.

Cables can freeze or the inner cable may bend or kink. A bad cable must be replaced. Never try to repair one—it's a waste of time. First, though, you should establish if the cable is causing the problem.

Disconnect the cable from the engine and lay it where you can watch it as you activate the control lever at the remote box through its entire shifting and acceleration range. If cables are working properly, you'll be able to see them move throughout the entire range of lever operation. You can also see if the cables are frozen or hampered in some other way. If a cable is bad, it has to be disconnected from inside the control box, which means you have to unbolt the box from its pad and open it up. Before you remove the cable, see if it has come loose from the lock setscrew that attaches it to the rack gear or cam. If it has, you have located the trouble and saved yourself the price of a new cable. Simply re-tighten the cable by tightening the lock setscrew.

If you've diagnosed the ailment as a lower unit malfunction (the motor won't shift into forward or reverse or neutral when operated manually), the lower unit must be disassembled and overhauled. However, an element enters here that may make disassembly impossible. That element is salt.

If a motor is operated primarily in fresh water, you should have no trouble taking the lower unit apart. But if a motor is operated mostly in salt water, disassembly may prove difficult. In the worst cases, the lower unit may have to be removed with a hacksaw and be replaced completely—costing $200 to $500, plus labor.

Naturally, if the unit will come apart, overhaul costs are much less. The professional you hire for the job should be the best you can find and should follow the sound procedures listed below. We cite these procedures because it would be a good idea where possible to look over the mechanic's shoulder as he does the job to make sure they are observed:

1. The work area should be clean. As they are removed, gears should be handled with dirt-free hands and laid aside on a workbench covered with a clean cloth or paper. If dirt gets on gears, it will cause severe damage when the unit is reassembled and used.

2. Old seals, O-rings and gaskets should be discarded. New seals, O-rings and gaskets for lower units are usually issued by manufacturers in kit form. Price is a couple of dollars.

3. All metal parts should be cleaned in a solvent, such as kerosene, and dried with an air hose. If compressed air is not available, parts can be air dried.

4. All parts should be inspected very closely for nicks, pits, grooves, discoloration—any symptoms of damage or excessive wear. Parts to check include the driveshaft, water pump impeller, water pump housing, drive gears, pinion gear, bearings, bushings and washers. Replace any part that is damaged. If there is doubt whether a part is damaged or not, replace it anyway. Don't take a chance that may lead to another overhaul.

5. If the gear case or motor leg extension shows damage on the inside (which could ruin adjacent parts coming into contact), the case should be resurfaced. This job will have to be done by a professional who has the necessary equipment, including surface plate, surface gauge and scriber. If the case is bent, get a new one.

6. In reassembling the skeg (lower gear housing) and upper gear housing, and upper gear housing and motor leg extension, the mating surfaces between them must be sealed with marine sealer. The screws holding these components must be dipped in marine sealer also.

If you watch your mechanic closely enough, you should gather sufficient knowledge to do the job yourself next time.

WILL SHE START? ...and what to do if she won't

By Mort Schultz

july & august

Not being able to start an engine at the dock is no special panic. You can always call in a professional to help you. But having your engine fail on the water is something else again—then you get to be the pro. It doesn't matter whether your boat's under inboard or outboard power, the sinking feeling you have when your motor doesn't respond is the same in both cases. To help forestall such an unwelcome possibility, here are on-the-water tips for troubleshooting your engine.

Outboards

To Start With

1. If your outboard motor is equipped with electric starting and the battery goes dead, use the normal rope starter to get going again.

2. Think a minute. Was the motor tilted out of the water? Was the fuel tank sitting in the sun? A buildup of pressure could have forced the needle valve in the carburetor to open, allowing fuel to flood the engine. You can prevent flooding by disconnecting the fuel line when the motor is not running.

Remove the sparkplugs and dry the tips with a clean rag. Turn off the fuel shutoff valve and crank the eingine to force excess fuel from the combustion chambers. Reinstall the plugs snugly by hand and give each a half turn with a plug wrench.

3. If the motor still doesn't start, disconnect the fuel-tank line where it connects to the engine and squeeze the primer bulb. If fuel does not squirt from the line (hold it overboard) a malfunction exists in the line or fuel tank.

Inspect the line for damage. Wrap friction tape tight around any breaks. Check the edges of the line connector to see if the "O" ring has chipped. If it has, the fuel system will draw in air, which makes the mixture lean and prevents starting. Cut the damaged connector from the line. Disconnect the line extension at the intake side of the fuel pump and hook the connectorless line directly to the pump.

The filter inside the fuel tank may require service if fuel isn't getting through the line. Remove the tank's connector-pipe assembly and clean the filter at the bottom of the pipe.

Things to Remember

Speaking of filters, a primary reason for outboard motors suddenly refusing to start is a clogged filter. Some outboards have the filter inside the fuel pump and it's necessary to remove the pump housing cover to get to it. Other motors have the filter at the carburetor. Learn where yours is by consulting the owner's manual.

Sparkplugs may fail, although there's usually some warning. As plugs wear the engine becomes more and more difficult to start. If you haven't heeded the warning, at least carry a spare set in your tool box that are gapped to manufacturer's specifications as spelled out in the owner's manual.

Checklist

- *Is the fuel tank sitting on the line? The tank's weight can squeeze the line closed.*
- *Be sure that fuel pump housing bolts are tight—air drawn in around the cover can make the fuel mixture lean.*
- *Make sure that high-tension wires are tight and sparkplug terminals firmly attached.*

• Out of fuel? Hope you brought along a spare can.

• Perhaps wires and connections are wet. Spray them with water displacing compound, such as CRO 6/66 or LPS2.

• Is the choke plate free? If not, clean it.

OUTBOARD TROUBLESHOOTING SUMMARY

Problem	Repair	Equipment Required
Wet wires and connections	dry	water-displacing compound
Stuck choke	free	
Flooded engine	remove spark-plugs and crank engine	sparkplug wrench
Bad sparkplugs	replace	new sparkplugs
Collapsed fuel line	remove fuel tank from top of line	
Ruptured fuel line	repair	friction tape
Damaged connector "O" ring	cut away connector; hook line directly to fuel pump	sharp knife
Clogged fuel filter	clean	
Loose fuel pump housing bolts	tighten	
Clogged gas tank filter	clean	
Loose ignition cables	tighten	screwdriver

Inboards

To Start With

1. Always carry a booster battery and jumper cables in case you have to jump a dead primary battery.

2. If the starter doesn't turn or turns too slowly the problem may be loose or corroded terminals. Before you go poking around air out the engine compartment for a few minutes to dispel fumes that might ignite in case you accidentally short the battery and cause sparks.

Disconnect the terminals and clean them and the battery posts with a piece of sandpaper or a battery cleaning tool that you can buy in an auto parts store for a couple of bucks.

Hook up the terminals tight and try the engine. If it still doesn't start, the battery probably is dead. If you have a dual setup with a crossover switch, simply switch to the other battery. Otherwise you'll need your booster battery to get back to shore.

Things to Remember

You don't need to buy a new battery to serve as a booster; get one from a junkyard—it's a lot less expensive—and be sure to keep it charged. Buy jumper cables from an auto parts store.

Be careful how you hook up the booster. Reversing polarity, even momentarily, will cause the alternator to burn out. Battery jumper cables are color coded. The red cable is positive. The other, which may be yellow, black, green or any color except red, is negative. Connect the negative post of the booster to the negative post of the boat's battery with the negative cable. Connect the positive posts together with the positive cable. Crank the engine. It will start if the problem is a dead battery.

If the battery is not dead reach beneath the flywheel and feel to see if the pinion is free. If it's jammed, loosen the bolts holding the starter and back it away from the flywheel until the pinion snaps back. Retighten the starter bolts securely.

If the ignition operates normally but the engine doesn't start check for an empty fuel tank, flooded engine or wet ignition system. A flooded engine is easily put right. Open the throttle full, close the choke, switch on the ignition and crank the engine about a half dozen times to draw air through the carburetor and mix with the trapped puddle of rich fuel. If the engine starts, shove the throttle closed immediately. If it fails, let it stand for a minute or so and try again. If it still won't start, flooding is not the trouble. Keep a can of water-displacing compound around to treat wet ignition parts. Spray the compound on all wires and connections, plugs, the distributor cap and ignition coil.

Checklist

• Give sparkplug cable terminals a firm push at the plugs and at the distributor cap. Also give the coil cable a push to make sure you have no loose connections that could prevent starting.

• Vapor lock occurs when engine heat makes a vapor pocket in the fuel line. Pour cold water over the fuel pump, fuel line and carburetor bowl, taking care not to get water in the carburetor.

• Fouled points may be preventing spark. Open

the distributor and slip a point file between points. File lightly—only one pass is needed. Remove file, open points carefully and blow the debris away.

- *Does the choke move free? If not, clean it.*
- *Is your fuel strainer clogged? If yes, clean it, too.*

INBOARD TROUBLESHOOTING SUMMARY

Problem	Repair	Equipment Required
Corroded battery terminals	clean	battery cleaning tool or sand-paper
Dead battery	boost	booster battery; jumper cables
Jammed starter pinion	free	
Flooded engine	crank engine with throttle full open	
Wet ignition	dry	water-displacing compound
Loose wires	tighten	
Stuck choke	free	
Vapor lock	pour cold water over fuel system parts	
Clogged fuel filter	clean	
Dirty distributor points	clean	ignition-point file

THREE WAYS TO PROTECT YOUR BOAT AGAINST LIGHTNING

By Manfred W. Meisels

july & august

Because lightning tends to strike at the highest point in a given area, every boat on open water, be it sail, cabin cruiser or outboard, is a potential target. If your boat isn't already equipped with a proper grounding system, here are three designs that will protect any craft against damage.

None of these will *prevent* one's boat from being struck by lightning, for lightning strikes where it pleases. However, a well-designed lightning rod system will divert the lightning along a path that is harmless to the boat and its crew. This is done by providing an easy electrical path for the lightning—instead of a more difficult path through the structure of the boat.

Sailboats, because of their height above the water, are most vulnerable to lightning, but at the same time, easiest to protect. Their wire rigging forms a natural lightning rod, which need only be well grounded to the water. Figure 1 shows a standby protection system for sailboats that can be lowered into the water at the approach of a storm or left immersed when the boat is moored.

It is particularly suitable for day sailers and other small boats without outside ballast.

Clamp securely one end of a bare, 8-gauge, stranded copper wire to an upper shroud or stay. Use a heavy wire clamp to assure firm, permanent contact to the rigging. Fasten the wire above the turnbuckle, as the heat generated by the immense electrical current of a lightning stroke could damage the turnbuckle. The clamping point should be high enough above toe rails or bulwarks to allow a reasonably straight path for the wire into the water.

The other end of the wire should be tightly fastened to a copper plate by a heavy brass nut, bolt and washer. Cut the plate to an area of one square foot in any size or shape and let the wire allow an immersion depth of two feet.

For automatic protection, the grounding plate can be epoxied to the bottom of the hull and the grounding wire connected to it externally or by a heavy bronze through-bolt.

If the boat has outside ballast, fasten the grounding wire under a keel bolt or drive a separate attachment bolt into the top of the keel. The top of a metal centerboard is also a good grounding point. Don't ground through the centerboard pin or lifting cable.

In metal-masted boats, the grounding wire can be led from the bottom of the mast instead of from the rigging. Again, fasten the wire securely to the mast with a heavy bolt. For easy attachment, the wire can be terminated with a press-on connector, but soldered connectors must be avoided.

Engines and other large metal masses (such as anchor winches, davits, etc.) should be at least six feet from the grounding wire. If this cannot be done, such objects should be bonded to the ground plate or wire with at least 8-gauge wire securely fastened for good electrical conductivity. Metal-hulled boats are naturally grounded, so the grounding wire can be led to any convenient part of the hull.

On power boats, the absence of rigging calls for a separate rod of some kind to achieve protection. The main problem here is to provide sufficient height to enclose the boat in the recommended 60-degree cone of protection. All parts of the boat must lie within this cone.

If the rod is midway between bow and stern, it should be at least 10 feet high for every 17 feet of boat length. For every foot of distance from the

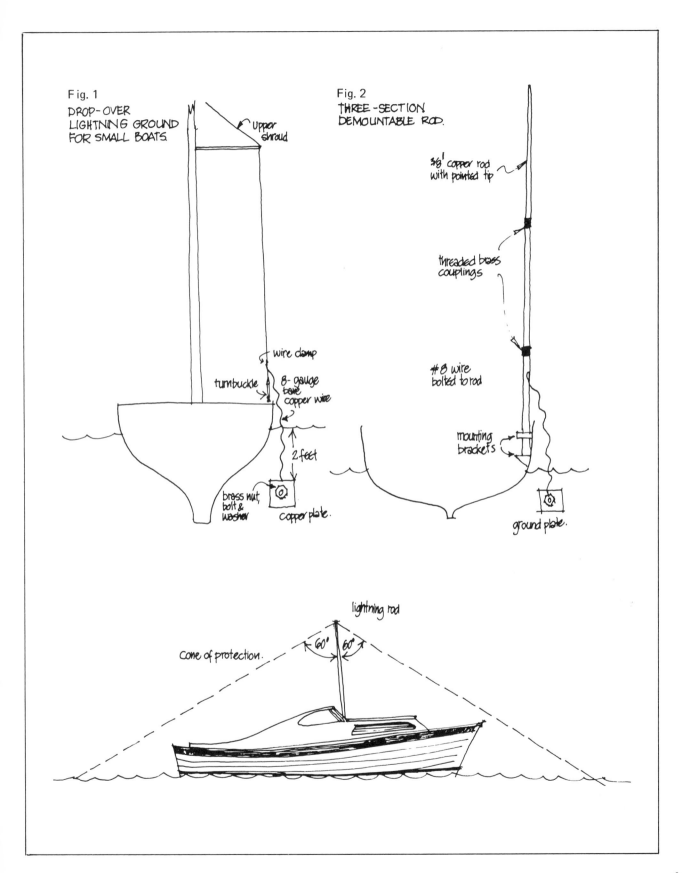

Fig. 1
DROP-OVER LIGHTNING GROUND FOR SMALL BOATS

upper shroud

wire clamp

turnbuckle

8-gauge bare copper wire

2 feet

brass nut, bolt & washer

copper plate.

Fig. 2
THREE-SECTION DEMOUNTABLE ROD.

3/8" copper rod with pointed tip

threaded brass couplings

#8 wire bolted to rod

mounting brackets

ground plate.

lightning rod

60° 60°

cone of protection.

midway point to the position of the rod, add another six inches of height.

Fashion the rod of at least ⅜-inch copper stock with a pointed tip. The rod itself need only be long enough to achieve the desired height when conveniently mounted. The remainder of the path to the grounding plate is covered by the copper wire as previously described. Either a permanent or dropover ground plate can be used.

Small, open power boats are best protected by a demountable rod, again high enough to form a 60-degree cone. Figure 2 shows an easily deployable rod, which can be made in one or more sections as required. A sectioned rod should be fastened by threaded brass couplings. Fasten the coupling permanently to one section and allow for at least five threads for attachment. Machine the threads loosely enough to allow assembly of the rod without a wrench. In computing the height of the rod for very small boats, the height should be above that of any person who might be standing in the boat during a storm.

The lower part of the rod is equipped with a permanently secured grounding wire and a drop-over grounding plate. At the approach of a thunderstorm, mount the rod in brackets provided, immerse the ground plate and you're protected.

Radio antennas can also be used as lightning rods if properly grounded and equipped with lightning arrestors, but the fiberglass whips in common use are not conductive enough for good protection. You'll end up with a splintered antenna and very poor lightning insurance.

What to do
without turning
on the engine

SEPTEMBER

This could be the best boating month in the year. After Labor Day, everyone with a commercial waterfront facility drains his swimming pool, closes his snack bar, and waits for winter. A lot of boating people take their cue from this peculiar ritual, and remain at their moorings. This means fewer craft on the water, and more leeway for you. If you are a fisherman, bass and bluefish should be running, as well as Spanish mackerel and—if you are a bottom fisherman—flounder.

The weather can be tricky—September is the traditional beginning of the hurricane season. But you are surely a listener to the FM weather station in your area, operated by the U.S. Weather Bureau, and will be warned of any unusual hazards. (Whatever your electronic accessories may consist of, they should include an am/fm receiver with the U.S. weather station.)

This is the best time to buy a boat. (Sid Stapleton tells you how starting on page 153.) And the last chance to sell one. If you are buying a used boat, the owner may be happy to shave the price to avoid the expense of lay-up, covering, and winter storage. The broker, if there is one, is often happy to throw in storage and lay-up just to make the sale. And you still have a month or two of boating ahead. The weather may not be predictable enough for extended cruises, but day cruising is a lot of fun. And if you are taking up boating for the first time, just spending weekends pottering around in port can be a delight.

And speaking of pottering, if you are considering buying a power boat, do not be deterred by the cost of fuel. Eighty-five percent of the fun of powerboating is without fuel. Maybe even 86 percent. Take a look around your local club, marina, or yard. Are most of the members' boats in their home port? Yes, they are. Do their owners look happy? Yes, they do.

For a powerboatman, the boat is itself a destination. He knows that all he has to do to get underway is to turn on the ignition (after sniffing the bilges, of course). He doesn't have to prove his machismo by going anywhere. He already is somewhere—on his boat—which includes him in an instant fellowship as old as Noah. He can wear faded khakis and a Block Island cap, and be more detached from everyday cares on a 17-foot runabout than on a 20-acre country estate.

What is there to do on a boat without turning on the engine? Lots. The natural inclination of a boat is to recycle itself into the great scheme of Mother Nature. A boat wants to crack, craze, corrode, tarnish, oxidize, electrolyze, polarize, dissolve, rust, disintegrate, and merge with the life cycle. The natural inclination of a boatman with a bank loan on his craft is to resist this ecological thrust. A minimum of 40 percent of his time afloat is spent in maintenance or recovering from it. He is constantly painting, caulking, waxing, patching, and spraying things with silicone to dry up moisture or with disinfectant to arrest mildew. He is dousing wood with curinol to prevent rot, repairing, lubricating, rebuilding, and looking for spare parts.

Real boatmen do not regard working on their boats as an irksome chore. It is a privilege. A man who evades fixing a dripping faucet in the kitchen sink will spend the entire month of August repairing a leaky exhaust line. I know one happy soul who devoted his entire summer vacation to adjusting his radar and then used it only to navigate as far as the port of his winter storage. Every boating book must include the observation of the Water Rat in Kenneth Grahame's classic: "There is nothing—absolutely nothing—half so much worth doing as simply messing around in boats . . . or with boats . . . in or out of 'em. It doesn't matter."

A LOT ABOUT ROT

By Gurney Williams

Sooner or later, every boat owner finds himself face-to-face with rotting wood in his craft—even metal and fiberglass boats are not immune to it, for they contain seats, reinforcements and other wooden parts. The wood in your boat can literally be eaten alive.

Wood is the natural food for certain species of fungi which send their roots into wood to feed on the cellulose which, along with lignin, is the basic building material for wood cells. As cellulose is withdrawn from the wood, it becomes soft and punky and eventually crumbles. It is then an easy matter for raindrops, ice and wind to complete the task.

Fungus spores are carried by the wind and lodge on the rough surface of any piece of wood. There they remain until conditions are favorable for germinating. Just as with any other kind of plant seed, temperature must be mild—there is little fungus activity when the average daily air temperature is below about 50° F., and many species require the temperature to average around 70°. Wood that is outdoors or in cold buildings just does not rot. If fungus is already growing in a piece of wood and is actively rotting it, it will become dormant when the weather becomes cold, and will reactivate upon the return of warm weather.

Spores and fungus plants also require moisture. Most fungus species require the wood to have a moisture content of 20 percent or more. Properly seasoned wood exposed to the atmosphere typically has a moisture content between 8 percent and 12 percent, and this is why unpainted wooden buildings, tool handles and innumerable other wooden items do not rot. At the same time, fungus requires oxygen. Because there is insufficient oxygen in thoroughly waterlogged wood, it simply will not rot. Wooden boats moored in the water do not rot from the outside of the planking inward. Rot begins inside them in places that are merely damp, and the last place it shows up is in the bottom planking after having progressed outward. Tree stumps stand in swamps for years because they are waterlogged, where logs resting on the forest floor rot quickly because they are merely damp.

Wood that is wet for a few days during a rainstorm does not rot, because it dries out when fine weather returns. Fungus spores must be kept damp for an appreciable time before they will start to grow. You find early traces of rot in a wooden boat not in the bottom planking but in crevices and corners of the internal framing, the decking and the cabin structure. Rain water and water from condensation gather in such spots, and the wood is kept damp but not soaked.

Most people use the term "dry rot," but there is no such thing because fungus must have moisture like any other plant. It's the combination of fungus spores, dampness, mild temperatures and the presence of oxygen that leads to wood rot.

The first sign of rot is a collection of scattered blackish spots on the wood. This might be some harmless mildew, so a rather rough-and-ready general rule is that if the suspicious spots are showing up on non-wooden as well as wood surfaces, it's likely mildew. But if the spots seem to be actually in the wood and *under* the paint or varnish (much easier to see them early-on when the wood is varnished!), it's a warning to suspect that rot is breeding. At this stage no harm has been done and you just have to dry out the area and keep it dry.

Once a fungus plant has gotten itself established and has started to withdraw a significant amount of cellulose, the average workman encounters his first tangible evidence that the wood is going bad. It has become "brash"; it still looks sound but it has become weak and brittle. When struck or bent, instead of breaking with a lot of sharp splinters it breaks more or less straight across, with a slightly zig-zag but notably splinter-free fracture line. Brash wood is dangerous because although it looks sound when inspected visually, it can break easily under normal operating stress in a boat. Should you be concerned about possible brashness in a piece of wood, take a large needle or a very small, sharply pointed knife and insert the point of the tool diagonally into the surface of the wood. Then lift up to pull out a splinter. If it is long and sharp, the wood is probably sound. But if the splinter is short and blunt-ended, the wood is most likely brash.

Experienced builders of wooden boats know that the rot resistance of various species of wood varies widely. One is tempted to jump to the conclusion that soft woods are more susceptible to rot and hard woods more durable. It doesn't work

this way in practice. Cedar is a soft wood but is very durable. Birch is a hard wood but it rots so readily that good boatbuilders have no use for it whatsoever. Rot resistance is based not on hardness but largely on a wood's chemical characteristics. Those that are high in natural oils and aromatics apparently repel fungus, just as the odor of cedar repels moths.

Observant seamen of long ago noticed that wood doused with salt water did not rot. From this grew the practice of "salting" large ships with piles of rock salt which gradually dissolved and seeped down into rot-prone spaces, usefully prolonging ship life.

Old ships were usually assembled with "trunnels" or "tree nails," dowels of wood driven into bored holes and locked with wedges much like a handle in a hammer. In today's small and medium-sized wooden boats, metal screws and nails are used because trunnels would have to be tiny, weak and extremely fussy to install. If a modern craft is salted, metal fastenings and also the engine, pumps and other metal parts suffer so rapidly and seriously that salting just doesn't make sense any more.

There are, however scientifically compounded wood preservatives available. Creosote is widely used today for railroad ties, utility poles, fence posts and other outdoor items made of wood, but it is miserable stuff to have on the wood in a boat. Its smell lingers indefinitely, and it rejects any paint one might try to put onto some wood to seal in the smell and stain. Modern wood preservatives are generally rather simple products—the liquid is a petroleum-base vehicle compounded to soak into wood quickly and thoroughly and then evaporate fairly rapidly, leaving little odor. Into this vehicle is mixed some kind of soluble chemical such as copper naphthenate, pentachlorophenol or any of several other substances with names generally reminiscent of these two. All are fungicides, which means they make the wood very unpalatable to fungus. When the vehicle has evaporated, the wood is impregnated with fungicide.

How well a wood preservative works depends on circumstances. A light brushing-on of the preservative will not encourage thorough penetration. The minimum recommended treatment is repeated and copious brushing-on of the product. Better results are had from giving each part of a boat several hours of soaking in a tank full of preservative, before being put in place in a boat's structure.

The combination of using rot-resistant woods, designing all joints to shed water, avoiding non-ventilated spaces inside a boat, plus treatment with preservative can make a wooden boat quite resistant to rot. Depending on how much the treated wood is exposed to immersion, preservative chemicals can eventually leach out and leave the wood more exposed to rot. There is no way to tell when preservative is gone from treated wood. A good treating should protect wood for several years at least, and sometimes for many years. Most modern wood preservatives can be painted over after a reasonable amount of drying time. Effect on glue adhesion varies somewhat with the kind of wood and preservative, drying time and kind of glue.

There are several epoxy-based "restorers" for rotten wood. These products come in small containers and when the ingredients are mixed, they will soak into dry, rotten wood like oil into a lantern wick. They harden in place and add rigidity to the rotten wood. Use of such products is an excellent way of fixing the small rotten spots often found in a boat. Let the wood dry thoroughly and then impregnate with the epoxy product. This process saves the often complicated and costly task of removing and replacing an important piece of wood. Such products are somewhat expensive, though, and when larger pieces of rotten wood are found, one has to decide intelligently whether it is cheaper to use a lot of epoxy or to remove and replace the bad wood.

An ounce of prevention is worth a pound of cure any time. On the topsides of a wooden boat, periodically inspects joints and seams and when you find a place where rain water or fresh water spray could get in and take a long time to dry out, wait until the wood is thoroughly dry, squirt in preservative, then go to work with sealers and compounds to seal up the gaps and keep water out.

Down inside, watch for places where condensation regularly forms puddles of water and open things up so condensation no longer forms, or cut drainage notches so it will flow away quickly. When the boat is in the water the bottom planking and bilge framing will normally be too damp to rot. But during storage open up all floorboards, lockers and cover plates so there is ample ventilation. When a boat is in service, people open and close windows and hatches constantly so there is good air circulation; in storage, a tightly-sealed boat is very susceptible to developing a hothouse atmosphere that leads to many cases of rot.

Never seal a boat up tightly in a plastic winter cover. Always leave ample ventilation openings at the ends of the cover. Although fungus is inactive in cold weather, a sweating boat gets its wood full of moisture and when mild weather arrives, it is a sitting duck for rot. If you have a fiberglass boat, explore the bilge area looking for places where water could get through cracks, opened seams and thin spots in the enclosing fiberglass, and beef up such places with more fiberglass. If necessary, drill small exploratory holes through fiberglass into encapsulated wood and feel the drill chips for suspiciously damp or even rotted wood. Should such bad omens be found, it is probably best to seek out a local fiberglass-boat expert and have him appraise the situation. Just what to do will require a knowledgeable evaluation of the location and extent of the problem, difficulty of getting at and/or thoroughly drying out the affected wood, and treating or replacing it.

HERE'S HOW TO PUT AN END TO MILDEW

By Gail Hoffman

september

Mildew is a form of fungus, a mold which attaches itself to and lives on suitable surfaces. Though always present in the air in the form of spores, to thrive mildew needs a damp, warm, poorly-aired and poorly-lit home. Your boat, of course, is a potential mildew paradise, but there are things you can do to make it less hospitable.

The mildew season doesn't really get into full swing until July or August up North, although it can attack even in the winter if other conditions of dampness, darkness and lack of air circulation are right. The farther south your boat, the more year-round the problem is, but no matter what your situation, it helps to be prepared. As the mold grows, it can cause considerable damage—discoloring fabrics, paper or walls and creating a distasteful, musty odor. It can cause fabrics to rot and fall apart or ruin pillows, mattresses, sails and equipment.

It's much harder to get rid of mildew once you've got it than to keep it from growing in the first place, and with a little planning, you can in-sure a mildew-free summer. The first rule is to keep things clean. Soiled clothing, bedding and towels can supply sufficient food for mildew to start growing when moisture and temperature are right. Most man-made fibers, such as nylon, acetate, acrylics and polyester are naturally resistant to molds, but even on these fabrics, soil can provide food for mold, and once it's there, it can destroy man-made fabrics as easily as it can cotton. Storage areas, particularly those for clothes, sails and line, should be scrubbed thoroughly at the beginning of the season.

Chris-Craft's accessories division makes waterproof zippered cases for blankets and bunks, protecting them from moisture and dirt.

Greasy films, the kind that form around galley areas, are also a breeding ground for the organisms and should be scrubbed regularly with soap and water or a commercial product like Marine Development & Research Corp.'s Mildew and Anti-Rot Spray.

The fashionable flat paint used in cabins is more attractive to mold than gloss paint because its surface is rougher and more porous, giving spores a better initial grip. And it's much easier to wipe mildew off gloss enamel. The Pettit Paint Co. of Belleville, N.J., makes a chemical to be added to cabin paint to keep growth off the painted surface.

The next step in mildew prevention is eliminating dampness. This may sound like an impossible dream on a boat but there are some things you can do.

Bob Whittier, *Rudder*'s maintenance editor, suggests keeping a household dehumidifier in the main cabin and plugging it in whenever 110V power is available. Many boatmen, according to Whittier, keep the dehumidifier plugged in Monday through Friday.

And, of course, never put anything away wet. A soggy life preserver, bathing suit or damp towel can ruin everything around it, and so can a perspiration-soaked shirt.

A long-time aid to on-board mildew prevention is the electric light bulb. Burned continuously in the small area of an enclosed cabin, head or closet, the bulb's heat will be sufficient to prevent spores from growing. A word of caution though: be sure the light is far enough away from clothing to avoid the danger of fire. Dampp-Chaser East of Oceanport, N.J., makes a number of heating rods in different sizes for this purpose.

A couple of chemicals available in hardware stores also absorb moisture from the air. Silica gel and activated alumina, harmless to fabrics, are porous granules that hold about half their weight of water and remain dry to the touch. Hang cloth bags of either chemical in storage areas, or scatter granules through layers of clothing to be stored for awhile. Both silica gel and alumina can be used over and over if dried in a vented oven at 300° for a couple of hours.

The Department of Agriculture has produced a booklet full of home remedies for mildew, one of which is calcium chloride, another moisture-absorbing chemical that you can buy in a hardware store. It comes in two forms: small white granules to be hung in bags like alumina and silica gel, and a porous clay-like material to be set on a rustproof screen over a pan which catches the accumulated moisture. Care must be taken not to let this chemical in its clay form come in contact with fabrics. It can eat holes in them.

Good ventilation can also be a preventative measure if you live or spend a lot of time aboard. Keep ports and head and shower doors open, except when you're under way, or put an electric fan in the main cabin to be hooked up to a battery or dockside power. And if the boat isn't to be used for long periods of time, remove things like sails, bedding, clothes and books.

If you spot signs of the dreaded fungus despite your efforts, work fast before it gets worse. Mildew is affected by variations in the weather, more of a problem in hot, wet springs and summers than cool, dry ones. It seems to run in cycles like fish and game, so growth can be more prolific one year than another. Sometimes all efforts to stop it will be of no avail.

As soon as the telltale odor and discoloration appear, walls and floors of the offending area should be scrubbed with soap and water and any of the commercial liquids or sprays. Check hardware as well as marine supply stores for these. Remember that most of these chemical products are poisonous and should be kept out of reach of children and pets.

If walls become discolored, they must be repainted or at least touched up. After scrubbing the area thoroughly, help it dry with a light bulb, heater or a little rubbing alcohol before repainting. Formaldehyde, familiar to us as that pickler of frogs in high school biology, can be used to bleach the stain before repainting. The chemical is usually available only through chemical supply houses, though, and must be used with caution because it's irritating to the lungs if inhaled.

Fresh mildew stains on fabrics can be removed by washing and drying fabrics in the sun and, if stains remain, bleach with lemon juice and salt. Sodium perborate is another safe bleach for anything washable, but first test a bit of the fabric to make sure it doesn't change color. Old stains can be dealt with by soaking the item in chlorine bleach for one minute, then dipping it in a weak vinegar solution. U.S. Continental Labs in Houston, Tex., makes a liquid called Minute Mildew Remover for sails, cushions and rubber.

The best single cure for mildew on upholstered things, life preservers, mattresses and rugs is sunshine. Take such articles outside, wash them with soap and water, and let them dry in the sun.

THE SPACE-AGE WAY TO STOP LEAKS

By Fred C. Clark

september

It is easy to get confused when shopping for a little gook to plug an annoying leak. The pages of marine catalogues and the shelves of vendors have a wide variety of acrylic, butyl, silicone and polysulfide sealants and compounds, all promising to stick to anything, not to shrink, fold, harden, fall out or go away.

Not all salesmen are helpful with technical questions, so with a considerable cost differential most of us will shop for price and hope for the best. Unfortunately, in the marine world price shopping isn't always the smart thing to do. The inexpensive caulking which did such a beautiful sealing job between bathtub and wall may fail when asked to caulk between deck and cabin of a sloop. The tub doesn't fall off five-foot waves, get twisted and knocked down by the wind, nor is it subject to alternate doses of boiling sun and ice-cold water. Marine sealants, like marine paints, take a beating and need the best of ingredients if they are to do their job, and last.

Some Facts and Comparisons

Before World War II, most pleasure boats were wood, and their seams needed caulking frequently. Rarely would the old oil-base compounds go more than two years. Today's top polysulfide seam compounds, properly applied, can last up to 20 years.

There are a few tricks with modern sealants, which aren't clearly spelled out in the directions. We'll detail these as we go along, but first let's see "which one" is best for your problem.

In the industry, there is general agreement that the thiokol-based polysulfides have no competition for seams and underwater use. Polysulfides have outstanding adhesion, superior to all other sealants, and the one-part compound is the only one that will stick to a damp or moist suface. Also, polysulfides have by far the best elastic memory. As wood boats swell and shrink, polysulfides can squeeze and stretch 10%–25% without losing their grip or leaking. Where watertight integrity or underwater use is involved, choose polysulfides, period. When cured, they can be sanded and painted. The cost of a small blister pack tube is around $3, around $6 for the cartridge. Super-cheap polysulfides have an excess of filler and will shrink to beat the band. Since polysulfides cure by absorbing moisture, there are no problems below the waterline. Above the waterline, however, they may take a long while to cure in dry, cool weather, unless you moisten them as we'll explain.

For bedding compound and for small deck and cabin leaks, the silicones are easier to use and do a fine job. The acrylics and butyls are also fine above decks, costing about half as much and giving about half the life expectancy of a silicone. Just squeeze these out of the tube onto a clean, dry surface. Without further ado, they start to skin over in 10 minutes to an hour; they cure ¼ inch deep in 24 hours. Acrylics can be painted; silicones and most butyls cannot. Silicones cost around $6.50 for the cartridge; acrylics and butyls around $2.50 but, as we mentioned, last only about half as long. Acrylic excess can be cleaned off with water. Silicones and butyls need special solvents. The cheaper acrylic and butyls cure to a harder rubber than the silicones. These compounds are very nearly

MB&S SEALANT GUIDE

Sealant	Silicone	Butyl	Acrylic	1-Part Thiokol Polysulfide	2-Part Thiokol Polysulfide
Cost (Approx.)	$6.50 Per Cartridge	$2.50 Per Cartridge	$2.50 Per Cartridge	$5.95 Per Cartridge	$10.00 For 24 oz.
Color Availability	Black White Mahogany Aluminum Clear	White	White	White Black	Black Only
Surface Preparation	Clean & Dry	Clean & Dry	Clean & Dry	Clean But Can Be Damp	Clean & Dry
Application & Method	Tubes & Cartridges	Tubes & Cartridges	Tubes & Cartridges	Available In Liquid Form (Boat Life)	Recommended For Professional Use. Needs Primer For Metal And Oily Surfaces
Can Be Painted Over?	No	No (Except Boat Life)	Yes	Yes	Yes
Below Water Use?	No	No	No	Yes	Yes
Cure Times	Skins Over In ½ Hour	Tack Free In 1 Hour	10 Minutes	1½ Days To 1 Week Depending On Moisture And Temperature	Varies Dependent On Amount Of Catalyst
Shrink Rate	Moderate	High	High	Not Measurable	
Longevity	10 Years	5 Years	5 Years	20 Years	
Above Water Use		All Good		OK But Needs Wetting Down To Promote Cure	OK

foolproof above water, if applied to a surface that is *really clean and dry.* A clean surface is obvious. But, considering that boat woods always have some moisture content, what is dry? If the surface feels dry to the finger, it is probably dry enough for silicone, acrylic or butyl. If it feels damp or moist to the finger, dry the wood if possible, or use a one-part polysulfide.

Emergency Usage

Although it is not recommended, in an emergency one-part polysulfide can be stuffed into a seam that is under water. You can also caulk a seam with one-part polysulfide, paint right over it with anti-fouling and launch immediately. Since one-part polysulfides cure by absorbing water, they set up nicely when immersed.

Polysulfides can also be used above the waterline, but take time to cure if they have to depend on drawing moisture out of the atmosphere. In cool, dry weather, one-part polysulfides could take as long as a week to cure, by themselves. However, if you take a hose or sprinkler can and wet them down a couple of times the day you apply them, you'll start them skinning over right away. Any further wetting down will hasten the cure further. Count on 1½–3 days at best for air cures. Even though the cure takes longer, one good above-waterline use for polysulfides would be for paying a deck seam or cabin leak in rainy or damp weather. One-part polysulfide would get a grip on the damp surfaces where no other sealant could. The rain or dampness would hasten the cure. If a seam is too narrow to stuff paste into, there is a one-part liquid polysulfide so thin it can be poured into narrow cracks.

To sum up, when painting over is unnecessary, pick the simple, easy-to-use, quick-curing silicones for above-deck seams, bedding hardware, portlights, hatches, and for making gaskets or weatherstripping. Below the water-line, it is always polysulfide—one-part where seams are damp, two-part where they can be dry and for better control of curing time. Topsides, count on three days to a week for one-part polysulfide to set up ready for sanding and painting, longer if the weather is cool and dry.

Silicone trade names you may find on your dealer's shelf are: Dow-Corning *Marine Silicone Sealant,* Valspar *Marine Silicone Seal,* General Electric *Marine Rubber Silicone,* Boat Life *Marine Silicone Rubber.*

The Polysulfide trade names are: Boat Life *Life Caulk,* Woolsey *Caw King,* Valspar *Valcaulk Polysulfide.*

While there are chemical differences between these products, all are essentially similar, work about the same way and will do a great job, *if the directions are followed closely.* The quickest path of grief we know is to short circuit the directions and out-smart the chemists who compounded these materials.

A Technique for Curing Cabin-to-Deck Leaks

Thoroughly clean the area using a wire brush chucked into a ¼-inch electric drill. The pros use masking tape to define the sealant limits. This will keep the sealant under control, save clean-up time and give a neat job. The tape must be carefully laid and thoroughly rubbed down into the adjoining surfaces. It takes time and patience to do a good taping job, but the end result is well worth it.

Both blister pack tubes and cartridges come with a conical spout. You cut off the spout for the size bead you want. Most first-timers cut too small a bead, and the stuff is so hard to force out through the tiny hole that placement of the bead is difficult. Cut at least a ¼-inch hole for starters. You can control the amount of sealant laid by the speed with which the nozzle is passed over the work. Lay down a good solid bead. If any area comes up short, just go over and lay on some more.

When the bead has been laid, press the sealant firmly into contact with the two seam surfaces. A wet finger is the ideal tool, but you must be careful to limit exposure, since the compounds contain lead. That means not wetting your finger with your tongue; use a damp rag. If you have a long job or skin cuts, a small plastic or metal spoon can be used. This tool should also be kept moist. Be sure to wash your hands before smoking or eating. And while the blister pack tube works well, the cartridge gun is far easier to control. For small sealing jobs the tube is ideal. For bigger ones, the cartridge is the thing. Either may be saved, for the material has a good shelf life.

A Reuse Tip

Put a big wood screw in the spout when you are through. When you want to seal again, pull the screw with slip joint pliers. Out will come a solid rubber plug which has cured and protected the rest of the contents. Since the compound will not stick to the special snout material, the remaining sealant will flow readily again.

With the sealant pressed into place, the tape should be lifted at once. Left down overnight it will make a ragged edge, or perhaps even have to be sanded away.

How to Use Sealants for Bedding Down

Whenever a cleat, chock, rod holder, winch or whatever is attached to a deck or cabin top, it needs bedding compound. Bedding plugs the gaps between the uneven surfaces, stops water from coursing down the attachment hole and protects the bolts from corrosion. Bedding compound must adhere to all surfaces, retain flexibility, resist sun and moisture and not shrink. With its quick set, silicone, along with acrylic and butyl, is excellent as a bedding compound. If you ever have to remove the fitting temporarily, you may have to cut the silicone apart with a knife, but when reinstalling in the same location, you can reactivate the old silicone with a fresh layer of same. It bonds to itself even years after it has cured. Except for one-part polysulfide, which can be applied to moist surfaces, we've stressed the need for clean surfaces, preferably barren and dry. There are several ways to do this, but one favorite is with a wire brush in an electric drill. This is quick and effective and goes into many of the awkward situations which crop up in boat maintenance. In addition to cleaning, the wire brush tends to leave a scratchy tooth to which the sealant can get a better grip.

Be generous in the application of the sealant. Apply some to the outer edge of the fitting as well as the surface to which it will be mounted.

Fasten in place and remove the excess with a wet finger or damp rag as described before.

In addition to one-part polysulfide, there is also two-part, which chemically cures with the addition of a catalyst. Once catalyzed, a batch must be used or stored in minus 40 degree temperatures to deactivate it. Two-part poly, like silicone, demands dry seams. The primary users are boatyards which can't wait for warm temperatures or good weather. By varying the amount of catalyst, experienced hands can control the time of cure. Once cured there is no difference between one-part, two-part or liquid polysulfide. Like most paints, sealants and adhesives, polysulfides won't adhere to oily surfaces, nor to oily woods like teak, cypress and cedar. For metal and for the oily woods, a primer is needed. If in doubt, always prime, for it greatly enhances the holding ability of the sealant. You can apply over tight old paint, but then your sealed joint is only as strong as the paint bond. If the paint fails, your sealant comes loose too. Clean, bare wood, free from oily spots, is the obvious way to achieve real success.

Customizing for Ports and Doors

One interesting use for silicones is to make a custom weatherstrip or gasket for a port or door. Clean the surfaces, then apply a generous bead of sealant to the surface to which the gasket is to adhere. Put waxed paper on the movable part, and close for 24 hours. After the sealant has set, you can trim the edges with a razor blade. When you open and remove the wax paper you will have moulded a perfect gasket, no matter how uneven the mating surfaces.

Insulating with Sealants

Silicones are useful in insulating aluminum hulls from dissimilar metals which could cause electrolysis. The trick here is to prime the metal, then lay down a pad within the confines of a taped area and allow to cure for 24 hours. Then lay down another bead and while wet, bed down the fitting. Since silicone adheres to itself, even after cure, you can build up a pad as thick as you want, with additional layers. This application is useful for mounting through-hull fittings.

Other uses could include the formation of a rubber gasket to protect any piping, wiring or tubing which passes through a bulkhead. This tough job is easy with formable, self-curing silicone.

Lose a rubber foot from a lamp, calculator or other appliance? You can squeeze out and form another with silicone sealant. There are many uses for instant rubber around a boat. With understanding of these products and a bit of acquired skill, your imagination is the only limiting factor in their utilization.

One Last Caution

Before using a silicone on any fitting or accessory of plastic, make sure it is not made of polypropylene. Silicone and polypropylene chemically react and the fitting will be cracked or crazed. If you are not sure what your plastic is made of, don't use a silicone.

BOAT BUYING AS AN INVESTMENT

By Sid Stapleton

september

 Today people of moderate means are plunking down hard-earned dollars for their dream boats and they want to be sure they are getting the best boat value for their cash. In fact, since a boat is normally the next largest purchase most people make after their home, the smart yacht buyer looks on the transaction not so much as blowing money on a luxury as investing his dollars in something that will return its cost at trade-in or resale and perhaps even make him a profit.

"You can't buy any utilitarian item as a true investment," cautions Walter Sullivan, whose BUC Used Boat Directory is the industry bible of current prices. "There are certain types of boats where you are buying materials and workmanship at current prices that will certainly increase in cost. As a result the rate of depreciation has slowed dramatically in recent years," Sullivan points out. For example, 15 years ago a typical boat was worth between 62 and 64 percent of its purchase price after six and a half years. Today that figure would be closer to 86 percent.

The average boat in the 30- to 45-foot class theoretically depreciates six to ten percent per year. But because inflation is pushing new boat prices up at about that same annual rate, used-boat prices are going up enough to offset depreciation. Thus, if you sensibly invest $30,000 or $50,000 in a quality new or used boat now—and take care of it—the chances are good that you'll at least break even when you sell or trade it. You might even make a profit.

Consider some examples:

• *A 1970 Pearson 30, which sold new for $13,000 to $15,000, held that value as a used boat in 1973 and today that boat will command as much as $24,000.*

• *A 5-year-old C&C 35, which sold new for $23,500 to $31,000, today will bring from $40,000 to $45,000.*

• *A well-maintained Bertram 38 or Hatteras 41 will sell today for 10 to 25 percent more than its original price, regardless of its age.*

• *A clean Morgan Out Island 41 today sells for $10,000 to $15,000 more than its original purchase price.*

• *A Triton sailboat which in 1961 sold new for $8,000 to $11,000 now brings $10,000 to $12,000. That's roughly a 25 to 30 percent increase for a boat that is 15 years old.*

"Every boat of quality has increased at least 25 percent in the last ten years," says broker David L. Fraser of San Diego, who specializes in big motor yachts. "Some have appreciated 50 percent; a lot have doubled in price. A 1966 Feadship which sold new for $600,000 recently went for $1 million."

Interviews with a wide range of boating-industry professionals ranging from manufacturers to dealers, from brokers to insurance agents, indicate there are no magic formulas that will put your dream boat in your slip at a fantastic bargain and eventually return your money or make a profit. The pros do say, however, that there is a logical, rational way to go about buying a boat and enhancing its quality as an investment. And the rules they cite apply whether the boat you yearn for is a sportfisherman or cruiser, is power or sail, is new or used, is a $7,000 trailable or a $500,000 motor yacht.

To the pros, buying a boat "right" means not necessarily buying it at the lowest possible price, but buying it at a price which gives you the best boating and investment value for the dollars you spend.

Your accountant will tell you whether you're in the market for a new boat or one that's been, as the Cadillac people like to say, "preowned." But with that out of the way, here's how the pros say to proceed.

Define Your Boating Purpose

Virtually every expert interviewed says the biggest mistake boat buyers make is in deciding what type of boat they really need.

"Before you look at the first boat," says Bob Fisher of Northrop and Johnson in Fort Lauderdale, "take a long look at how you are really going to use it. Will you be using it on an inland lake, in protected coastal waters, or offshore? Will it be a day boat or will you be taking it to the Caribbean? How often will you use it, for how long at a time, and how many people will you normally have aboard? Know your purpose and make sure you're not trying to buy a Ferrari when what you really need is a Mack truck."

Begin, then, by shutting out those entrancing visions of gleaming chrome, burnished brass, oiled teak and graceful sheers and, instead, define your purpose. Put it down in writing, in detail. You'll find that the harsh reality of that purpose spelled out in black and white will be a useful checkpoint when you're hypnotized by the lovely lines of a boat totally unsuited for your purposes. And be specific. "A big sportfisherman" doesn't help much. "A sportfisherman of 38 to 42 feet in length with twin diesels of not less than 225 hp each, a generous cockpit . . ." and so on will save you from looking at boats that won't suit you and keep you from falling in love with a boat that won't do what you want.

Also know your pocketbook, which will help define your purchase. A boat is no fun if buying and maintaining it leaves you with no time or money to enjoy it. Decide, based on a factual consideration of your own finances, how much you can really afford to spend. If you plan to pay cash, how much can you plunk down on the barrelhead? If you plan to finance, how much can you put down and what kind of payments can you afford?

In rummaging about in your budget, allow for the fact that in the first year you will probably spend an additional 10 to 15 percent of your boat's purchase price on the gadgets and comforts which will make her truly yours. And don't forget to figure upkeep costs. Allowing $100 a month to keep up a $10,000 boat may seem high, but when you include insurance, dockage or mooring fees, fuel, normal maintenance, etc., it's not out of line.

After you have narrowed the list down to the boat you really want, talk to owners and note their comments. Check consumer literature and try to spend some time aboard each one. Does the layout really suit you? Will the galley be usable at a 20° angle of heel? Does the boat have enough power to go where you want to? Does it have too much?

In making your final selection, the pros offer this advice: Stick with the established brands. Some new, small or regional boatbuilders make excellent craft and you might get in early on the beginning of a trend. But if you go with a boat whose manufacturer is not well-known, you run the risk of winding up with a boat four or five years from now that will be tough to resell. The pros also advise you to stick with boats that are well-known and popular in your area. Importing some exotic creation from abroad or another part of the United States may give you a real kick when you operate it, but it will give you a kick of a different kind when you go to sell it and a prospective buyer greets your mention of its builder's name with a blank stare.

Once you pinpoint the boat for you, shop several dealers who handle it. "This is especially important if a trade-in is involved," says Gordon C. Woodland, general manager of Pearson Yachts. "Your current boat may be more valuable to one dealer than to another. One may have a buyer looking for just what you're trading. If he knows he can resell it quickly, he's in a position to give you a better deal."

Some price dickering is expected, but be reasonable. A dealer in quality boats has a markup of around 18 to 20 percent in smaller boats and 10 to 15 percent in larger boats. Out of that he has to meet his overhead, maintain a service department, pay his salesmen commissions and make a profit. He may be able to offer 3 to 5 percent off the list price of the basic boat, and 10 to 12 percent off major accessories. He might be able to do a little better on a boat already in his inventory since he probably borrowed money to "floor plan" it and is paying interest. In some cases, the factory will offer him a special discount on a model that's being phased out of the line or something extra off on a display model at a boat show. Some dealers will pay all or part of the cost of freighting the boat from the factory. In slack seasons he may offer savings on rigging or throw in some extras like cushions, life jackets and fire extinguishers.

But if a dealer tries to sell you on price alone and his price is much below what you know other dealers are asking for the same boat, be cautious. Whatever you save up front on a deal like that will usually be made up for later in poor service and frustration.

Once you find a dealer who seems genuinely interested in working with you, check his service record. Ask for the names of customers to whom he has sold boats in the last year and ask them if he backed up service warranties or gave them the run-around. You can probably expect the same treatment.

Once you've selected make, model and dealer, spec the boat out the way you want it. But here the pros counsel you to put your money in hull, engine, sails and *basic* accessories—not gadgets. You'll probably come out better including basic electronics and any instruments which require through-hull fittings in the initial order for the boat. The dealer probably can give you a better price on a "package" than you could get buying accessories separately; you'll have only one place to go for warranty service, and you can finance the entire deal. But limit the accessories you add to what you will really use, and save frills for later.

Now that we've got the new boat buyer started off right, let's see what the pros suggest for the guy who wants a good buy on a used boat.

Start with a Broker

In the used-boat market, the pros suggest you start by looking for a good broker rather than a good boat. As for type and builder, the advice on new boats applies here as well. Bob Fisher suggests you visit several brokers, then make your selection based on "how your chemistry works together. Find a guy you can trust," he says. "Develop trust and everything else will fall into place. If trust is lacking, nine out of ten times you'll come away unhappy."

In considering brokers, don't hesitate to ask for

references of former clients and check them. A reputable broker will be delighted at the chance to parade his satisfied customers for your inspection. If a broker shies away from such a request or appears offended, say thanks and leave—fast. Also be cautious about the broker who offers to cut his commission "to help you out." A good broker is worth every dime of his commission, usually ten percent, which he collects from the seller.

Three surprising points emerged from talking to the professionals who know boat buying.

First, most agree you don't really save by going very far from home to buy a boat. Says one broker, "By the time you figure up all the phone calls, the long trips to look at boats which can involve air travel, meals and hotels, and the cost of getting the boat back to your home waters, you'll eat up whatever you save on the purchase price itself."

Second, there's really no "best time" to buy a boat. "Seven or eight years ago," says Bryan Waters of United Yacht Brokers in Fort Lauderdale, "summer was the time to buy a boat at a bargain down here. You could fire a cannon through the streets and not hit a soul, so sellers were happy with any offer they could get. That's just not true anymore."

"Prices around Long Island Sound might drop a little in the fall," says Dean Matthews, "but the drop is not enough to make a significant difference."

Third, in dealing with a broker, the experts say you're better off to select one and stick with him rather than trying to play several off against each other. "Some people will write 10, 20, 30 brokers," says Bryan Waters. "Chances are, eight out of ten listings they get will be for the same boats." "Any reputable broker," echoes California's David Fraser, "has access to any boat for sale anywhere in the world. By trying to deal with more than one broker at a time, you just wear yourself out."

Once you've found a broker you can work with, be scrupulously honest about the amount of money you're willing to spend, and listen to his advice. If he tells you the type of boat you've decided on isn't right for you, go back over the basics to see if you missed anything. If he says your budget just won't buy the kind of boat you want, decide if you can go higher or should scale down your expectations. Sure, the broker wants to make a sale at the highest dollar figure he can. But brokers live on referrals and a good broker will want to sell you not just one boat but several. If he can't keep customers singing his praises and coming back with their repeat business, he won't last very long. So listen to what he tells you.

Get a Survey

Never buy a used boat without a competent marine survey. It will cost you a couple of hundred dollars, but it's well worth it when you're on the verge of spending thousands. The trick is to find a good surveyor to do the job. Reputable brokers will be hesitant about pushing a particular surveyor's services too hard, but they will give you a list of two or three they consider reliable. As with brokers, if a surveyor offers you a cut-rate deal, keep looking.

Once you've found a boat that meets your original specifications, that is endorsed by your broker and is passed by your surveyor, seek guidance from your Ouija board as to what

would be a reasonable offer. First, make sure the asking price is in line with boats of comparable type, size, quality and age. If that seems about in line, you can usually figure an offer of six to ten percent under the asking price will buy it. But even that general rule should be flexible.

"You're not only buying a boat," points out Bryan Waters, "you're buying a set of circumstances. It may be an estate sale or the owner may need cash quickly, and you may stumble onto an exceptional deal. Or you may find a real cream puff that is worth the full asking price, even though it's a bit higher than other boats of its type."

So that's what the experts say about boat buying. Their advice is not infallible. But if you follow their suggestions—even if you have to bend them a bit to accommodate the tug at your heart for that 20-year-old Trumpy or Alden—you stand a better than even chance of buying a boat that will suit your needs, provide you endless hours of pleasure, and pay back its cost—maybe with interest—when you move on to something else.

And that's a tough combination to beat in any game.

INVESTMENT TIPS FROM THE PROS

Like the stock market, the key to buying a boat as a financial investment is to buy low and sell high. Here are some ways to do it:

1. When a new boat is introduced that strikes your fancy, seriously consider it. A few companies still have "introductory" prices that are, in fact, bargains. More often, however, the initial price for a boat may reflect what a manufacturer *thinks* he must get for the boat before he goes into production. Since most manufacturers are trying to deliver the most boat for the money, occasionally they err to the benefit of the buyer. The industry is full of stories of companies that actually shipped scores of boats at a loss before discovering it.

2. Watch what OPEC is doing with the price of oil. If OPEC jumps the price of oil significantly, as it did in 1974, you can bank on two reactions: First, the price of resin and fiberglass will go up, which will be reflected in boat prices six months later; second, some powerboat owners may overreact and fire sale their boats below market value. Powerboats are here to stay.

3. When shopping for a boat, keep an eye out for the boat that has been in inventory the longest. The chances are good that if it has been sitting in the dealer's shed for six months it has the old sticker price, which may have already been superseded by one or two price increases.

4. Keep an eye on the used-boat market. Pick one or two boats of the type you are interested in and keep mental track of their asking prices, much as you would follow a stock on the New York Exchange. When a boat comes on the market significantly below what you know to be the going rate, investigate. It could be that there is nothing at all wrong with the boat, but simply that the owner doesn't know the value or that he is in a forced-sale situation.

5. When you go to sell your boat, determine its realistic market value, and then hold out for your price. Be patient. Don't sell your boat short.

Land ho!

Where are you going to be in October? If you are a boatman with a flexible work schedule and a passion for the Inland Waterway, you could be following the wild geese to a warmer climate like Sloan Wilson (see page 159). If you are an imaginative spirit like Arthur Rosien (see page 165), you could be preparing to spend the entire winter snugly aboard your boat with a few necessary improvements in weatherproofing and heating.

But if you are not the type for a long cruise south or the long winter north, you may find that a strange thing is happening in the affair between you and your boat.

Until now, everything was fine. But one chilly Saturday morning, around the middle of October, as you're driving to your boat, you suddenly realize that some of that old passion is missing. You notice . . . trees. Right around your boatyard, they're turning all variations of red and gold and russet. You've rediscovered land! You remember the time when you were little and your father took you hiking.

But don't worry. It's all only temporary and really quite normal. Lots of boatmen feel this way with the frost in the air and the football season under way.

In another few weeks you'll be laying up your boat, whatever your feelings. And this is the time to plan ahead. Will you winter right where you are, or do you have to find a winter berth? Should you choose dry storage (hauled out) or wet (in the water)? See "November." For those who can't tear themselves away from the deck, stay awhile with Sloan Wilson and Arthur Rosien, who follow.

A LOVE LETTER TO THE BIG DITCH

By Sloan Wilson

october

I love the Intracoastal Route to Florida.

In many quarters this confession will be considered naive; sophisticated sailors summon up their *machismo,* call the Route the Big Ditch to indicate how unchallenging and boring they find it.

But the ICW is a lot more than a big ditch—it is some of the loveliest rivers, bays, and sounds in the world. I cannot see how anyone with eyes can be bored with the Intracoastal Route.

For me, familiarity has bred increased appreciation. I have sailed it more times than I can count. I used to go back and forth on it with my father decades ago; this year I have already made the trip once and I plan to do it again. No matter how many times I take this voyage, I always regard it as a challenging adventure.

Technically the Intracoastal Route starts in Norfolk, Va., but I always think of it as starting in New York, where we begin our journey South. I like to start in mid-September, when the first cold rains of fall begin to make the golden beaches of Florida and the Bahamas a goal worth pursuing.

I save a full month for the trip, not because it can't be done in less, but for the same reason I don't like to hurry through a good meal.

Besides, rushing leads to carelessness: one reason so many people run aground, I believe, is that they stay at the wheel long after they are tired. It takes concentration to follow those narrow, winding channels. The faster the boat goes, the more concentration it takes. Our 54-foot cruiser, the *Pretty Betty,* cruises at little better than ten knots, but even so, I am tired after six hours at the helm, and exhausted after eight. Even if my energy lasted longer, I would not want to steam at night in these inland waters where there are many floating logs. And in pleasant ports I like to tarry for several days. (If for some reason I absolutely had to hurry south, I would make sure I had another person aboard who could help pilot the boat. We would start at dawn every day and by taking turns at the wheel could average a hundred miles a day before dark. That way we could make the trip with a ten-knot boat in about two weeks.)

For us, me, my wife, and six-year-old daughter, the voyage begins when we go into one of the bays in Brooklyn to take on fuel, water, and stores. We change the oil in the engines, put in new filters, and check the radio. I then start listening to weather reports, waiting for the right day to go down the New Jersey coast. Just the right day is important to me because once, long ago, my father got caught in a fall gale off Atlantic City aboard his 60-foot ketch. My mother and younger brother were so seasick and scared that the moment they got ashore they took a train to Florida. For years, it was difficult to get them aboard a boat again; I don't want that to happen to my wife and daughter.

During my boyhood we had no choice but to take the open ocean from New York to Cape May, N.J., a distance of well over 100 miles. Nowadays a boat which draws less than four feet and which has a mast lower than 35 feet can duck inside at Manasquan Inlet, only 26 miles south of Sandy Hook. Such a boat can stay in the New Jersey Inside Route all the the way down to Delaware Bay. I have never taken this route because an inspection of the charts and the advice of friends has led me to believe that it would be slow going for the *Pretty Betty.* There are a lot of bridges, some of which are said to be slow to open, and many areas have both low speed limits and aggressive sheriffs. If my boat were smaller, or if the weather were bad and I felt committed to start on a given day, I would try the New Jersey waterway. As things are, I generally wait for a nice day and go from Sandy Hook outside to Atantic City, a nice day's run of about 75 miles, with the automatic pilot doing most of the work. After an evening of wandering down the boardwalk and a good night's sleep, we run outside the remaining 30 miles or so to Cape May. There we have a celebration because the open ocean part of the voyage is done.

Atlantic City and Cape May are somewhat alike, both resort towns on the open sea. Both give the yachtsman a choice between an old harbor crowded with commercial fishing boats and a new marina. I usually pick the old harbor because of its charm and its easy access to good restaurants. Cape May is far less crowded than Atlantic City, and someday I'd like to spend a couple of weeks there. Up the creek at the southern end of the harbor is an authentic Gloucester fishing schooner, the *American*. Although she has been turned into a barroom, she has lost none of her grace. The modern fishing vessels which surround her also give a photographer or painter much to admire.

One of the reasons I never find the trip tiresome is that every hundred miles or so, the whole nature of it changes—occasionally even for the worse. For instance, what comes next, the run up Delaware Bay, the Delaware River, and the Chesapeake and Delaware Canal, is one of the parts of the trip that I don't much like. Delaware Bay can get sloppy, and it's so wide that there isn't much scenery to admire. We try to pick a good day, and don't stop till we get to the head of Chespeake Bay, where I like to anchor. There is a place where one can tie up in the middle of the C & D Canal, but the currents are swift there, and little of interest exists within walking distance of the pier. We regard the day's run from Cape May to the southern end of the C & D Canal as sort of payment we have to make for the great privilege of cruising Chesapeake Bay.

In the summer Chesapeake Bay can be hot and "sea nettles" can make swimming painful, but in the fall there surely is no better place in the world for a man with a boat. Indian Summer lasts longer in the Bay than in most other places. For about 180 miles it stretches south, and on

each side are bays within bays and countless rivers fingering into picturesque creeks. There are fishing villages with fleets of skipjacks, quietly expensive resorts with coveys of gold-plated yachts. In October especially, when the fields are golden and the Canadian geese are swooping down to steal corn, all those little villages with white churches and the last fleets of working sailing vessels are difficult to leave.

If I had time to visit only two ports in the bay, they would be Oxford and Annapolis. Annapolis is, of course, a sort of shrine to any American who loves the sea; and Oxford, where we bought the *Pretty Betty* four years ago, is a lovely town with excellent yards for any sort of repair. There is also a fine old inn within walking distance of the docks which serves the best crab cakes I have ever eaten.

Although Chesapeake Bay can be almost as rough as the open ocean, there are many protected harbors all up and down both shores. When the wind pipes up we head for the nearest snug cove. In September and October the weather is generally good, and I have even had grand days in November. I wouldn't want to linger much longer than mid-November, because I have vivid memories of my days in the Coast Guard, when we often had to break ice in Chesapeake Bay, and the winds were almost Arctic.

If it is late in the year, we are always glad to get to Norfolk, because the wide waters have been left behind and hundreds of miles of sheltered rivers and canals lie ahead—here we stop tapping the barometer and get out the strip charts which cover the Intracoastal Route.

Just as the Jersey Coast is nothing like Chesapeake Bay, the next segment of the trip is another complete change. With strange abruptness the great city of Norfolk disappears the moment one enters the canals, and one is smack in the middle of the Old South. It doesn't make much difference whether one takes the Dismal Swamp Canal or the Virginia Cut route. This is deserted country, swamps and lowlands which have changed little since the day George Washington worked there as a surveyor.

Because there is a feeling of safety to the glistening black water of the canals south of Norfolk, there is a temptation to sit half dozing at the wheel as the miles of tawny marsh and green pastureland roll by. When I catch myself doing this, I remind myself that each time I have gone down the Route I have seen at least one yacht sunk or badly damaged.

There are two classic ways to run aground on the ICW. If you are simply following the markers without keeping track of your position on the chart, it is easy to miss a turn in the channel, and then to try to cut across a shoal to reach a marker that should have been approached by a more circuitous route. To guard against this mistake, I check off each marker we pass with a colored pencil. A glance at the chart then shows exactly where we are. This is hard on the charts, but by marking with a different color each trip, we can use the same charts several times; anyway, charts should be renewed every year or so unless one has the time to keep them up to date, which I don't.

The other classic way to run aground on the Intracoastal Route comes from being lulled by seemingly broad rivers, in the center of which there often are narrow channels. Because those channels are dredged, the deep water often runs between spoil banks which are only a few inches under the surface. If one takes the Virginia Cut route, one passes a section immediately north of Coinjock where the chart warns of sunken pilings just outside the channel. Last June we saw a cruiser about 55 feet long which had disregarded that warning. Although only about 30 feet out of the channel, she was sitting on the bottom with the water lapping around her decks. On a dry spot near the stern her captain was sitting in a canvas chair reading a book while he waited for a salvage barge. We took a photograph of this sad sight and pasted it on our chart table to keep us on our toes.

The way to stay in the channel is to keep glancing astern and to each side, instead of staring straight ahead. The breaking wake of the *Pretty Betty* gives me ample warning if we get too close to the edge.

Instead of taking the Virginia Cut route or the Dismal Swamp Canal, one can go out through Pamlico Sound soon after leaving Norfolk. For the sake of variation we plan to take this third option this fall. Pamlico Sound is wide and I wouldn't want to take it if I didn't have good weather reports, but I have wanted to see Roanoke Island and the country around Hatteras Inlet ever since I read years ago that they had wild horses there. If the wild horses have disap-

peared, please don't tell me about it. I want to go and see for myself.

If we do take the Pamlico Sound route however, I shall be extremely sorry to miss Belhaven, which both the other routes pass through, and which is one of my favorite stops. Belhaven is a small North Carolina town on the banks of the Pungo river. When we were at the Jordan yacht basin there last June, an old man who had been trimming the garden of a manor house nearby strolled down to the boat and gave my wife a huge basket of flowers. When my wife thanked him effusively, he came back with a dozen freshly picked gardenias. "I often bring flowers down to the boats," he said to me. "When there are women aboard, they generally like them. One thing we have in Belhaven is plenty of flowers."

Another thing they have in plenty is friendliness. When our 12 volt generator broke down, a man gave me a free ride to a town some 30 miles away, and waited there for an hour to take me back.

Within walking distance of the docks at Belhaven is a very good restaurant in a huge old manor house. Last June, a fine vocal group from a nearby college performed there. When they had finished their concert, they came down to our boat, where they sang and played guitars until early the next morning. Do you see why I am so seldom bored on this trip?

Part of the fun of this voyage is meeting people aboard other boats. Often vessels of similar speed find themselves tying up in the same port night after night. One fall a man who didn't want to bother with problems of piloting followed us all the way from Norfolk to Miami. A retired fireman who was traveling with several friends from inland states, he had stocked his small cruiser with bottles of homemade whisky and sacks of homegrown potatoes. Every fifty miles or so, they dropped an empty bottle overboard, and every evening they gave us a full one as a sort of piloting fee. This came in handy in Virginia and the Carolinas, where they don't serve hard liquor in bars, and where the package stores close at sundown.

Within an easy day's run south of Belháven there are several interesting places to stop. This fall, if weather prevents our Pamlico Sound passage, we plan to go from Belhaven to the town of Oriental, which I have not seen in more than a decade. I remember it as a fishing village with few facilities for yachtsmen, but with great friendliness and charm. Millions of oyster shells were piled up to provide protection from southerly gales. There was a general store and an active fishing fleet. There was no electricity at the wharf where we stayed, but since no one charged me for dockage, I did not complain. I hope the town has not changed.

Most people push on from Belhaven to Morehead City, N.C., or to Beaufort, N.C., which is adjacent to it. According to all the guidebooks, these two cities, which are connected by a bridge, have a great deal to offer people on boats, but from the water the area there just looks industrial to me. If they do not have a big fertilizer plant in Morehead City, they have something in the air which makes me think they do, so I generally hurry through. The current in the harbor there is swift, and the channel twists and turns even more erratically than is usual on the Intracoastal Route. Several times I found that the buoyage doesn't correspond exactly to that on my chart. I am always glad to get to Spooner Creek, which is only about five miles farther on.

Spooner Creek is an elaborate harbor constructed especially for yachts. An excellent restaurant and a ship's store are run in conjunction with it, but there is no grocery store within walking distance. When we were there last June our dachshund, Underdog, gave birth to six puppies. The people who ran the restaurant donated a half gallon of milk for her, and a fine collection of steak scraps.

Wrightsville Beach is the next place we look forward to. This is a busy little North Carolina seaside resort. Unlike many of the towns which incorporate the name "beach" into their names, this place actually has a fine stretch of sand open to the public and within walking distance of the Intracoastal Route. My daughter, Jessica, loves to swim in the surf there, and the beachcombing is excellent. Last spring she found, in addition to a fine collection of shells, the handle of an old knife imbedded in a piece of coral.

A day's run from Wrightsville Beach is Georgetown, S.C., a rather unattractive town with a pool hall on the main street; like something out of an old Western movie. We had the good luck to meet people who live there, however, and discovered that there are many charming plantations nearby. Incidentally, in June of 1970, when Wall Street was talking depression, this whole

section seemed unusually prosperous. I talked to one man who bought a shrimp boat for $62,000 and had paid for her in one year of fishing, and an ancient gentleman in overalls told me he had sold his crop of tomatoes for $110,000. Maybe these folk were exaggerating, but they sure weren't talking poor.

Charleston, S.C., did not seem as prosperous as the smaller towns around it, and there seemed to be much more racial strife there. "The bigger the city, the more misery there is," the skipper of a shrimp boat explained to me. Nevertheless, Charleston has a good big municipal marina. The rise and fall of tide is so great there (about 8 feet), that it is wise to try to get a berth at one of the few floating docks.

In this part of the South, my wife and I like to combine the sports of bicycle riding and walking with cruising. We try to save an afternoon for walking along the Battery in Charleston, which is surely one of the most handsome streets in the world, with the wide harbor on one side and a row of great stately homes on the other.

Beaufort, S.C., another day's run south, is even better for walking or riding bicycles. Huge mansions in walled gardens and groves of majestic live oaks with Spanish moss make a large part of the town look like a set for "Gone With The Wind." The Isle of Hope, a few miles farther south, continues this kind of scenery in a more rural setting. The hills are gentle enough for even a middle-aged bicycle rider and each bend of the road holds promise of new gardens and orchards.

It seems to me that the Old South ends at the Isle of Hope, and one enters a noble and lonely land of swamps and forests which the Indians of five hundred years ago would still find familiar. Here it is difficult to believe in the population explosion. Between the Isle of Hope and Fernadina, Fla., a long day's run for us, we saw almost no human habitation last June. If it had not been for a few passing boats, we could have imagined ourselves to be entirely alone in the world. When a thunderstorm broke over the swamp, the tall grass waved like big ocean swells, but the black creeks were unruffled. There are islands in the swamp which I would love to explore with a kayak; the next time I go South I hope to have one aboard. Sometimes on the banks of a canal or river one sees the chimney of a burned house, or the outline of a foundation covered with vines. This part of the country was explored very early by Englishmen and Spaniards—it would be a great place to explore with a metal detector.

Fernadina, the first port in Florida, has little to recommend it. The marina is unsuitable for vessels as big as ours, and it is unprotected from swells from the inlet and the wake of passing trawlers. There are giant factories nearby which spew filth into the air and water. Nevertheless, this is Florida, and like so much of Florida, its waters teem with life. When we were last there we counted more than a dozen huge sea turtles which had apparently come into the harbor to get the heads of shrimp which were being thrown overboard from the trawlers. The fact that the harbor was sudsy with detergents being discarded by the factories did not seem to bother the turtles a bit. The sight of giant sea turtles churning around in a harbor full of suds is something we are not likely to forget.

If we are too tired for a long run, we go next to St. Augustine. St. Augustine is supposed to be the oldest town in America, and it is said to have the oldest house in America. I don't know much about that, but I suspect it is the oldest tourist trap in America, and I stay clear of it when I can. The municipal yacht basin there is conveniently located in the center of town, but it is swept by swift currents, and there is a shoal between the docks and the land which is strangely marked by pilings painted to resemble barber poles. The slips were so tight for the *Pretty Betty* last June that we had to warp her out big-ship style, a maneuver which is exhausting when one is short handed.

Daytona is better. There are several elaborate private marinas, but the city marina is so good and so cheap that I always go there. Last June the dockage was a nickle a foot, the cheapest on the whole voyage. (The most expensive was 30¢ a foot near New York, and the most usual rates were 15¢ and 20¢.)

In Daytona the city marina is right in the middle of a big shopping district. There is a baseball park next door. Usually I am not much interested in baseball, but the local teams and the audiences who cheer them on seem to me to have much more spirit than anything in the big leagues. When the home team came from behind to win last June, I thought the youngsters were going to tear the entire grandstand apart.

A bit south of Daytona is the Indian River; I used to sail small boats on it when I was a boy, and I have always loved it. On both banks of the stream stretch miles of orange groves. On small islands cast up by dredges are crowds of birds—pelicans, herons of many kinds, and a profusion of egrets; I have counted as many as 50 white-plumed egrets in one mangrove tree. The river abounds in mullet. Occasionally I have seen them so thick that one could scoop them up by the dozen with a dip net. A friend of mine has taken to casting for mullet here with a trout rod, using a small pellet of dough instead of a dry fly. Folk lore has it that mullet will never bite a hook because they eat no fish or insect, but they will bite on bread.

There are more porpoises in the Indian River than I have seen in any other inland body of water, and they are friskier. Often they swim alongside our boat, occasionally leaping as high as the rail. It is sentimental, I know, but I always consider the porpoises of the Indian River a kind of welcoming committee to the sunny south. They greet us every year between New Smyrna and Eau Gallie.

Our immediate destination when we leave Daytona is Eau Gallie which has a naturally formed land-locked harbor with splendid houses on the banks—just the sort of places which deep-water sailors dream of buying in their old age. The yard there does repairs at cheaper rates than will be available farther south. The whole Cape Kennedy research complex is only a few miles down the road, and the Eau Gallie Yacht Basin pursues the pleasant practice of lending a car to visiting yachtsmen free of direct charge for a visit to the Cape.

From Eau Gallie we make a long day's run all the way to Ft. Lauderdale. By that time we're getting close to home, and the old boat seems anxious to go. Ft. Pierce and Stuart are pleasant places, but they can offer nothing like the facilities farther south. Palm Beach and West Palm Beach are towns which I have never liked—fishing cruisers roar up and down Lake Worth with even less regard for the effect of their wake than is usual. Palm Beach, with its opulent houses and gardens, is interesting to inspect on foot and there is a nice bicycle path along the lake shore, but there seems to me to be something oppressive about the wealth, the ostentation, and the age of most of the inhabitants.

Ft. Lauderdale suits us better. The most elaborate marinas I have ever seen exist there. The dock boys courteously help a visitor to tie up and they immediately place a telephone aboard. A fine beach and a variety of swimming pools are nearby, as are suitable restaurants and shops. The newspaper is delivered free each morning. These marinas are a little more expensive than average, but in view of the fine service they offer, I believe them to be a great bargain. They are less expensive than many marinas in Lond Island Sound which offer almost nothing but the use of a wharf, water, and electricity. The Port Everglades Inlet, just south of Ft. Lauderdale, is deep enough for huge ships as well as small yachts. Bimini and Gun Cay, the gate to the Bahamas, are only about 55 miles across the Gulf Stream. It is small wonder that Ft. Lauderdale is one of the greatest yachting centers in the world. One reason I love to stay there is that I enjoy watching the constant parade of boats of all kinds on the waterway.

Miami and the end of the Intracoastal Route is only about 25 miles south of Ft. Lauderdale. The city is building an elaborate new marina in the downtown area which should be finished this year. I don't know what life there will be like, but I hear they will cater more to transients and charter boats than to live-aboard yachts which want to stay for the season.

The city owns another large marina at Dinner Key in Coconut Grove. Protected by small islands from the broad waters of Biscayne Bay, this is a pleasant place to lie. Unfortunately, there usually is a big waiting list for season slips. Perhaps because so many people want to get in, the city does not seem to waste much time on courtesies to yachtsmen. The dock men seem more interested in police duties than in helping the people to tie up, and there is a long list of regulations which the visiting yachtsman must promise to observe. Anyone who wants to stay at Dinner Key should be warned that it is dangerous to own a cat there. For some reason people get very upset over cats at Dinner Key, and I know of two fine yachtsmen who were summarily ordered out of the place because the management received complaints about cats having invaded other boats. Dogs must be kept on a leash at Dinner Key, and people on boats are not supposed to hang up clothes to dry. Although there are many pleasant people who live year after year there, and the winds from the bay, as well as the view of surrounding waters, make evenings there unusually attractive, sometimes, when I leave, I feel as though I have just been let out of boarding school.

In Biscayne Bay, just east of Dinner Key, the Intracoastal Route ends, 1,095 land miles south of Norfolk, Va. (Why the strip charts use land miles, I have no idea, but they give me the illusion of traveling faster than we do.) Often when we reach the end of the route, however, we wonder why we hurried even as much as we did. Of course, our daughter has to get back to school and I have to get to work on my typewriter, but it still seems a shame to have rushed through Chesapeake Bay or Pamlico Sound just to sit at a dock, even though it may be part of an attractive marina. The more one travels the Route, the more places one wants to explore, and the more friends one acquires at the familiar stops. We laugh when people ask if we don't find it a great bore to take this trip as often as we do. No, we never weary of the Intracoastal Route. As Samuel Johnson said of London, anyone who gets tired of it is tired of life.

"LIVE ABOARD? ...OF COURSE YOU CAN!"

By Arthur H. Rosien

There really is no esoteric mystique about living aboard full-time through a northern winter, even though you won't learn much from so-called boating experts. Most manufacturers, dealers, and marina operators seem to have absolutely no interest in the matter, are completely uninformed, and really don't want even to discuss it. Talk to the owner of a marina where there are some boats that are lived on all winter and he tends to go to the other extreme of assuring you that it is done and apparently is no problem. But don't expect any detailed answers to your questions. Evidently he, too, shares the common opinion that this is a madness fortunately confined to the very few, and feels that it must be akin to camping out in a pup tent in the Rockies.

Let's get right to the point and ask key questions: Can you live aboard full-time in the North comfortably, and find the life-style both practical and normal in the everyday sense? After two winters aboard our boat, my wife and I can assure you that the answer for us is an unequivocal "yes!" Given careful planning and assuming that you have honestly analyzed the criteria for living aboard successfully—you can face winter without fear and trembling. It really is much simpler than it appears, and doesn't require either the expertise of an engineer or access to a secret ritual handed down by the chosen few.

The logical starting place is to decide where the boat will be stored. We believe that if you are going to live on your boat she will have to be in the water. Right off the bat, that brings up all sorts of involved arguments—even among the knowledgeable—about whether this is a good idea. Live aboard or not, keeping your boat in the water year-round is unquestionably the best thing for her. Consider this: A boat is designed and built to have her weight supported in the water; any other medium is simply a poor substitute. No matter how good a job the yard does of blocking up your boat—or even if you use the manufacturer's cradle—the hull must, by definition, be under more strain than when it is evenly supported throughout its length by water. So, keeping her in the water is simply keeping her in the milieu for which she was designed. Incidentally, there are no special valves or other gear needed to do this, despite what some marinas try to tell the uninitiated; if your boat is safe in the water all summer, she will be safe in the winter too.

"Ah," you say, "that seems reasonable. But what about ice damage to my hull?" Believe it or not, ice need *not* damage your hull, even if the marina doesn't have a bubbler system. So long as the water around your boat is calm—that is, passing boat traffic does not cause enough movement to break up the ice—the ice will not affect your hull. We have walked around our boat on four inches of ice—and have talked to owners with up to eight inches of ice around their boats—and none of us has had any damage whatsoever. The ice will not crush your hull, and will not cut it unless, as pointed out, the ice is broken up by outside forces.

If you can install a bubbler system, so much the better; but don't worry if you can't. Note that your insurance policy disclaims any liability for ice damage, but don't let that stop you; simply be sure of the water conditions where you will have your boat. You will find—if you do your research carefully—that many manufacturers and dealers store brand-new boats in northern waters through the winter, waiting for spring customers. If they don't worry about ice, why should you?

Winter storms are common, and you must be prepared to handle them. This is simply a matter of being sure your boat is properly made fast—good lines of proper diameter for the boat's size, extra lines for a margin of safety. It is wise, too, to choose a marina where there is some weather protection from the direction most winter storms take, and to keep your boat rather close to shore. We have weathered high winds with no discomfort or worry, simply by observing the same simple rules we observe during the regular boating season. Oh yes, be sure you have enough depth of water for safety where you dock, to cope with the abnormally low tides you'll inevitably encounter; we have seen sailboats heeled over against the dock, their keels grounded because of a low tide that left too little water to float them upright.

Should you cover your boat during the winter? We originally decided not to, feeling that the ravages of winter were exaggerated, especially in view of those brand-new boats stored out in the open at factories and dealerships. However, a few months convinced us that being covered is essential to comfortable living aboard, whatever the merits of protecting the boat against the weather. You will find that heat loss from the interior, and the effect of cold wind on the exterior, are too great to ignore. If you do ignore them, you will waste heat, and even though the temperature is reasonably high the boat will never be as comfortable without a cover as with one.

We feel very strongly that the usual covers you see—either fitted ones from manufacturers, or canvas you throw over a frame—are highly inefficient, a waste of money, and generally unsuitable for living aboard. The average cover over a wooden frame is cheaply made whatever its cost, and long before winter is over it lands in the water, tears to pieces, or both. Additionally, both types let in too much cold air and often at the same time build up excessive dampness because of improper air flow. Usually the canvas is of a type that cuts off all light, and living in a dark bag is hardly conducive to a cheerful existence.

What's the answer to this? We believe it's a custom-made cover, utilizing a strong metal frame and a special type of canvas. We found ours at the Castaways Yacht Club, in New Rochelle, N.Y., where we keep our boat in the winter. They design a special package, fitted to the boat, that eliminates all the problems of makeshift covers; one look at it and we were sold. The main frame is made up of hollow, anodized-aluminum tubing, ¾" in diameter, with ½" tubing for the horizontal cross braces. Attached to a traditional wooden spine by screws, the entire framework is held together by metal clamps. With each piece coded by number, the framework is literally a gigantic Erector Set that can be put together and taken apart simply and easily.

The canvas cover, made by DiGioia Sails Co. of City Island, is a type of canvas that both breathes and lets in lots of light. Even on an overcast day, it is nearly as bright under the cover as outside. The entrance door is a double-zippered flap that can be opened and closed from either side. For living aboard, we strongly recommend a clear vinyl window or two—both to dispel a closed-in feeling and to allow you to view the scenery every so often. We have a large one opposite our salon facing shore, and one by the dinette facing seaward. This type of cover is efficient, strong, prevents moisture accumulation, and keeps things light and bright. Speaking of strength, ours has weathered an 80-mph wind storm with no trouble at all; you couldn't ask for more than that!

Surprisingly, under our cover the temperature is quite moderate, even on a very cold and windy day. It is no chore to fill the water tanks, run the engines or do odd jobs under the cover; protected from the wind we are quite comfortable. It's very nice to have a roof over your head in a blizzard while you put the groceries down and unlock the cabin door.

This cover, we feel, is ideal. But is there any other satisfactory though less-expensive kind if your budget is rock bottom? We have seen a heavy-gauge clear vinyl used, but it does have some drawbacks that in the long run cause it to be less effective and more costly. When you use vinyl, even with a good wooden frame, high winds usually wreak havoc on it and it ends up torn. Heavy snow deposits put quite a strain on it too, and it creates a hothouse effect that causes heavy condensation to gather on the inside. Most vinyl covers must be replaced each year. There is a reinforced vinyl, with strong cord imbedded in it to form squares, which does stand up to the job if properly installed with a good frame. This type is translucent, though not clear, and lets in a lot of light. But it's difficult to fasten the vinyl around the bottom and to prevent it from wearing through where it rubs against the frame. On an older boat, the vinyl can be secured at the bottom by nailing or taping it, without regard for damage when it is removed.

Assuming you use some sort of weather-proof cover, another good way to help keep out the cold is to buy regular house-type insulation, such as 3½" fiberglass with a foil backing. This can be applied against any window that seems to let in a lot of cold air. We do this on all windows in the forward stateroom (which is our closet area), the heads, the aft stateroom, and the windshield in the salon. It makes a big difference on a cold, windy day. A word of caution, however. Fasten the insulation with a good quality, two-sided tape *on the glass*. If you use *any* kind of tape on your woodwork or painted surfaces, you'll find that by spring it is nearly impossible to peel off, and when it does the paint will come with it.

We also bought very clear, high-quality vinyl and taped it onto our inside window frames; this gave a kind of storm window effect, with an air space between vinyl and glass. It added a lot to our comfort, but we wouldn't do it again! We used a good masking tape, and taped the vinyl to the teak window frames; by spring we went out of our minds trying to get it off the woodwork. It took hours with a putty knife, working carefully to avoid damage to the wood.

Now we come to the real heart of the winter problem, and the question that probably stops more would-be boat tenants than any other: How do you heat a boat, and can you be truly comfortable? There are quite a few possible answers to this, though we will spend time only on those we consider practical and efficient.

You can, of course, approach the matter rather scientifically by figuring an approximate Btu requirement for your boat. This involves knowing how many cubic feet of space is to be heated, and multiplying this by a factor of 10 to 15, the exact figure depending on such variables as the range of outside temperatures to be encountered, the heat level you wish to maintain, and

the heat loss of your boat. If you use electric heaters, figure that 1000 watts equals about 3400 Btu. At best, this is but a general guide—since you probably cannot estimate all these variables accurately. In the main, you will find that experience plus trial-and-error will provide a solution to the problem.

You *can* use a pot-bellied stove or a fireplace-type unit burning either wood or coal. Neither one is really a viable solution for winter-long heating. Both give off heat in their immediate area, but can do little to distribute it throughout the boat. At best they are good for spot heating for a short time, and for "atmosphere." Frankly, we simply don't trust either one, despite the fact that such units are faily common in some areas up North. You certainly wouldn't want to go to sleep or leave the boat with them burning, because of the fire hazard; not to mention the possibility of coal gas or a serious depletion of the oxygen in a covered boat.

Some people install home-type furnaces, fed from either propane or oil tanks on the dock. Assuming you have the room for these rather large units, don't mind running a vent pipe somewhere through your deck, and don't feel it takes up too much room or spoils your interior decor, fine. But if you live on a relatively modern boat in top shape, we doubt that you would want to go this route from an appearance standpoint alone, quite apart from any other objections you might have.

The two main alternatives left—which we recommend and prefer—are electric heaters, and combustion heaters specifically designed for marine use. At the time we outfitted our new boat, we had three electric heaters built in: one in the after stateroom, one in the salon, and one in the dinette area. These were of the usual blower type found on most of today's boats, each with a capacity of 1250 watts and controlled by a built-in thermostat. Prices range from $40–$125 per unit.

A few weeks of use revealed a major defect in the standard electric heater—it will not operate reliably or accurately on its simple thermostat. We purchased—on the advice of the heater manufacturer, who admitted the units were not made for much more than taking the chill off on a cool evening—high-quality, household-type thermostats. Each unit's built-in thermostat was bypassed, and a new remote thermostat hooked into the circuit. One thermostat was placed in the after stateroom, and one in the salon to control the two heaters in the salon/dinette areas. This worked beautifully, and gave highly accurate zone heating. We made sure to install the heaters near the cabin sole, since heat rises, and put the thermostats on an inner bulkhead about four feet above the sole.

Despite the manufacturer's reservations about using electric heaters for heavy-duty heating chores, they have worked remarkably well for two winters. Completely trouble-free, they maintain the interior at a comfortable temperature. On those rare occasions when a near-zero outside reading combined with a high wind, a 750-watt Thermolator heater was added for spot duty in the forward area. The Thermolator, incidentally, is an exceptionally good unit that gives off more heat for its wattage rating than any other we have tried. It's very reliable and rugged, and can be obtained with a separate thermostat.

A very inexpensive but useful idea is to burn a 100-watt bulb in the engine compartment during the winter; with the bulb burning, ours never went below 40° even on the coldest nights. In case you wondered, the water tanks never came close to freezing, and even in the coldest part of the bilge up forward—where there is no heat at all below the sole—the little water in the bilge stayed liquid.

Electric heaters, we concluded, can do a very good job of heating a boat, and at little more than an investment in some moderately priced units plus remote thermostats. The only real drawback is the operating cost; We had an electric bill that ranged from $40 to $100 per month for our 38-foot boat, depending on the severity of the weather.

A word to the wise about your power cord, plugs, and receptacles. Never use anything but equipment rated adequate for the job. Otherwise you'll not only waste money on material that won't work properly, but you'll also be plagued with constant plug and line failures. If you have a 30-amp system on your boat, use a cord rated at that output; be sure, too, that both your plugs and the marina's receptacles are also rated at a full 30 amps. You should make sure that the marina is supplying you with a full 30-amp service and sufficient voltage; some *say* they do,

but bitter experience sometimes proves otherwise.

A smart investment in security and convenience is to have a spare for each type of plug you use. You'll appreciate it some freezing-cold night when one lets go and you have a spare handy for replacement without losing power, heat, or your temper. Use nothing but twist-lock plugs; even these can occasionally burn out after extended year-round use has built up salt corrosion. We use electrical devices made by Harvey Hubbell, Inc., as do most marinas; we've found that their higher cost pays off in the end.

The combustion heater, we believe, is without question *the* best solution of all. It is professionally engineered to do the job efficiently, with reserve capacity, and built-in reliability at an economical operating cost. The ideal situation, in our opinion, is to have a good electric heating system *plus* a good combustion heater. This allows you to heat with inexpensive fuel, using a battery power source for a back-up or, if that should fail, a shore-power electric system. Surely this combination is the best of both worlds!

For a combustion heater we chose a 12-volt Shaw Marine Air Heater, manufactured by Hall Industries of Pittsburgh, Pa. It has a rated output of 15,000 Btu. The recommended fuel is kerosene, and consumption is a mere 1/7th of a gallon per hour—at 35¢ per gallon that's real economy! The installation isn't difficult if you want to tackle it on your own, though we chose to have it done, simply because we didn't have time to do it ourselves.

We bought the complete package, which included a master control panel, outside exhaust muffler, thermostat, and all necessary ducting and heat outlets. A suitable filter should be placed in the fuel line to cut contamination to a minimum. We draw fuel directly from two 55-gallon tanks on shore; if you use gravity feed, a solenoid valve must be installed to prevent flooding the unit.

This works beautifully, providing us with a warm, comfortable boat at a reasonable operating cost. Most important of all, there is enough heat radiation from the unit (located in the engine compartment) and the ducts to keep the engine compartment in the 60s. This means that we needn't winterize our engines—another source of savings. Besides, we hate to deactivate the engines when we know they have been running well at the end of the season. We would, however, recommend that you do winterize your engines *unless* you have the combination of both electric heat and combustion heater, so in the event one fails the other can take over. One system is too risky—it could go out for a lengthy period during freezing temperatures.

The other big benefit of combustion heating is that it keeps the sole in every cabin warm; 70° with the combustion heater going is far warmer and more comfortable than the same temperature with the electric heaters. We should add, too, that built-in saftey features make the combustion heater absolutely safe under *any* conditions; if anything goes wrong it simply shuts off automatically. The cost of this unit—depending on number of outlets, feet of ducting and options purchased—runs to about $600. A much larger unit, for bigger boats, puts out 60,000 Btu.

There are other combustion heaters on the market. For example, the Smith-Webasto forced-air heating and ventilation unit comes in five different models rated at 12,000 to 50,000 Btus. Prices run from about $500 to $1000, plus the cost of ducting, etc. Diesel fuel is used, with consumption running from 0.13 gallons per hour to 0.45, depending on size. These units are manufactured by Smiths Industries, North America Ltd., Don Mills, Ontario, Canada.

Way-Wolff also offers a line of excellent combustion heaters, but the main drawback to their units is that they are engineered for large boats. The output of their smallest unit is 50,000 Btus; it uses ½ gallon of fuel per hour. Another major manufacturer of marine combustion heaters is the Robert Bosch Corp.; this German company has an American distributor in Broadview, Ill.

Their units are quite similar to the Smith-Webasto models.

One word of caution in regard to any of these units: It is difficult in most areas to find a local dealer who handles them. You usually end up purchasing them directly from the manufacturer—which does have the handicap, sometimes a major one, if you have serious operating problems, of finding someone qualified to trouble-shoot and repair it. You'll find yourself learning to do routine maintenance, which is easy if there is no major trouble. Whichever unit you buy, and regardless of cost, you must be prepared to follow a more precise maintenance schedule and expect more minor troubles than you would experience with a home heating system. Why? We don't know, but we do know that is the experience of everyone we have talked to who has such units. Still, they are excellent and do a good job; you simply have to be a little more aware of their operation and somewhat handy in doing minor maintenance and repairs.

So, there you have it. Winter abroad is not an ugly, uncomfortable life, fraught with fears of ice damage, lack of heat, and other unspecified dangers ready to pounce on anyone foolish enough to tempt fate. It's just as normal and comfortable as a life ashore; the only thing you need to do is plan it out carefully, then proceed accordingly. Perhaps one of our nicest winter moments came with our first New Year's Eve afloat, when friends dressed in heavy sweaters and boots arrived in a driving blizzard to celebrate with us. To their surprise, after a short time inside our boat, they shed the sweaters and had their shoes off as they toasted the New Year in. Both their surprise at and delight in the comfort of our boat gave us, their hosts, a great feeling of satisfaction.

Lay-up time

If you have not gone south and are not planning to live aboard, your remaining choice is to winterize your power plant and plumbing and lay up. This is *not* fun. But since most damage occurs to a boat's engine when it is out of use during the winter months, you can save yourself spring headaches by following Bill Duggan's step by step instruction (See page 172). (If you engage the yard to do the job for you, specify what you want done.) Follow his advice on the head as well. Do not simply pour antifreeze into the bowl and flush it through the system. Do what the man advises if you want to protect the pump in the head from Jack Frost.

More and more owners are leaving their boats in the water all winter. Water is the ideal support, and a freeze should not damage your hull unless you start breaking up the ice. Some owners keep their boats in the water all winter and leave them uncovered. One man I know calls winter covers "boat killers" because condensation plus poor ventilation encourages rot, corrosion, and mildew. People who leave their boats uncovered frequently give it a coat of paint in the late fall, to minimize wear and tear, and they show up at the dockside from time to time to sweep off accumulated snow.

But most owners in the northern climes cover their boats. There are two reasons for this: ice crystals, blown by high winds, can give exposed surfaces a bad beating. And fresh water, seeping into seams and other crannies, can freeze, then swell, thereby causing damage.

The ideal covering for a boat is a shed on the water. Second best is a custom-made frame made of light tubular metal and a custom-fitted cover with windows and ventilating ports—the kind under which the Rosiens spend the winter. Third best is a homemade frame of scrap lumber, covered with whatever material catches your fancy. As long as it's pitched to keep the snow off the cover and allows for plenty of air to circulate—there's no reason why it should not work very well.

What now?

When you've covered your boat and time lies heavy on your hands, one way to keep them busy is with ropework. It's almost Thanksgiving and how-many-days-to-Christmas—and if you get started now, you can get some marlinespike gifts made for your boating friends. I first discovered the satisfactions of marlinespike seamanship at age 14, when I made a few Turk's heads to ornament my bamboo fishing-rod. It didn't catch any more fish, but it excited a few words of approval on the pier at Venice, California, where I daily tried to augment the evening meal with a halibut or two.

To start you off, in this chapter you'll find some magnificent illustrations by Hervey Garrett Smith for a rope ladder and a monkey fist (see page 177). There are fifty more items you can learn to make if you can lay your hands on *The Marlinespike Sailor,* which in itself is a great gift for any yachtsman.

WINTER LAY-UP

By Bill Duggan

november

Maybe you've never thought of it this way, but when you lay up your boat in the fall, you're also doing some of the fitting out she'll need next spring. By doing more of it now, you can spend more days next summer on your boat instead of beneath it.

You can't really begin planning your lay-up too soon, especially in heavily populated boating areas where storage space gets tighter every year. If you're a newcomer to a yard, reserve space well in advance and at the same time get their charges for hauling, storage, and other work. And remember to check with your insurance broker about the coverage you'll need during storage—most yards, for example, don't carry fire insurance on the boats but leave it up to the owners.

Wet or Dry Storage?

This is a question you may want to ask yourself in planning your lay-up. More owners of cruising boats are laying them up afloat or giving it

serious consideration. You'll notice more bubbler systems in use at yards and marinas, as well as at yacht clubs and private docks. There are pros and cons for both types of storage, so don't rule out the possibility of wet storage for your boat until you've checked it out in your area.

Before Hauling Out

When you've got a firm date from the yard for haul out, try to get as much loose gear as possible off your boat before she's hauled. This is usually a lot easier alongside a dock or float than buggy-lugging the stuff down a ladder in a crowded yard. Just remember to leave aboard the essentials for the run to the yard. Getting off the nonessentials will give you more working room for lay-up jobs and also reduce the possibility of theft.

Bottom Cleaning

This job is an important part of your lay-up so whether you do it yourself or have the yard do it, make sure it's done right. The bottom of your boat should be thoroughly cleaned within two hours after she's hauled. Some yards steam clean the hull while it's still in the lift or crane slings. You can use a stiff broom and a hose to get off marine growth while it's still soft and mushy. Don't make the mistake of putting it off until later or it will be like cement and nothing short of blasting will remove it.

On wooden hulls, some pros recommend sanding the bottom lightly, then after it's clean, applying a coat of bottom paint. This helps keep the wood from shrinking and the caulking from drying out, and it acts as a prime for a final coat of bottom paint before launching in the spring. On fiberglass hulls, be careful cleaning the bottom to avoid damaging the surface. If you sand a fiberglass bottom, wear a face mask to protect your eyes and lungs. A nylon scrub pad and elbow grease may help and you can also use liquid, non-scrubbing type algae removers.

Blocking and Shoring

How well the hull of your boat is supported is probably the most important single factor in winter storage. Unless the job is done right, a boat may be sprung out of shape and weakened when she gets afloat. Most yards do a careful job of this but here are the points to watch—or to follow if you're doing it yourself.

For small to medium-sized boats, a cradle well-made of husky timbers and shaped to fit the bottom of the boat will usually give enough support. On sailboats with a deep hull, fin keel, spade rudder, etc., the cradle should support the hull all along the bilges, and match the underbody. The drawback with most powerboat cradles is there's not enough room under them to work on the bottom.

For boats without cradles, bow and stern blocking should be placed under the keel first so the waterline is level, then the intermediate blocks placed. All blocking should be set up with wedges so each block can be removed for painting. Make sure the center blocks aren't higher than the end ones or you'll have trouble. Long overhangs need bow and stern supports to the ground. Always try to have your boat blocked high enough to get at the bottom without belly crawling.

While blocking supports the keel, heavy shores should keep the hull erect. These should rest on ground timbers to prevent settling. Pads on top of the shores should spread the load over the planking. Don't let anyone run shores to the underside of the sheer molding or rub strake. These can push up the sheer and start deck leaks that are hard to fix. The blocking and shoring of houseboats requires a little extra care because of their broad, flat sections and low deadrise V-bottom.

Hull Care

With your boat blocked and shored, begin at the highest point on deck washing off the seagull mess, and keep cleaning right down to the keel. Give bright work and light colors special care. If you've kept up the bright work during the summer, all it should need is a light sanding and a coat of varnish for protection. Don't let it go untouched or it will darken and discolor, requiring stripping and complete refinishing.

Draining the bilges should be your next job, knocking out the bottom plugs in a wooden hull or unscrewing them in fiberglass. This is also a good time to clean out the bilges, using a detergent or chemical bilge cleaner, then flushing

it out with a hose. Sponge up any water that may be left so it doesn't freeze and damage the hull.

If yours is a wooden hull, now is the time to check for cracked or sprung planks or loose fastenings. Make a note of their location so they can be repaired before launching. It's also a good idea to check on the caulking so you'll know how much work needs doing in the spring. On fiberglass hulls, check for cracks and deep gouges so they can be fixed before someone slaps on a coat of bottom paint, when they'll be out of your sight and mind.

While you're checking the hull, remember to inspect the hardware—the shafts, props, rudders, trim tabs, and anodes. Start with the anodes, if any are on the shaft or rudders, and work your way forward. If any of the zinc is eaten away, note the size and shape for replacements. Check the propellers for nicks or bent blades and if you find any, have the wheels pulled for reconditioning or, if too far gone, replacement. Check the rudder action for excess play in the linkage or cables. Trim tabs can be damaged backing into a dock or piling, so look them over for bent or broken parts. And while you're back there make a mental note to seal the exhaust tubes after the engines are winterized.

The depth sounder transducer and ground plate are small items, but important. Make sure the fitting on the transducer is secure, and that the ground plate hasn't pulled away.

Sterndrive Unit

If you have this type of power, have the yard carefully follow the manufacturer's instructions for winter storage. Some yards recommend removing the units and storing them under cover. In any event, here's a checklist of the major points to watch in winterizing sterndrives—and these may vary slightly depending on the engine manufacturer:

1. Check entire unit for damaged or loose parts that may need repair or replacement.

2. Drain all water from the sterndrive unit.

3. Check the oil in the housing for any water contamination. If there is any, the leak should be found and repaired—it may be a leaky seal.

4. Check and refill the lubricant in the upper and lower gear cases, making sure the sealing gaskets are in place.

5. Check the boot (rubber seal at transom) for brittleness, cracks, and wear. If you find any, have a new boot installed before launching. Some yards install a new boot every season, regardless—a good idea.

6. Remove the propeller and check for damage. Lubricate shaft.

7. While it's off, check the condition of the zinc anode collar and replace it if necessary. Put the prop back on.

8. Lubricate the tilt, shift-booster assembly, and steering linkage. These may vary for different sterndrives.

9. If the sterndrive is removed by the yard, make sure the transom opening is covered and sealed against the weather.

10. Clean the entire unit and touch up any damaged or corroded areas with matching paint.

With most of the outside work on your boat done, you can now move aboard and get the interior ready for winter storage. It's a good idea to plan these jobs in logical steps, working down from abovedeck to the bilge.

Abovedeck Care

Begin with the flying bridge and take off as much of the electronics—depth sounder, radiotelephone, etc.—as can be disconnected. Store it ashore, and have any necessary repairs made during the winter. Remember to protect the instrument panel and engine controls on the bridge with covers, and take off seat cushions.

On the deck, clean out all loose stuff from lockers and under seats—lines, fenders, life preservers, etc.—and store them ashore in a dry place. Leave locker doors and seat covers partly open (chocked if necessary) for ventilation. If you're a sailor, protect the winches with canvas covers or plastic containers that fit upside down over them.

If any hatches on deck, or ports, have leaked during the summer, add them to your list of essential repairs.

Engine Lay-Up

With the abovedeck work done, you can now move below. Begin your lay-up with the engine—

a major part of the investment in a powerboat and something that should get all the winterizing necessary to protect it. While you may not do the job yourself, here's a brief rundown on what most yards usually do, depending on the power aboard and the manufacturer (his lay-up instructions should be followed to the letter).

Gasoline Engines

1. Change oil and oil filter using an engine oil supplement for a short run-in time before the change and another after it to circulate new oil.

2. Shut off the fuel line at the tank, remove the flame arrestor and "fog" the engine by running it at a fast idle while pouring a half can of rust preventive in carburetor. Pour in rest of can to stall engine.

3. Remove the spark plugs and ignition coil wire and squirt *no more than* one ounce of crankcase detergent/rust inhibitor in each cylinder, replace plugs. (Adding any more inhibitor may cause hydraulic lock, resulting in bent connecting rods and piston damage.)

4. Clean the flame arrestor core in kerosene, replace it on the carburetor, and seal the screen of the arrestor with waterproof tape.

5. Drain the fuel tank, fuel line, and carburetor—unless you're adding a fuel conditioner to them. Some yards recommend topping off gas tanks to prevent condensation, so check your insurance and the yard.

Diesel Engines

1. Drain engine oil and replace lube filter, then refill and run engine.

2. Rustproof the lubricating system by squirting rustproofing oil into the blower inlet and cranking the engine with the starter.

3. Drain all fuel from tanks and filter, put a gallon of rustproofing oil in each tank, and seal the vent with tape. Replace the filters, prime the fuel system by operating feed pump, and run engine with starter.

4. Remove injectors and spray ¼ pint of lubricating oil in cylinder bores, dividing oil among all cylinders. Crank engine a full turn with starter. Replace injectors.

5. Remove air filter(s) and any piping. Seal air intake with tape, clean out breather pipes, and seal ends. Remove exhaust pipes at engine manifold and seal manifold ports.

Engine Cooling System

Raw Water Cooling System

1. Flush system with fresh water—especially on boats that operate in salt water.

2. Drain system completely by removing drain plugs on block and manifolds.

3. Replace plugs, refill system with 60% water, 40% antifreeze (alcohol type, not glycol). Run engine to circulate antifreeze.

4. Remove impeller from raw water pump to avoid damage in lay-up.

Fresh Water Cooling System

1. Drain fresh water side, flush with clean water with rustproofing agent in it while running the engine with the starter to circulate.

2. Drain raw water (sea water) side and reverse flush, drain again.

3. Refill both sides of system with 60% water, 40% antifreeze as above—run engine again to circulate.

4. Remove impeller from raw water pump. (Fresh water impeller isn't removable.)

Auxiliary Generator Sets

If you have one aboard give it the same treatment as the main engine, including draining, refilling with antifreeze, changing oil, etc.

Batteries

Store all storage batteries in a warm dry place ashore. Many yards have a room for battery storage and an automatically-regulated charger for keeping them up.

Seacocks

All those inside the hull should be opened. Make sure no water has collected around them. After cleaning and using graphite on them, make sure they operate smoothly and are closed when you finish the lay-up.

Galley, Head, and Cabin

These are the places where a little more time spent on the lay-up will help get you afloat sooner next summer. By removing and storing ashore as many of the furnishings it's convenient to transfer, you'll have more working room in the spring for painting, or improvements. Things like deck chairs, tables, cushions, lamps, television, and radios can be stored ashore. This is also a good time to have your fire extinguishers checked and recharged. Remember to clean out all foul weather gear and extra clothing from lockers and leave the doors open for ventilation. Take ashore all bedding and foam mattresses for cleaning and laundering. And don't forget the lockers under the berths.

If your deckhouse or cabin sole is carpeted, take up the carpet for cleaning ashore. Then remove the floorboards for ventilation during the lay-up.

Galley Lay-Up

Get the ball rolling here by removing all the stuff that piles up during the summer—clean out all food from lockers and the refrigerator. Wash the refrigerator out with a bicarbonate of soda solution and leave the doors open to vent it. Dishes, glassware, pots, and cutlery belong ashore for cleaning and storage.

The stove should be laid up by shutting off the fuel line. If you're using butane or propane gas, remove the tank from the boat. For alcohol, drain the tank and don't leave any fuel in containers aboard. Give the sink some care, draining it and the faucet pump, then closing the outlet seacock and filling the pump and sink trap with antifreeze. Break the unions on the water supply line to the sink and drain your freshwater tanks completely. If you have a pressure water system, drain the tank then pour in a non-toxic antifreeze like "Winter-Gard" (blue color) and run the pump until you get "blue" from the faucet. Hot water heater systems, purifiers, and distilling systems should all be drained.

The Head

Start your lay-up here by cleaning out lockers and especially cans from under the sink—they'll rust. Open the outlet seacocks from the sink and shower (if you have one) to drain them, then close the seacocks and fill the sink pump and trap with antifreeze.

Toilet and Sanitation System

Winterizing these depends on the kind of system you have aboard. The best way is to follow the manufacturer's instructions for lay-up. The major cause of most marine toilet failures is improper winter lay-up. Here are some simple but effective steps you can follow to avoid trouble next spring:

1. Close the inlet seacock. Remove the inlet hose from the pump housing and temporarily attach a short hose to the inlet.

2. Pour a quart of antifreeze (not anti-leak type) into an empty coffee can, insert the open end of the temporary hose in the can, and pump the head until fluid runs down the inside of the bowl. This means the fluid has been circulated and is being pumped out the outlet seacock.

3. Close the outlet seacock and leave the antifreeze in the head all winter.

These steps will protect both the inlet and discharge sides of the pump. Just pouring antifreeze in the bowl protects only the discharge side.

Don't put oil, kerosene, gasoline, or alcohol in the bowl or pump of a marine toilet or you'll ruin the valves.

Forepeak and Sail Locker

Take all lines and gear ashore for checking and replacement if needed. All sail bags should be taken ashore, the sails examined, and any repairs made during the lay-up.

Framework and Covers

If you're putting a winter cover on your boat, you'll get a better fit and the job will be easier if you first take down the whip antenna, cruiser or light mast, searchlights, etc. These can be stowed belowdecks or ashore. The same thing is true for abovedeck canvas, such as awnings, cockpit curtains, and dodgers.

With the investment in your boat and the blood, sweat, and tears you may put in its lay-up, you should keep it carefully covered during the winter. It will pay to have a light but strong, easily-erected framework that fits the deck structure of your boat exactly. This should have a husky ridge pole with well-braced cross pieces and an overhang at bow and stern for ventilation. Make sure there are no sharp edges to chafe through the cover.

You can rent a cover from some of the larger yards. If you're supplying your own, it should fit over the framework without hard stretching but be tight enough to avoid sagging that forms pockets to collect rain water and snow. A cover should be at least two feet longer than your deck length and four feet wider than the beam. The sides should be carried down to the waterline if possible.

Canvas is still the most popular fabric for covers because it breathes—permitting free air circulation that reduces condensation inside the boat. A good cover fabric is 13 oz Army duck which comes already treated to resist mildew and rot—but it should be fireproofed. You can use synthetic fabrics like the new laminates of nylon and vinyl but these require more ventilation than canvas.

Ventilation

No matter what the cover material, make sure there is enough ventilation. The great enemy of a boat during lay-up is dampness created by condensation in the hull. With a wooden boat, this can produce dry rot, and with fiberglass, sweating inside the hull can warp joiner work, damage electronics, and mildew fabrics. Whatever ventilation system is used it should allow a free exchange inside all spaces, otherwise the cover acts like an incubator for dampness. Make sure there's space between the cover sides and the hull. The cover itself should have vents built in at the highest point as well as at the bow and stern.

With all the time and effort you spend on a lay-up, it's a good idea to see that it's doing the job by making an occasional inspection of your boat during the winter. You may be able to spot and fix something that could cause trouble come spring.

GIFTS TO MAKE FOR XMAS

By Hervey Garrett Smith

november

The Monkey's Fist

"Capt'n Al," asked the small boy, "what's a heaving line?"

"Why that's a lifeline for sailors when they's seasick," the captain replied.

"But what's the ball on the end for?"

Capt'n Al shifted his pipe to the port side of his other tooth. "It's a gag, son, just a gag!"

Believe it or not, there are a surprising number of yachtsmen who do not own a heaving line, have never used one, or do not even know what it is. It is true that one may sail for a dozen seasons without meeting a situation requiring its use, but when that day comes the heaving line may save a life and every well-found yacht carries one on deck where it is handy. Every yachtsman should know how to make one and how to use it. An hour's practice on the lawn is sufficient to acquire the proper technique in throwing it.

Bradford's *Glossary Of Sea Terms* defines a heaving line as "a light line weighted at its end to aid in throwing to a pier or another vessel, as a messenger for a heavy line." In my opinion most yachtsmen can lay their craft in to a pier close enough to toss a dockline ashore, and those who cannot probably are inexperienced and could not throw a heaving line anyhow. But even the expert has been known to stall a motor or get in stays, and when that happens a heaving line can prevent serious damage to both his pride and his yacht.

More important, to my mind, is the use of the heaving line in going to the aid of craft in distress. It generally happens in foul weather, a capsized sailboat with three kids hanging on her rail, or a motor boat with dead engines and wallowing broadside in the trough. You want to put a line aboard without damaging either your or the other fellow's boat, and with rough seas and a high wind such a task calls for seamanship. While approaching, the heaving line is bent to a cable or towline and then coiled carefully, the coil held loosely in the left hand, and the weighted end swinging in the right. You come up to windward of the disabled craft, thus making a lee for him, and the wind helps to carry the line straight to him. An underhanded swing does it, and do not swing it around your head like a cowboy if you want an accurate throw.

A proper heaving line should be about seventy-five feet long for a yacht of moderate size, longer for a large vessel. It should be light enough to throw easily, yet strong enough to haul a man through the water, and five-sixteenths inch manila is about right. In order to give weight to the end of the line so that it will carry some distance a knot of considerable size is required. Since time immemorial the monkey's fist has been the standard knot used for this purpose, and no one has been able to come up with a better one.

To make the monkey's fist lay a bight of the line across the fingers of the left hand, about three and one-half feet from the end, holding the standing part with the left thumb. Take three turns about the fingers, which are separated as shown in the first illustration on the following page. Now take three turns at right angles, as in illustrations 2 and 3, through the fingers and about the first three turns. At this point the knot is removed from the fingers and a third set of three turns is made about the second set, and inside the first set. The fourth illustration shows this final

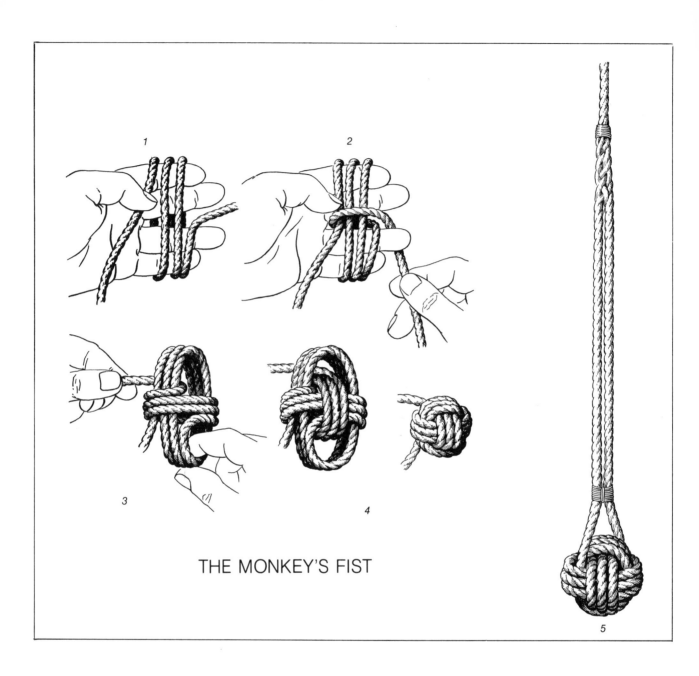

THE MONKEY'S FIST

step, and alongside is the finished knot with all the slack taken out.

Now this results in a knot that is roughly cube shaped and rather small, hollow inside. It lacks the weight necessary for throwing any distance, so it is necessary to load it. This is accomplished by placing a rubber ball, a smooth round stone, or similar spherical weight inside the knot before it is worked taut. A ball of lead foil is ideal, for it can be made as heavy or light as you choose. This is a problem calling for serious thought and delicate judgment, as the heavier the weight, in reason, the easier it is to throw, but out of consideration to the man on the receiving end who will catch it in good faith there is the question of how much weight shall be called sporting. So be sure it is heavy enough, but do not lay yourself open to charges of premeditated mayhem.

When the knot is loaded and drawn up firmly it assumes a spherical shape, and you should have an end about eighteen inches long left protruding. This end is brought down alongside of, and side spliced into, the standing part. Then a seizing is clapped on both parts close up under the knot, and don't forget to put a palm-and-needle whipping on the other end of the line.

A Rope Ladder with a New Twist

Almost every yachtsman at some time in his career feels that he must have a rope ladder, primarily for swimming from his boat. This is a perfectly logical desire which can be satisfied in two ways. He can walk into the nearest marine supply store and buy a serviceable rope ladder for less than ten dollars, or if he's so constituted he can take some salvaged material and spend seventy-five dollars worth of time making his own. It is to the man who chooses the latter method that these remarks are directed.

Common rope ladders have wooden rungs or steps and are called Jacob's ladders, have been used for centuries as boarding ladders, and in modern times as swimming ladders. Generally speaking they are bulky and awkward to stow, although otherwise very practical. However the ladder I am showing here is definitely not a Jacob's ladder, but an honest-to-codfish rope ladder, made with a single length of rope and nothing else. It is a very ancient form, yet strangely enough few yachtsmen are familar with it. As a swimming ladder it is excellent since the rope rungs are large in diameter and comfortable to bare feet.

I would like to suggest another use for it which

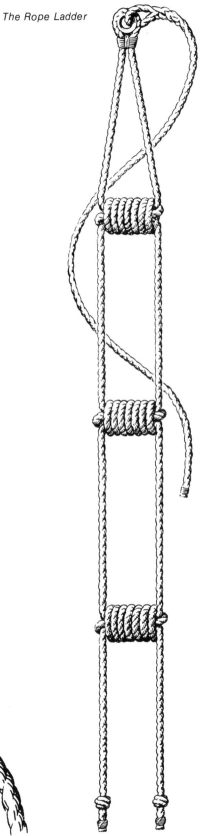

The Rope Ladder

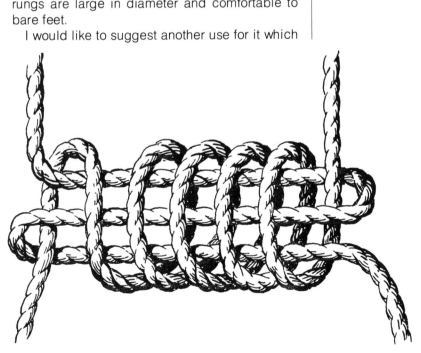

is strictly my own idea and as far as I know original. Instead of going aloft in a bosun's chair why not use a long rope ladder for an easy climb? It need be only as long as the luff of your mainsail, and when hoisted aloft by the main halliard, with the lower ends secured to the boom or gooseneck, you can quickly reach any part of your spar with little effort. On a recent afternoon I made ten trips to the mainmast head in a bosun's chair on a luff tackle, hoisting myself up and lowering away laboriously. Each time I seemed to gain in weight, and on the last trip I went aloft slowly and came down rather fast, finally collapsing on deck like a ruptured jellyfish. Now had I used one of Smith's Patent Mast Climbers the job would have been easy. Of course there's nothing beats a bosun's chair if you are going aloft to stay awhile, but when you go up to take off a fitting, bring it down to bore a hole, go up and put it back, come down on deck for the tool you forgot to take on the first trip, and so on ad infinitum, it sort of wears you down.

However you wish to use it, this is an easy ladder to make. First decide how long you want it and the number of steps required, about fifteen inches maximum or twelve inches minimum for spacing. You will need a piece of half inch manila twice as long as the ladder, plus about three feet for each step. Better add a little extra to be sure. Middle the rope and put in a thimble with a stout round seizing. To start the first rung or step, pass a bight of the left hand leg to the right around the right leg, then pull another bight across to the left. Now take the right hand leg and make seven or eight round turns about the three parts of the two bights just formed and finally pass the end down through the lower bight at the left. The illustration, I think, shows the sequence fairly clearly. Draw the parts up as tight as they will go and you will see that the step just formed is stiff, bulky and just wide enough to fit your instep. While I don't doubt that it could be made wide enough to stand on with both feet, the step would undoubtedly sag to an uncomfortable degree. To the best of my knowledge this ladder has always been made as a "one-footer."

Measure down the left leg for the next step. Again start from the left side with two bights as before, but notice that what is now the left leg was originally the right leg. The reason I call your attention to this is that you thus are expending the same amount of rope in each leg, and when you reach the end of the ladder it comes out even. So always work from the left side.

To finish off the lower end of the ladder you have your choice of several methods. The legs should extend at least twelve inches below the bottom step. They can be finished off with a palm and needle whipping, or a fancy manrope, lanyard or Matthew Walker knot, or the two ends can be short-spliced together to form a loop.

To my mind the most important feature of this ladder is the ease with which it can be stowed. Being made entirely of rope, and not over five or six inches wide at the most, it can actually be coiled down compactly and crammed into almost any shape of compartment. The rope rungs will not loosen or slip and are safer than wooden ones, since your foot is in effect held in a stirrup.

Armchair cruising

Last month, with the wind whistling up your sleeves, you may have felt a touch of coolness toward your boat, you brute. You couldn't get away from her winter berth fast enough after pouring the last drop of antifreeze.

But by now, that old call of the sea has returned, and you find yourself spending more and more time with your charts, parallel rulers, dividers, and cruising guides. Julius Wilensky, the cruising connoisseur, plots his summer passages during the winter months, down to the last ETA (estimated time of arrival) and guest. It's a good way to make the most of your boating time and to spread a little of the sunshine into the bleaker season.

For escape reading, there is nothing more intoxicating than a chart. Especially an old sea-sprayed chart, with special pencil notes that mean something only to you. Next are charts that take you into unfamiliar waters, and books and yachting magazine articles about exotic cruises you'll never take . . . but who knows?

For the biggest armchair powerboat cruise of all, take a look at *Voyaging Under Power,* a book by Robert P. Beebe, which you can order from Seven Seas Press, 32 Union Square, New York 10003. Upon his retirement from the Navy (where he was the navigator of the carrier *Saratoga* in World War II), Captain Beebe decided to design a "retirement boat" capable of making an ocean passage. Nothing remarkable about this, except that what Beebe had in mind was "a seagoing motorboat." Now, while there is literature galore about long-distance voyaging under sail, there has been almost nothing published about voyaging on small boats under power. (Nonetheless, there were four ocean crossings by small powerboats between 1902(!) and 1937.)

Beebe set about designing a powerboat with unique capabilities to make use of the long-distance environment. For example, where the sailing vessel looks for strong winds, Beebe's craft exploits the calms and doldrums. In the 50-footer, *Passagemaker,* Beebe and his wife cruised three-fourths of the way round the world in an ambience much different from that of an ocean sail. Beebe writes:

> The ideal crew for an extended sailing voyage would all be experienced in sail, young enough and rugged enough not to mind months of standing watch-and-watch, steering in an open spray-drenched cockpit, setting and taking in sail in the middle of the night. It is an activity for youth. . . . This is where the seagoing motorboat comes in. Stabilized against rolling—the curse of the ordinary motorboat—she steams along in the calmest weather she can find at a rate that exceeds the average possible for a much larger sailing vessel. With the autopilot performing all the work, her single watch-stander is essentially a lookout. For this, no experience is necessary, because the only duty, until the watch-stander is qualified, is to call the captain when sighting *anything.*

Read on, and you will see that another man's voyage can be a trip for you.

OPERATING A SEAGOING MOTORBOAT

By Robert P. Beebe

december

"Operating" is a very broad term that covers just about every activity aboard a seagoing vessel once it gets underway. We cannot even begin to list *all* the captain and crew should know or should have done before they leave the dock. Instead, we will make comments on certain activities and functions which experience has shown to be important, or in which we differ from the standard texts, or where we can offer a better way of doing things.

The great majority of yachtsmen who acquire a motorboat with real seagoing ability have already had years of experience. Many have switched to power after years in sail. At any rate, they have long since graduated from "basic training."

But there are some skippers coming into the field without this basic training and without prior experience at sea. What advice can we give them?

While there is no substitute for time at sea in the making of a competent seaman, the vast store of knowledge built up over years of experi-

ence by mariners of all nations is available in books. These books should be part of the boat's "equipment" from the start. The skipper should be so familiar with their contents that he knows just where to look for any information he needs. Courses in navigation and seamanship are available commercially, and free from such excellent organizations as the U.S. Power Squadrons and the Coast Guard Auxiliary. By volunteering for and becoming proficient as an observer in predicted log racing, a good deal of "underway time" can be acquired quickly. This activity is particularly valuable for the example experienced operators will give in operating at the highest standards of navigation, steering, and speed control.

As for the sea time, there is just no substitute for getting out there. Experience as a crew member should be actively sought. If a power voyage is not available and a sail voyage is—grab it. You will learn much on either. Four of the people who have made long voyages in *Passagemaker* now skipper their own little ships.

With the commissioning of your own vessel, you should lay out a definite program for advancing your experience, doing a little more each time you go out, until a passage of several days is no longer a novelty or a cause for concern.

In observing neophyte skippers, I've noticed that they generally show wisdom by starting slowly, with respect for the sea and an understanding of their own limitations, but when finally they are qualified to take off on a passage of some days, they are somewhat reluctant to do so. This is largely a reluctance to trust their navigating ability out of sight of land. As this seems to be a common affliction, it is a good starting point for our comments on navigation.

Navigation

These days, the paperwork required to work out celestial navigation fixes has been so simplified that there is quite literally "nothing to it." This is in marked contrast to the days of my initial instruction in the art, when the only connection between the earth and the stars was a horrendous term entitled "The Right Ascension of the Mean Sun Plus 12 Hours."

New, shorter methods of navigation came into use during World War II. It might be supposed that in such a huge ship as the *USS Saratoga* we would navigate in very formal fashion to the greatest accuracy. Actually, the reverse was true. The navigation department of an aircraft carrier is under tremendous pressure for accurate fixes day and night on a continuous basis to support air operations. So we concentrated on the quickest methods—which were also the easiest. The routine we developed then is the same one I use today and have taught to many students aboard *Passagemaker*. In each of her voyages, the navigating students made all the landfalls with no assistance from me. If they could do it, you can do it.

This reluctance to "take your foot off the beach" is sometimes hard to understand. It is near the shore that a vessel is in danger. The tales are legion, especially on the Pacific Coast, of vessels lost while hugging the shore for no good reason.

It is well for the reluctant navigator to remember that the only fix that *really* counts is the last one before landfall. In fact, the only difference between a 24-hour passage and one of several days is that instead of coming back in, you just keep going. The navigating done is to show you how well you are doing and what small adjustments have to be made in your courses and speeds. So even if that long voyage seems formidable, just take it a day at a time and it will not be an overwhelming problem.

The power vessel has advantages over sail cruisers when taking sights, because it is high-sided, steadier, and usually offers better shelter for sight-taking. We found we always could rely on getting good results, regardless of weather, when stars were visible. Because of the superior accuracy of star sights, it was our practice to use them almost exclusively, turning to sun lines only when necessary. I do not agree with the statements made in certain cruising and navigation books that star sights are too difficult to take from small craft: I have taken them often in a 36-foot yawl. The watch-standers, being relieved of steering duty or sail tending, have plenty of time to do their own navigation. When taking sun lines has to be the main reliance (as on *Passagemaker*'s trip from the Azores to Ireland when we never saw a star), it was easy for the watch to get the five to seven sun lines needed for a good day's fix.

I have worked a good deal on organizing

sight-taking so a single person can do it without having a recorder to help. This is essential with a one-man watch for morning stars, and desirable always. Recording is not easy and requires training to do properly. It is a good idea to dispense with a recorder, so you know where the responsibility lies.

The latest setup is shown in the accompanying photo. It consists of an 8″ × 3¼″ piece of plywood that is provided with two elastic straps to hold it to your forearm. The Huer 24-hour-dial, stop-second action clock is fastened at one end, and 3″ × 5″ index cards are held by rubber bands at the other end (cards stand wetting better than paper and are less affected by wind). The other item of special equipment is a penlight worn around the neck.

The drill goes about like this: The clock is set to correct GMT just before taking sights, a step much facilitated by the stop-second action. When a sight is taken, you say "Mark!" to yourself and start mentally counting seconds until you have your eye on the clock and can read the second hand. Subtract mentally the seconds you have counted and record the reading—always seconds first, then minutes, and then the hour, the body, and the altitude. At night hold the penlight in your mouth to point at the watch and sextant. A two-cell penlight gives just enough light to read by, yet not so much as to spoil your night vision.

For star sights, it's a good idea to make up a diagram showing the altitude and azimuth of selected stars as taken from the star-finder *HO 2102D,* or its commercial equivalent. The bearings are shown relative to the ship's bow for the course you are on as indicated by the central double-line arrow. You can then preset your sextant to the approximate altitude and look in the right direction. That gives you the maximum chance to spot the star quickly while it is still too light for general sky search in the evening. Of course, the lighter the sky the better the horizon. I always use the above method and as a result have never really learned any constellations at all. I am convinced that the emphasis placed on learning them by many navigation books is wasted effort. If you wait until you can find stars by constellation in the evening, you are bound to have horizon trouble because of darkness.

A most useful aid is a table that combines the various corrections for sights for the height-of-

Passagemaker *on trial trip off Singapore.*

Passagemaker's *Data Board. Linford Beebe at the helm.*

eye you will use. You thus have a single correction for each sight.

Enough on navigation. As was mentioned earlier, these days the paperwork involved is so simple anyone should be able to navigate anywhere with a few weeks of drill and a little practical experience.

Communications

Passagemaker did not have a radio transmitter during the time I owned her. There was little point in having one when we left Singapore because once you leave the U.S. coast, with the 2–3 MHz type of transmitter, nobody is listening. There are supposed to be stations in the Mediterranean and elsewhere, but I never heard of anyone getting a message through to one of them.

Today, the shift to VHF and Single Side Band (SSB) changes things considerably. The bridge-to-bridge capability of VHF is useful. On *Mona Mona* we discussed weather with several ships, for instance. But not all the ships we called answered at sea. VHF was useful in harbors, in Panama, and at some marinas. I would certainly have it nowadays.

As for SSB, a high-seas set with capabilities from 3–22 MHz would assure your reaching a marine operator in the U.S. from anywhere. There has been a marked rise in the number of amateur licensed operators on cruising yachts where the SSB sets have been particularly successful. Active nets exist in such areas as the west coast of Central America where they contribute to safety and convenience in such matters as ordering spares. The SSCA has details on these nets. Altogether the shift to VHF and SSB will be a boon to the long-range voyager.

We had a regular Aldis signaling lamp aboard *Passagemaker* and we used it quite a bit on our first voyage from Singapore to Suez as we were almost constantly in sight of shipping in the busy sea lanes. While most of our use was just for gossip, especially with lonesome third mates on the midwatch, it would have been handy if we had had any real need to communicate. As a standby for VHF as well as the Xenon flasher discussed later, it is my recommendation that an Aldis lamp be included in the ship's outfit, and that you practice sending and receiving flashing light.

Safety at Sea

Collision Avoidance

Anyone who goes far to sea these days should be aware of two things: First, the number of ships transiting the oceans is increasing by leaps and bounds; second, the speed of ships is increasing.

What does this mean to power voyagers running at eight knots in a 40- to 50-foot boat? Obviously, it means the watch-standers must be more alert as the time available for evasive action is shortened, and there is the real possibility that the ship you've spotted will not sight you at all.

All this is compounded because many ships of all nations are running with a one-man watch, a watch that has other duties besides looking out. Even following good procedure—before taking his eyes off the sea to do something like writing up the log, the watch-stander should sweep the sea ahead very carefully with binoculars—the lights of a yacht most probably will not be visible from the distance the ship will cover while the watch-stander is not on the lookout.

You will have no trouble seeing the ship; the range lights of ships these days are much brighter than the law requires. They come up over the horizon looking like searchlights on a clear night. What is needed is some way *the ship* can see *you* as soon as possible. There is only one light available to a yacht that will do this—the Xenon flasher. I strongly recommend that you equip your vessel with one. The flasher should not be used except for its intended and legal purpose: as the "flare up light" allowed by the rules "in order to attract attention."

Even with this equipment, the only safe policy, in my opinion, is to assume *nobody* can see you, and act accordingly. This means staying out of everyone's way by early and extensive changes of course if there is any possibility of another vessel coming close. In fact, any changes in course or speed should be large so they will show up quickly if you are being watched on radar.

For radar and reduced visibility it is essential you have some really good radar reflectors. It is not generally appreciated how sensitive "corner reflectors" are to the slightest deviation from a 90-degree angle. The sides must be rigidly held to this. The folding type of reflector is hardly more useful than a big tin can.

If you have a radar on your vessel, you owe it to your crew to obtain training in plotting, both on the maneuvering board and the scope so you will have a clear picture of what is happening, and can instruct the rest of the crew in this skill.

The Man-and-Wife Boat

Here, we are concerned about the safety of this type of operation.

Sailing yachts with crews of two, or even one, have been sailing the seas for many years. By and large, their casualty rate has not been great enough to cause concern, but they do go missing occasionally. There are good reasons to suspect some of these casualties were run down by large ships which never saw them. The problem of taking evasive action in a small sailing vessel can be compounded by sudden calms or wind shifts. So from this point of view the full-power craft is safer.

The danger of being run down varies in different parts of the oceans. For instance, from Los Angeles to Panama, the coast has an almost constant curve toward the east, causing everyone to hug the coast most of the way. On a passage I made in 1973 there was almost always traffic in sight. In the South Pacific, the traffic is still quite light. In the North Pacific, and to a lesser extent in the North Atlantic, new routing services to take advantage of weather have resulted in some scattering of shipping away from the traditional (and direct) great circle routes, so ships can be found all over the area.

With only two watch-standers, alertness is bound to deteriorate when a passage lasts more than a few days. There are some things that can be done to assist in this matter. Small radars are available that will sound an alarm if there is any contact within a certain minimum distance of the vessel. It is expected that this feature will soon become more common and cheaper. Although electronic experts keep saying it is difficult and costly, it still appears possible that without owning a full radar set, you can have a relatively cheap receiver that would alert you to the fact a radar is operating nearby. If this receiver had a reasonable bearing capability it would be a good substitute for radar on many small craft.

As another alert, a clock could be rigged to sound an alarm at any interval desired unless a reset button was pressed regularly. If this is rigged also to stop the engine, believe me, it will bring all hands up, all standing!

The idea that a fully alert watch should be stood in the dark with less alertness during the day has been advanced in several places and appears to have some merit as making the best of a bad situation. Of course, a full watch list of at least three watch-standers is even better. It is worth some inconvenience and added expense to achieve this on long passages.

Maneuvering

Some prospective owners, while conceding the superiority of the single-screw vessel in range and propeller-protection, still want twin screws to make the vessel easier to maneuver around docks. The twins do this, of course, but not by much in a proper vessel, and by proper vessel we mean one without an excessive A/B (above water/below water) ratio. The chief use of twin screws is to neutralize maneuvering problems caused by windage. Many popular makes of coastal motorboats have A/B ratios of 4.5 and higher, and are practically unmanageable in a good breeze of wind; *their* twin screws are a necessity.

But a seagoing vessel with an A/B ratio of about 2.6 should handle easily with a single screw under all conditions. The owners of single-screw vessels whom I know all have developed great competence in putting the ship right where they want it, and they take considerable pride in this ability. As one said to me, "Twin screws take all the sport out of it."

Heavy-Weather Handling

The literature of sail cruising is loaded with advice and examples about handling vessels in heavy weather. For power voyaging there is not nearly as much advice available and what there is seems largely concerned with coastal motorboats and "recreational" boats—such as fishing launches. Some of this advice is applicable, particularly about running inlets and handling in thunder squalls. But for a small motor craft a thousand miles at sea, not much has been written—the experience is just not there.

Passagemaker's experience may be of some

use, though her gales were not too severe. Her first hit us at the south end of the Red Sea with winds of just about gale force, around 30 knots from astern. The problem was that we had to head about 20 degrees across the wind to avoid going ashore somewhere near Mocha. And we were uncertain about how far off downwind we could safely go without tending to broach. It soon became clear that we could head as far off as we needed, except before the very biggest waves. As a matter of prudence, we took these from dead aft. It was not until this wind died out after sunset that I realized it had never occurred to me to slow down: We ran at 7.5 knots the whole time.

Our hurricane off Bermuda was a strange experience. The sky became overcast and it started to rain, the barograph went down like a rock and the wind increased. The trouble was that to us the wind appeared to be from the wrong direction for a tropical storm. It turned out later the storm had formed *over* Bermuda and headed northeast so it was already north of us. At the time, we had sail up and ran off with the wind on the port quarter, which of course is the wrong tack for a tropical storm. The rain was so heavy it flattened the waves, but as closely as we could determine, the wind reached 55 knots. It had been 85 knots at Bermuda but was dying rapidly. We eventually entered what must have been the remnants of the storm's center because the barograph started back up as rapidly as it had gone down. We were able to go to power only and head directly for Bermuda in a dying sea.

A day ahead of us, a yacht (a 77-foot motorsailer) had a very hard time of it, but she came through undamaged.

Our second hurricane was encountered on the passage from Sandy Hook, New York, to Delaware Bay; this storm was coming up the coast. The weather bureau said we could beat it if we started *right now;* but what they didn't tell us was that conditions were building up for a typical nor'easter, in addition. The result was plenty of northeast wind all night as we ran down the coast. At about 0200, when I took over, we took down the sail and continued to run with the wind and sea on the quarter, our only choice. She rode the big swells easily, and we had no real problems in a wind that got as high as about 50 knots.

Our worst gale, which I noted earlier, was encountered off Cape Mendocino, California. After a summer in British Columbia, we were going down the Pacific Coast toward San Francisco where we had an on-board party planned for the next day. The night before, the wind started to increase from astern. By 0300 it was bad enough for me to be called. I was on the bridge for the next 27 hours. Conditions were not too bad until dawn. After that, the winds gradually increased in strength until they reached full gale. This was not a storm but a gradient wind, powered by the hot interior valleys of the West making a "thermal low," while the cold ocean air rushed in to fill the vacuum. It soon became so strong I felt it advisable to take the wheel and head off directly before the waves at low speed. Around sunset, the waves began to "roll," giving them a most frightening aspect. I was concerned about being able to stay dead before the waves after dark on a moonless night. Much to my relief, I found this was no problem: The waves could be seen well enough to achieve this.

Thus we kept on southward. The trouble was San Francisco was southeast, getting more easterly the farther we went. I had visions of the gale sweeping us right past the Golden Gate and putting us back in Monterey again. But after midnight, the wind gradually started to slacken and we could steer across it a bit more each hour, until the course was attained for San Francisco. Shortly after dawn we were steaming through a windless sea. The party was a great success. We were on schedule despite a difficult night.

Now, in all these incidents we ran off before the weather; in the last, dead before it, in the others, across the wind to varying degrees, at all times using flopperstoppers. Would it be possible to do this in winds of higher velocities, say in the 65–75 knot range? The answer is, I don't know. I rather suspect that in those conditions, the recommendations for sailing vessels under such "survival conditions," found in books on the subject, would be applicable to power vessels as well. But the essence of the argument—and there is an argument—about the best methods of meeting heavy weather is that running off raises the danger of "broaching," while lying "a-hull," that is, with engines stopped and the drifting vessel allowed to take what attitude she will to the seas, raises grave danger of heavy damage from breaking seas because, in this situation, almost every vessel will lie broadside to the seas.

Broaching means the boat turns uncontrollably beam to the wind and sea. It is caused by going too fast down the face of a wave that is coming up from astern. The bow buries deeply with enormous increase of resistance forward. The rudder is unable to provide the force necessary to stop the turning motion that results. The turn is so quickly made that large centrifugal forces are generated which, combined with a breaking wave pushing against the side, can capsize the vessel. The same forces in extreme conditions have also caused some vessels to "pitch-pole," or turn end-over-end.

It is these end results of "broaching" that have caused some experts to urge "lying a-hull." They point out that the forces acting on a hull lying broadside to the seas are very much less if the vessel is stopped than they are with the addition of centrifugal forces from the sudden broaching turn. This should make the vessel less liable to capsize. If it does, it would be better to be rolled over from the broadside position, with inertial forces helping to bring the vessel upright through a full roll, than it would be to chance the damage from "pitch-poling." Actual incidents are cited to show the difference in danger and damage.

All of this sounds quite grim, and of course it is. Although many professional seamen have gone to sea all their lives without meeting such conditions, nevertheless one must realize that it can happen. What is really needed in this case is something like a submarine. Vessels going far to sea should have extensive preparation for preserving their water-tight integrity under any condition. The roster of sailing vessels that have pitch-poled or been capsized, yet righted themselves and returned safely to port, is quite lengthy. So we can see such an incident need not mean certain death—no matter how traumatic the experience. The key, of course, is keeping the sea out of the boat.

Our experiences with *Passagemaker* showed she had less tendency to broach than I had hitherto experienced. The "rooting" tendency was there—you could feel it as she put her bow down and accelerated before a wave. But her big rudder proved to have enough "command" to keep her from actually running off course. The drill was to watch the waves astern, and when a particularly vicious one appeared, to put the stern dead before it. As the bow went down, the helmsman's line of sight was shifted to dead ahead. If the bow showed the slightest tendency to turn to either side, the rudder was immediately slapped hard in the opposite direction. This always worked, yet I hesitate to imply that it always would, the sea being so full of surprises.

Paperwork and Officials

"Going foreign" means inevitable contact with the maritime officials of countries much different from your own. This is nothing to worry about, provided your papers are in order and your heart is pure.

For a vessel built abroad, a consul may issue a "Certificate of American Ownership." If he does not remember what this is, tell him it is in his form book. Ordinarily, permission to issue the certificate must be obtained from Washington after the sale is completed. But for a brand-new vessel obviously being built for an American citizen, it is possible to obtain permission in advance from the State Department for the consul to issue the certificate when he is satisfied all conditions are fulfilled. We did this, and were able to leave Singapore immediately after completion of the sale. Be sure to invite the consul to your christening party.

See that the consul binds all your papers with yards of red tape and the biggest seal he has. I think this does more good than anything. You will often be asked for gross and net tonnage figures. If you don't know them, give displacement for gross and half that for net. I had *Passagemaker* measured by the British, and although the paper was clearly marked "not for British Registry" this impressive form seemed to do a lot of good. The yard's hull number was mentioned on this form and in the certificate and was successfully pointed out as the "registry number" more than once. A consul can issue a "Temporary Certificate of Registry," but this document is only good for six months and hardly any owner would want to return home in that short time.

All hands should have passports; don't fool with "seaman's papers" on a yacht. The only place we went where a visa was required in 1963 was Yugoslavia. That country, Greece, and possibly other countries have a restricted list of ports where a yacht can enter and clear. If there is any doubt, you should plan your entry into a country at a port that has facilities for regular shipping.

Every port will want crew lists with passport numbers, dates of birth, and so on. Make up plenty of them in advance on a typewriter. I have been asked for as many as six. Be sure all hands have International Immunization Certificates and that shots are up to date. Have a locker where "spirits" and cigarettes can be sealed up in case Customs thinks you have too much.

The best time to enter port is 0900 on a working day. I had reason to regret the occasions we did not follow this rule. Overtime charges are quite high in some places.

Flying a good-sized national (not merchant) flag of the country, steam right into the port. If no one tells you what to do, it is always legal for the captain to go ashore and make his presence known. But *only* the captain.

If, as is usually the case, the officials come on board for check-in, have everything ready in advance: all papers and passports laid out in an area such as the dinette where writing can be done. The area should be cleared of all crew members except the captain, with one other member prepared to come if the captain summons him to serve coffee or beer. During the time the officials are on board, no crew members other than the captain should speak to them. If questions are asked they should be referred to the captain. He alone should speak for the ship, and he should limit himself to answering questions. After all business is concluded, it is in order to offer some refreshment. It is surprising how often this will be refused. Even if no one on board smokes, it is a good idea to have cigarettes on board to offer to the officials.

This may all sound a bit formal and stuffy, but it is a good idea to exhibit a brisk, businesslike manner, be dressed in clean clothes, and have the yacht all ship-shape in order to make a good impression. Unfortunately, there are enough sailors who *don't* make a good impression to raise suspicion of yachts among customs men, and to lead to remarks like this in an SSCA bulletin: ". . . and find some freaked-out creep in a sailing pasteboard box has queered it for everybody else."

Fire

Fire is an ancient terror of seamen. Many of the sea's great tragedies have been caused by fire, not by the sea itself. The possibility of fire must always be present in the captain's mind and every precaution taken against it.

What I want to emphasize here is something these books neglect: The diesel-driven vessel, while much safer than gasoline, is *not* immune to fire caused by fuel. Carelessness in handling diesel fuel or control of leakage is no more tolerable than it would be with gasoline. Under certain conditions the fumes from diesel oil *can* explode. And high-pressure fuel-injector leakage that can drain into the sump has caused "base explosions."

I personally know of two small vessels that were destroyed by diesel-fuel fires. A 50-foot twin-engine (in the stern), long-range yacht burned and sank while underway in the Mediterranean when it was about three months old. During the short period the crew was able to fight the fire with ordinary fire extinguishers before they were driven off the vessel, no investigation could be made of how or where the fire started.

In the second instance, the engine room was equipped with a CO_2 flooding system. It was also equipped with powerful engine-room blowers which were in operation. The cause was a fuel-line break right over an uncooled section of exhaust line, a situation that should have been foreseen. The CO_2 automatically functioned—and the engine-room blowers automatically blew the CO_2 out the vents! Result: an uncontrollable fire. This gives you something to think about.

Diesel-fuel fires can be fought using techniques the Navy developed during the war. The principal reliance was on the "fog nozzle" at the end of a "wand," a section of pipe about seven feet long. The fog nozzle can be approximated by the ordinary adjustable spray nozzle used on rubber hose. The main point is to get it into action as quickly as possible. On *Passagemaker,* the hose with nozzle was always hooked up with the valve open. Full pressure could be obtained instantly by flipping a switch that was outside the engine room in the galley. Some such arrangement is recommended.

I will personally not ever have propane or butane gas aboard for cooking. There are enough things to worry about at sea without the threat of explosion, which is inherent in propane. In certain areas, it is now possible to buy compressed natural gas which, being lighter than air, is much safer.

If gas is to be used, the vessel's whole design should be drawn with this in mind, rather than being a tacked-on afterthought. For instance, in one yacht, belonging to a very experienced seaman, which uses propane for cooking and heating water, the appliances are confined to one compartment of the vessel which is completely sealed off from the rest of the ship and has a blower in the bilge running constantly.

Keeping Time

Your vessel should be run on zone time, using the numbered zones as described in *Bowditch*.

The time we use to regulate our own routines is called local time, and usually corresponds nearly to the ancient idea that noon is when the sun is highest. In the U.S.A, what we call Eastern Standard Time is the time of zone +5, while Eastern Daylight Time is time of zone +4. But what happens when we leave our home boundaries to go out on the sea and disappear into the distance? What is the *local* time then?

Well, the answer is perfectly simple. *The local time aboard a ship is what the captain says it is.* This is literally true. In the old days, before accurate time pieces, when the captain observed the sun at its highest, he would say "Strike eight bells." This would be done and the hourglass turned over to start another cycle of watches.

So it ill behooves me to tell you, the captain of your vessel, what time to use. But let me respectfully suggest, as the result of my experience, that you do what we did on *Passagemaker:* Run your ship on zone time.

To handle this, the data board shows four things: the local time in the form of the presently used zone description; the local date, which means just that; the time of sunset; and the time of sunrise, which is for the next day.

Sunrise and sunset are useful for several reasons. They show when star sights will be taken when combined with the duration of twilight you experienced the previous day. (This is more accurate than the tables in the almanac.) And they show how the local time being used works in

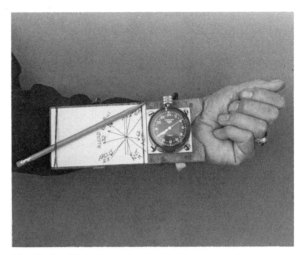
The Beebe Sight Recorder attached to the wrist.

with the ship's routine. For example, steaming steadily eastward across the Atlantic, if you do not change your zone time, you will eventually find all the navigators on deck taking star sights just when the cook announces supper at the scheduled hour of 1800. And there is nothing madder than a cook who has fixed a masterpiece and finds no one to eat it! As one of the basic principles of cruising is to keep the cook happy, you are due for a time zone change, but quick!

Another thing to keep in mind is that it is desirable to arrive at your destination using the time zone *there.* For instance, in going from Bermuda to Horta you would change three hours on the way to be on Horta time. So as a practical matter you are limited to three changes of one hour each in a passage of about 10 days. The timing of the changes is arranged with consideration of the factors mentioned.

On vessels with varnished woodwork rather than *Passagemaker's* blackboard paint, the data described above was kept on cards and posted near the wheel.

Watch-Standing Rules

The position of watch officer (or officer of the deck as it is called in the Navy), is unique among duties in that a single person is solely responsible for the safety of the ship and its crew. It is quite true that in a vast majority of cases, when a situation arises it can be solved by calling the captain to bring his experience to bear on the problem. Nevertheless it must be kept in mind that situations will arise that demand the watchstander take immediate and correct action on his own. Thus a certain amount of training of watch-standers is a vital ingredient of safety. Each person on the watch list should be able to perform such maneuvers as stopping the engine, changing course or speed, using autopilot "dodgers," taking bearings on approaching ships, and so on, as each vessel's makeup demands. Each watchstander should also have specific instructions about log entries, inspections to be made, and degree of alertness required.

I know from our experience that the crew does appreciate having things spelled out, and appreciates even more the opportunity to maneuver the ship. As to what rules you should have, I can only give for the reader's consideration some we have followed.

One traditional emergency is "man overboard." I recall being taken to task by a sailing man because I did not have the ocean-racer's two horseshoe life preservers on *Passagemaker's* stern, ready to be thrown over by the helmsman. Perhaps they would be useful, but I pointed out to this gentleman that in the first place, the helmsman was about 25 feet from the stern, and in the second place, our orders were immediately to turn the rudder hard over *toward* the side the man fell from and proceed in a full circle back to the place he was, a maneuver that took only a few seconds and something the sailing vessel cannot do. I note that the new owner of *Passagemaker* has put horseshoe preservers on her stern where they do look very salty.

As regards degree of alertness, we allowed the watch-stander to read during the day when there was clear visibility and no traffic. At night, this was not possible, as we emphasized protecting night vision by eschewing all light other than small penlights which give just enough light to read dials without spoiling your night vision. I have been on vessels that were quite slack about this, and I thought it a mistake.

We had the engine room inspected each hour. On *PM,* this was done from the pilothouse, looking down the hatch with a five-cell flashlight that was trained on certain spots, such as the one place you could see the bilge. For the purpose of visiting the engine room, using the head, etc.,

it was permissible for the watch-stander—after examining the whole horizon with binoculars—to go below for not more than 10 minutes since it takes about 18 minutes for a freighter to pass after first seeing its range lights. With the increases in speed of ships, already mentioned, perhaps this is now too long.

Each watch-stander should be trained as a helmsman to the point where he can steer the course by hand easily. One of the most common mishaps on the long-range seagoing motorboat is autopilot trouble. While it is being fixed, hand steering is required. This is particularly necessary if any of the crew are novices or if the compass reads from the rear, as in *PM,* where people trained in steering with a forward lubber line have a terrible time at first.

Ports

In 1966, while *Passagemaker* was crossing the Trades north of Hawaii en route to Seattle, a combination of two or three small waves on the face of a larger swell interacted to produce what for want of a better term I called a "jet break," striking her side in a limited area. In this area was a Wilcox-Crittenden 8" x 18" "marine window." The glass in this port shattered into literally a million pieces with the major ones looking like daggers. These were propelled across the ship onto Linford's bunk and she was cut in several places, luckily not very severely, though she carries a scar on her cheek to this day.

Now I was remiss in assuming that a marine port advertised as "built to meet the severe conditions of marine use," was actually that. Instead, it was equipped with the cheapest sort of plain glass, dime-store stuff. My complaints to the company were met by the statement that competitive conditions in the industry made it impossible for them to use better and more expensive glass because they would be priced out of the market. This incredible statement is probably true—*caveat emptor* is still the rule.

Subsequently, *Passagemaker*'s forward ports were refitted with quarter-inch, heat-tempered safety plate. In 1967, off Nicaragua, that same port was struck again in the same manner—the blow so severe that the man on watch stopped, thinking we had hit something. While water spurted in around the port, it did not break.

It is up to the individual, apparently, to see that his ports are safe and matched in thickness to their size. Large "picture windows" of quarter-inch glass, even if safety glass, give me the shudders. *Passagemaker*'s ports, other than forward, were all half-inch, heat-tempered safety glass. In a gale in the Aegean, we were seeking shelter by going alternately 45 degrees upwind and downwind to reach a destination across the wind. By my own mismanagement during one of these turns, we were struck broadside by a breaking sea. The pilothouse ports were covered entirely with green water—no foam—yet we suffered no damage or inconvenience, just a good scare. After that, we had every confidence in our glass.

Plastic ports are now appearing and use of plastic in metal-framed ports has been suggested. Certainly it would be a lesser hazard if it did break, but it also lays claim to being stronger than glass. *Mona Mona* is equipped in her hull with the Fuller Brush Company plastic ports. They work very well, being tight and easy to open and close. They took a few good blows during the three months I observed them, but have not yet been tested by the extreme "jets" we had in *Passagemaker*.

Because *PM*'s stern cabin ports were made up of simple panes of glass held in a frame that could be tilted open 15 degrees at the top for ventilation in rain, we provided covers for storm use. The covers were bolted on from the outside. This was not easy to do in a rough sea, and such ports should be provided with covers that can be put on from the inside—an easy thing to arrange. After our first gale, we never again applied the port covers in the actual stern as they were not necessary.

Conclusion

Writing these notes has forced me to review all that happened over a period of years in order to insure that nothing of prime importance to successful passage-making in seagoing motorboats has been forgotten, or misstated, or is not found somewhere in the recommended reading. In the course of this review, both Linford and I had many nostalgic memories about our cruising. Like our first cruise with just the two of us in Greece, from Athens to Rhodes with the *meltemi* blowing furiously. And how Linford got seasick for the first and last time—bravely trying to brown slices of delicious Yugoslavian fillets in the galley below. And how our new stabilizer pennants began to unravel, and we took shelter briefly behind a rocky reef to put safety lines on the wires in case the pennants let go. And how we spent half a day making up new ones, with Linford learning to "pass the ball" as I served. And how the wind shifted and chased us out of our harbor before we swung onto the shore. And how we then took refuge in what was just a cleft in a sheer cliff on the south side of Nis Nikouria and got the anchor to hold after four attempts. And how Linford hoisted me up the mast so I could install the new pennants with the winds whistling down the gully, almost pushing us against the rocks, first one side then the other.

One lesson is most important of all—we are glad we have done it and hope to do more. And so we will leave you with one simple thought: *"Go!"*

Index